BASICS OF STRUCTURAL EQUATION MODELING

*To members of my family, who made this project possible,
I dedicate this book:*

*my parents, George and Helen;
my wife, Barbara;
and our children, Kristie and Dan.*

BASICS OF STRUCTURAL EQUATION MODELING

GEOFFREY M. MARUYAMA

SAGE Publications
International Educational and Professional Publisher
Thousand Oaks London New Delhi

For information:

SAGE Publications, Inc.
2455 Teller Road
Thousand Oaks, California 91320
E-mail: order@sagepub.com

SAGE Publications Ltd.
6 Bonhill Street
London EC2A 4PU
United Kingdom

SAGE Publications India Pvt. Ltd.
M-32 Market
Greater Kailash I
New Delhi 110 048 India

Printed in the United States of America

Library of Congress Cataloging-in-Publication Data

Maruyama, Geoffrey M.
     Basics of structural equation modeling/by Geoffrey M. Maruyama.
         p.   cm.
     Includes bibliographical references and index.
     ISBN 0-8039-7408-6 (cloth).—ISBN 0-8039-7409-4 (pbk.)
       1. Multivariate analysis.   2. Social sciences—Statistical methods.
     I. Title.

     QA278.M374   1997   97-4839
     519.5′35—dc21

98   99   00   01   02   03   10   9   8   7   6   5   4   3   2   1

Acquiring Editor:	C. Deborah Laughton
Editorial Assistant:	Eileen Carr
Production Editor:	Diana E. Axelsen
Production Assistant:	Denise Santoyo
Typesetter/Designer:	Marion Warren
Cover Designer:	Candice Harman
Print Buyer:	Anna Chin

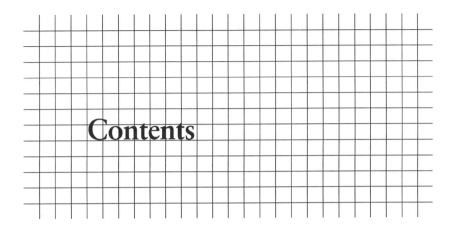

Contents

Preface   xi

Acknowledgments   xv

▮ PART 1: Background

1. What Does It Mean to Model Hypothesized
Causal Processes With Nonexperimental Data?   3

Methods for Structural Equation Analyses   9
Overview   12

2. History and Logic of Structural Equation Modeling   15

History   15
    Sewell Wright   15
    Path Analysis in the Social Sciences   17
Unidirectional Flow Models   17
Moving Beyond Path Analysis in Structural
    Equation Modeling Research   20
Why Use Structural Equation Modeling Techniques?   20

**PART 2: Basic Approaches to Modeling With
Single Observed Measures of Theoretical Variables**

3. The Basics: Path Analysis and Partitioning of Variance   29

   Logic of Correlations and Covariances   30
   Decomposing Relationships Between Variables
      Into Causal and Noncausal Components   35
      Direct Causal Effects   39
      Indirect Causal Effects   40
      Noncausal Relationships Due to Shared Antecedents   41
      Noncausal Unanalyzed Prior Association Relationships   42
   Approaches for Decomposing Effects   44
   Determining Degrees of Freedom of Models   48
   Presenting Partial Regression and Partial
      Correlation as Path Models   49
      Partial Regression   49
      Partial Correlation   51
   Peer Popularity and Academic Achievement:
      An Illustration   53

4. Effects of Collinearity on Regression
   and Path Analysis   60

   Regression and Collinearity   62
   Illustrating Effects of Collinearity   66
   Confidence Intervals for Correlations   70
   Ridge or Reduced Variance Regression   73

5. Effects of Random and Nonrandom Error
   on Path Models   79

   Measurement Error   79
      Background   79
      Specifying Relationships Between Theoretical
        Variables and Measures   81
      Random Measurement Error   84
      Nonrandom Error   87
   Method Variance and Multitrait-Multimethod Models   88
      Method Variance   89
      Additive Multitrait-Multimethod Models   92
      Nonadditive Multitrait-Multimethod Models   96

Summary   97

6. Recursive and Longitudinal Models: Where Causality
   Goes in More Than One Direction and Where Data
   Are Collected Over Time   99

   Models With Multidirectional Paths   100
   Logic of Nonrecursive Models   100
   Estimation of Nonrecursive Models   103
   Model Identification   105
   Longitudinal Models   108
   Logic Underlying Longitudinal Models   109
   Terminology of Panel Models   110
   Identification   111
   Stability   112
   Temporal Lags in Panel Models   115
   Growth Across Time in Panel Models   117
   Stability of Causal Processes   118
   Effects of Excluded Variables   119
   Correlation and Regression Approaches for Analyzing
   Panel Data   120
   Summary   122

PART 3: Factor Analysis and Path Modeling

7. Introducing the Logic of Factor Analysis and
   Multiple Indicators to Path Modeling   131

   Factor Analysis   132
   Logic of Factor Analysis   132
   Exploratory Factor Analysis   136
   Confirmatory Factor Analysis   139
   Use of Confirmatory Factor Analysis Techniques   140
   Constraining Relations of Observed Measures With Factors   147
   Confirmatory Factor Analysis and Method Factors   148
   *The Basic Confirmatory Factor Analysis Path
   Model for Multitrait-Multimethod Matrices*   148
   *Confirmatory Factor Analysis Approaches to
   Multitrait-Multimethod Matrices and
   Model Identification*   152

Summary of Confirmatory Factor Analysis
    and Multitrait-Multimethod Models   154
Initial Testing of Plausibility of Models: Consistency Tests   154
    Number of Indicators and Consistency Tests   155
    Costner's Original Consistency Model   158

▌PART 4: Latent Variable Structural Equation Models

**8. Putting It All Together: Latent Variable
Structural Equation Modeling**   **177**

The Basic Latent Variable Structural Equation Model   178
    The Measurement Model   178
    Reference Indicators   181
    The Structural Model   184
An Illustration of Structural Equation Models   187
    Model Specification   187
    Identification   188
    Equations and Matrices   192
Basic Ideas Underlying Fit/Significance Testing   195
    Individual Parameter Significance   195
    Model Fitting   196
    The Measurement Model   201
    The Structural Model   201
    The Variance/Covariance Matrices   202

**9. Using Latent Variable Structural Equation
Modeling to Examine Plausibility of Models**   **203**

Example 1: A Longitudinal Path Model   204
Example 2: A Nonrecursive Multiple-Indicator Model   209
Example 3: A Longitudinal Multiple-Indicator
    Panel Model   214

10. Logic of Alternative Models and Significance Tests   **234**

Nested Models   235
Tests of Overall Model Fit   238
    Absolute Indexes   242
    Relative Indexes   243
    Adjusted Indexes   245
Fit Indexes for Comparing Non-Nested Models   246

Setting Up Nested Models   247
Why Models May Not Fit   249
Illustrating Fit Tests   250

11. Variations on the Basic Latent Variable Structural Equation Model   255

Analyzing Structural Equation Models When Multiple
   Populations Are Available   257
   Overview of Methods   257
   Comparing Processes Across Samples   259
   Testing Plausibility of Constraints   261
   Constraints in the Measurement Model   261
   Constraints in the Structural Model   262
   When and How to Impose Equality Constraints   262
Second-Order Factor Models   265
All-Y Models   268

12. Wrapping Up   271

Criticisms of Structural Equation Modeling Approaches   272
   "Internal" Critics   272
   "External" Critics   275
   Emerging Criticisms   277
Post Hoc Model Modification   278
Topics Not Covered   280
   Power Analysis   280
   Nonlinear Relationships   280
   Alternative Estimation Techniques   281
   Analysis of Noncontinuous Variables   282
   Adding Analysis of Means   282
   Multilevel Structural Equation Modeling   282
   *Writing Up Papers Containing Structural
     Equation Modeling Analysis*   283
   *Selecting a Computer Program to Do Latent
     Variable Structural Equation Modeling*   283

**Appendix A: A Brief Introduction to Matrix Algebra
and Structural Equation Modeling**   285

   What Is a Matrix?   285
   Matrix Operations   288
   Inverting Matrices   291

Determinants   292
Matrices and Rules   293

Answers to Chapter Discussion Questions   294

References   299

Author Index   306

Subject Index   309

About the Author   311

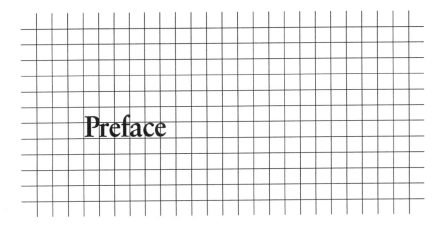

Preface

This book is intended for researchers who want to use structural equation approaches but who feel that they need more background and a somewhat more "gentle" approach than has been provided by books published previously. From my perspective as a longtime user of structural equation methods, many individuals who try to use these techniques make fundamental errors because they lack understanding of the underlying roots and logic of the methods. They also can make "silly" mistakes that not only frustrate them but also invalidate their analyses because writers have assumed that readers would understand basics of the methods (e.g., what are called reference indicators).

Because I came to these techniques fairly early (in the early 1970s), what now is history was what was current then. I learned about methods such as path analysis as contemporary methods, and they evolved into the current methods over time. I hope that I effectively transmit the strengths and limitations of these techniques as well as the ways in which they led to current methods.

I began teaching about these techniques in the spring of 1977 by default, for I was the only person in my department who had used the latent variable methods and understood them, and I also was one of the few who had access to the programs. For years, I patched together my course and looked for a book that I liked. Finally, I decided to write about what I taught. The product of that decision is this book.

I wrote this not as a statistician on the cutting edge of the approaches but rather as a user with strong interest in methods. The book reflects the way in which I came to these methods, namely, beginning with theory and a data set from a school desegregation study and looking for methods that could use the nonexperimental data from that project to examine plausibility of different theoretical views. In fact, I practically advertise the substantive problems that led me to these methods, for they appear repeatedly in examples and illustrations. As I will say again in the text, I do not use my data as examples because they are great data sets or because the models fit perfectly. They are not and do not. At the same time, they are the kinds of data that researchers find themselves having, and the substantive problems are ones that are accessible to readers. If they are as accessible as I think they are, then I am likely to get notes and comments from readers about the alternative models they generated from the data sets!

Throughout the book, I tried to present topics and issues in a way that will help readers conceptualize their models. In particular, I tried to spend time discussing logic of alternative approaches. One example is the discussion of nonrecursive versus longitudinal models. Although I have my preference, it is a relative one rather than an absolute one, and my own ultimate decision in any instance would be driven by a combination of methodological and conceptual issues.

As I progressed into the writing of the book, I found out quickly how hard it is to describe some of the more complex methods in simple terms. I suspect that there are instances in which I did not manage to stay "gentle" despite my best intentions. I would appreciate feedback from readers about where the complexity is too great or where the descriptions are unclear.

The book is divided into four parts: background, single-measure approaches, factor analysis and multiple indicators, and latent variable structural equation approaches. Readers with strong quantitative skills and backgrounds should be able to sample selectively from the first three parts of the book (Chapters 1-7) and focus on the remaining chapters, which present latent variable structural equation modeling. All readers, however, should be sure that they understand the logic underlying the methods. Furthermore, they should look at the examples and illustrations, for those make concrete many of the issues presented in more abstract ways.

Finally, once readers get to the end and go on to try to use the techniques, they should be able to go back to the illustrations and compare their analyses to those I report. I have appended LISREL control statements for most of the examples. Comments and queries can be sent by e-mail to geofmar@vx.cis.umn.edu.

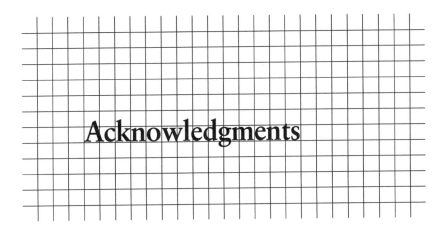

Acknowledgments

First, I have to thank my former students, who used earlier drafts of this book in my class as I refined it. Their feedback was very helpful, and I hope it results in a book that will be kind to future students. Second, thanks are due to those who helped me learn structural equation modeling (SEM) techniques: Norman Miller, my graduate school adviser who gave me my first SEM problem and helped me think about conceptual issues; Norman Cliff, who happened to have the Educational Testing Service publication on LISREL and focused me away from multiple regression approaches to latent variable SEM; Ward Keesling, an earlier developer of SEM approaches who provided advice and served informally on my thesis committee even though his university was different from mine; Peter Bentler, who allowed me to sit in on a class of his (at that same other university) as he explored SEM issues; and my colleagues here at Minnesota—George Huba, who shared the first SEM class with me as we stayed ahead of our students, and Bob Cudeck, who provided support, feedback, ideas, and resources as I worked on this book. Third are the array of colleagues and students who came to me with their problems, for they enriched my views about what comes easily and what is difficult to understand in SEM. Fourth, this book would not have been done were it not for the encouragement of (or was that prodding by?) my editor, C. Deborah Laughton, and the excellent and helpful group of reviewers that she found. Reviewers whose good advice I did not follow should know that I tried to incorporate their feedback, and where the advice was consistent and clear, I did. At the same time, I found instances in which there was not agreement among them, which gave me license both to pick and choose and perhaps to stay close to the views that I had acquired over time.

PART

1

BACKGROUND

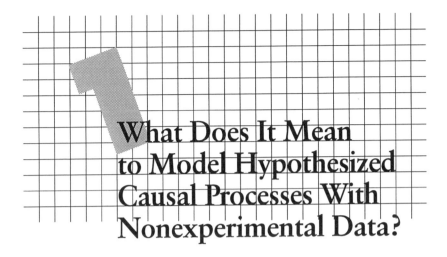

What Does It Mean to Model Hypothesized Causal Processes With Nonexperimental Data?

The purpose of the statistical procedures is to assist in establishing the plausibility of the theoretical model and to estimate the degree to which the various explanatory variables seem to be influencing the dependent variables.

Cooley, 1978, p. 13

The above quote captures in a nutshell the essence of techniques for modeling hypothesized relationships among variables using nonexperimental, quantitative (i.e., correlational) data. The techniques described in this book are intended to allow researchers to examine the plausibility of their notions about relationships and impacts when data are nonexperimental. Through these techniques, hypothesized structures, typically called **models** or (less accurately) **causal models,** can be either rejected as implausible or tentatively accepted as consistent with the data. The techniques to be described are not restricted to nonexperimental methods, for these techniques can be used to model experimental data (e.g., Bagozzi, 1991). In experimental research, they are most valuable for studies hypothesizing mediating variables that transmit the effects of the manipulations.

Unfailingly, structural equation methods need to start from a conceptually derived model specifying the relationships among a set of variables. Theory provides the centerpiece for structural equation methodologies; they were designed for use by researchers with substantive interests in understanding complex patterns of interrelationships among variables. Without theory, there is little to distinguish among the numerous alternative ways of depicting relationships among a set of variables. For most groups of variables, many different models can be specified, with very different consequences. Most important, in contrast to reality where cause and effect exist independently of our ideas about how they work, in models cause and effect are totally dependent on the way in which the relationships are specified, and the results at best speak to plausibility about the way in which relationships are specified.[1]

Structural equation methods provide estimates of the strength of all the hypothesized relationships between variables in a theoretical model. They therefore provide information about hypothesized impact, both directly from one variable to another and via other variables positioned between the other two. Those other variables are called **intervening** or **mediating** variables. If one can assume that the hypothesized model is true, then the information will accurately represent underlying (causal) processes.

So, one might ask, "What is the catch? The methods sound both interesting and promising. Why isn't everyone using them?" The catch comes from the repeated use of terms such as *hypothesized causal impact* and *assuming that the model is true*. They alert readers about the potential weaknesses of the methodology. If the model is wrong, then the analyses may be misleading or even just plain wrong. As was already mentioned, there are for most sets of variables many alternative ways of specifying their relationships. Even "small" errors in positioning variables or including paths can create havoc all over

---

1. In some ways, it is unfortunate that the **methods** are complex, for there has been a tendency for the techniques to focus too much on technical issues tied to methods and too little on substantive ones related to cause and effect. As will be discussed much later in this book, there have been tensions between researchers who argue for using the methods for testing a priori models and researchers who advocate for post hoc changing of models, called model modification, to produce models with good fits (e.g., MacCallum, Roznowski, & Necowitz, 1992).

a model and result in the solution suggesting erroneous inferences. One potential consequence could be to design an intervention that, based on inferences drawn from an incorrectly specified model, actually manipulates an effect and not a cause.

Consider as an example modeling the relationship between popularity with peers and achievement in school. This example is an important one for this book because the topic is used with a single data set to illustrate and compare different structural equation techniques and is used with various data sets in a number of illustrations. Furthermore, to the extent that readers can draw on their personal experiences in schools to conjecture or hypothesize about whether or not and how the variables are related, it hopefully also will prove to be an example that is easy to follow and understand. To limit the range of developmental or age-specific hypotheses that may be generated, this example assumes a focus on elementary grade students.

Imagine that a research team has decided to investigate the plausibility of a conceptually driven model investigating the nature of the relationship between being accepted by peers in school and doing well in school. The research question could be "Does an individual's popularity affect his or her achievement?" As should be true for all models, this model starts from a conceptual one specifying the nature of the relationships between the variables. Interest in the model comes from a large number of correlational studies that have found peer acceptance to correlate positively with academic achievement (see, e.g., Maruyama, Miller, & Holtz, 1986). First, the research question implicitly states two alternative views about the impact of popularity on achievement (does affect, does not affect). Second, there also is the question of the impact of achievement on popularity (does affect, does not affect). In past research, there has been theorizing supporting each direction of influence, and either one could account for the relationship between the two variables that has been found by correlational research. Thus, we should want to generate a model that allows us to examine hypothesized relations from each variable to the other, that is, going in two directions. Both views could be supported, one or the other could be supported, or both could be found to be implausible (see, e.g., Maruyama & McGarvey, 1980). The last possibility could occur, for example, if some other variable or variables influenced both popularity and achievement and thereby accounted for their association.

The first view about impact could be called a "social star" model in which popular children over time come to do better in school (popularity affects achievement). The processes could operate in a fashion such as the following: By virtue of some positive attributes they possess, popular children are liked better by teachers who expect more from them and also are liked more by and helped more by peers, with the result that their rate of learning will increase. The reasoning draws from teacher expectancy effects (e.g., Brophy & Good, 1974) and from the attraction and attractiveness literatures (e.g., Byrne & Griffitt, 1973; Maruyama & Miller, 1981).

A second view, which could be called the "academic star" model, hypothesizes that high-achieving children will be better liked because of their capabilities and accomplishments. This view also can be drawn from the similarity and attraction literatures, which suggest that we are attracted to others who reward us or have the potential to reward us (e.g., Byrne & Griffitt, 1973).

Figure 1.1 depicts pictorially a model that hypothesizes a set of causal processes linking acceptance by peers and achievement. The model would consist of two structural equations, one for each variable that has arrows going to it. It tentatively hypothesizes that popularity affects achievement (the arrow from popularity to achievement) and that achievement affects popularity (the arrow from achievement to popularity). It also articulates other variables—the social class of the student's family, the student's academic ability, and the student's social skills—that are hypothesized as affecting either popularity or achievement or both.

Because the model is complex, further discussion of it is left until later in the book. The important point here is that models provide a means by which to articulate patterns of hypothesized relationships among variables. Plausibility of the model could be tested if we were to collect measures of the variables described and use the techniques and methods to be described in this book to analyze the data. Of course, if the hypothesizing is flawed, then we likely would learn little regardless of what the analyses suggest.

The techniques and methods described in this book do not try to do the impossible, namely, to establish causality in the absence of an experimental intervention. They cannot prove that any variable causes another variable. At the same time, however, they also do not

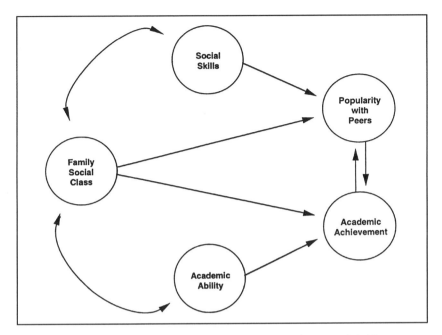

Figure 1.1. Model for the Relationship Between Popularity and Achievement

accept as truth an assertion that causality can and should be examined only through experimentation. Rather, they provide an alternative and complementary methodology to experimentation for examining plausibility of hypothesized models. The approach is particularly valuable in situations where, for various reasons (e.g., the variables cannot be manipulated ethically, comparison groups are not and cannot be made equivalent, a rich correlational data set is available to provide guidance for future research), experimentation was not done. In Figure 1.1, for example, each relationship described by a single-headed arrow hypothesizes the existence of a cause-effect relationship linking two variables, which means that analyses of the model provide information about plausibility of those relationships actually existing.

With the development of powerful computers and accompanying software that make the complex mathematics of the most effective techniques no longer a daunting obstacle, the methods described in this book have made great strides in the past 20 years. Within psychology, for example, they have gone from being generally unknown and being discounted as very limited to being widely accepted. They even have been viewed as exciting and as having great potential to transform or at least extend research across the social sciences, education, business, and health. After all, as has already been discussed, we all know about variables that cannot be manipulated ethically but about which we have ideas about causality. For example, neither race nor ethnicity can be manipulated, nor can gender or even social class, yet there are numerous conceptual models articulating ways in which those variables are related to other variables. Some of the models even hypothesize causal impacts of demographic types of variables. Furthermore, most researchers have ideas about causality irrespective of whether they use experimental or nonexperimental techniques. If theory drives a research study, then the analyses should be conducted in a way that does the best possible job of examining plausibility of the theory, and structural equation techniques provide a useful tool.

The availability and acceptance of structural equation techniques should not lead readers to underestimate the difficulty of using them. They have become so easy to use that there is now greater danger of such techniques being misused by researchers who really do not understand them than there is of such techniques being overlooked. The prominent computer programs for doing structural equation modeling (SEM) have reached the point where they can be run by creating a diagram of the model (e.g., the AMOS and EQS programs that will be described later in this text). Once models are specified, they can easily be modified, even from a diagram (e.g., the LISREL program, also described later).

At present, there is available an array of techniques for conducting structural equation analyses. These techniques include "ordinary" regression, multistage least squares regression, panel analysis, and latent variable (often maximum-likelihood) analysis of structural equations. These approaches are not without controversy. Some critics think of their use with structural models as representing GIGO (garbage in, garbage out); others view them as trying to accomplish the impossible—to prove causality from correlation. By contrast, experience using these techniques suggests to me a much different conclusion, namely, that they serve a valuable function in the social sciences and should be part of the repertoire of tools available to researchers.

Perhaps part of what leads to the range of divergent views such as those just described is the way in which one thinks about these methods. If the view is that users of these methods are trying to "prove" causality, then skepticism (if not rejection) of these approaches is reasonable. (We also could discuss how and whether or not experimentation actually establishes causality, but that is a discussion for a different book.) If, on the other hand, the view is that there are many alternative ways of thinking about causality among any set of variables *and* that data in many circumstances ought to be useful in distinguishing between or among alternative perspectives, then these approaches provide important information. More specifically, the way in which one distinguishes between various models is by finding **disconfirmation** of one or more alternative models. In other words, as is a central theme of this book, a particular data set may or may not "fit" or be consistent with a particular model. If the data and model are inconsistent, then that model can be rejected as not plausible and the theory that generated it is put at risk. Once implausible models are discarded, research can focus on remaining plausible models and develop ways of using various methods to pit them against one another.

Methods for Structural Equation Analyses

The approaches described in this book have been given a number of different labels including path modeling, path analysis, causal model analysis, causal modeling, structural equation analysis, SEM, and latent variable analysis of structural equations. Some are even referred to by the names of computer programs, for example, LISREL analysis. The particular term used reflects both the philosophy of the user about the approaches and the time period in which the user learned about the methods. Initially, these techniques usually were called path analysis, using the name given to the approaches by Sewell Wright in his early works on decomposing the relative importance of different genetic paths (Wright, 1921, 1934). That terminology remained most common throughout the early years and well into the period during the 1960s, when the approaches were imported into the social sciences by Blalock, Duncan, and others. By the 1970s, when advances in computers and in computer applications made more complex analyses possible and practical, the term "causal modeling" was used. That term fairly quickly fell into disfavor in the minds of at least a subset of social scientists, who objected to any use of the term "causal" with nonexperimental data. The term "causal" was replaced by the less controversial and very descriptive term "structural equation"; the relations between variables in these approaches are defined by a series of equations that describe hypothesized structures of relationships, thus **structural equation analysis** or **structural equation modeling**.

Figure 1.2 provides an illustration of a hypothesized causal structure. Note that the model's structure hypothesizes that Variable 1 (family social class) influences Variable 2 (one's successes at school), which in turn influences Variable 3 (one's first job). There is one structural equation that predicts Variable 2 and a second that predicts Variable 3.

Even the simple model of Figure 1.2 allows a test to be conducted. In this case, the relationship between Variable 1 and Variable 3 is **mediated** or transmitted by Variable 2. If the model is true, then, as will be explained more fully in Chapter 3 when path models are described, the correlation between Variable 1 and Variable 3 should be the product of the correlation between Variable 1 and Variable 2 and the correlation between Variable 2 and Variable 3. (That is, the equality $r_{13} = r_{12} \times r_{23}$ or $r_{13} - (r_{12} \times r_{23}) = 0$ should hold. Readers familiar with partial correlation or partial regression formulas will recognize the latter form of the equality as the numerator of those formulas for three-variable case partials between Variable 1 and Variable 3.) If the correlation between Variable 1 and Variable 3 is not similar to the product of the other two correlations, then the model can be rejected as not accurately representing the data, at least for the data set. If the correlation r_{13} is similar to the product of the other two correlations, then the model is viable. There are important issues in determining what constitutes "similar." Because issues of similarity are much easier to understand in the context of statistical tests of model fit, the discussion will be left for later. For now, assume that by inspection we might be able to make approximate determinations about similarity.

Even if the model "passes" our tests of similarity or fit, there still are limitations about what conclusions can be drawn. As will be discussed in detail in a later chapter, there are alternative theoretical models that predict the same pattern of relationships among measures. For example, in Figure 1.2, the "reverse" model formed by

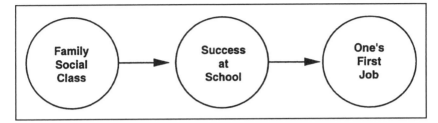

Figure 1.2. Simple Structure Model Interrelating Three Variables

reversing the direction of the arrows, namely, from Variable 3 to Variable 2 to Variable 1, is mathematically equivalent, as are a number of other models, including ones in which variables are related but do not cause one another. Thus, failing to reject a model as implausible means only that it is one of a number of viable remaining models. At the same time, however, inspection of the substantive variables in Figure 1.2 illustrates the point that not all alternative models are necessarily of equal viability; it makes little sense to argue that a child's first job causes the social class of his or her birth family. In other words, some mathematically viable models are less logically viable than others, and researchers need to take advantage of logical as well as mathematical and theoretical information in assessing viability of models and competing models.

In summary, the methodologies to be described in this book are intended to encourage and allow formalized presentation of the hypothesized relationships underlying correlational research, to test the plausibility of the hypothesizing for a particular data set, and to complement other methodological approaches. Because structural equation methods have become a part of the array of tools that graduate students today are taught, developing a sound under-standing of the techniques and the logic underlying them is of critical importance, and this brings me to the goal of this book.

The goal of this book is to provide readers with a good basic understanding of how and why structural equation approaches have come to be used. Providing that understanding requires ensuring that readers have the opportunity to learn about the logic underlying the use of these approaches, about how they relate to techniques such as regression and factor analysis, about their strengths and shortcomings as compared to alternative methodologies, and about the various methodologies for analyzing structural equation data. This book will not try to cover the entire field of structural equation techniques, for that field currently is a fertile one that is expanding rapidly. Explanation of the more complex issues will be left for other writers such as Bollen (1989), Hayduk (1996), and Hoyle (1995).

▮ Overview

This book is divided into four sections. The first section, Chapters 1 and 2, is an overview and history of methods for path models. The second section, Chapters 3-6, covers basic approaches to structural modeling with single measures of theoretical variables. The third section, Chapter 7, introduces exploratory and confirmatory factor analysis techniques and discusses measurement issues when multiple measures of theoretical variables are available. The final section, Chapters 8-12, covers latent variable SEM.

The book attempts to cover background information that often has been overlooked by other authors but that needs to be understood if one is to be an intelligent user and take maximal advantage of the approaches. Because the focus is on appealing to a general audience, technical language and equations are avoided whenever possible. As will be seen, however, technical language, equations, and matrix algebra are integral parts of structural equation approaches, and I found it impossible to cover the issues without including them. When technical language and equations are used, they are complemented with both narrative explanations and illustrations that apply to them. In some instances, this approach may gloss over technical issues of importance, but such instances are few.

Chapter Discussion Questions

1. Are the methods described in this book only for quantitative data?

2. Can econometric data be analyzed using these techniques?

3. In the model in Figure 1.2, is Success at School both moderating and mediating the relationship between the other two variables?

4. What does it mean to say that there are models that are mathematically equivalent to the one in Figure 1.2? What are some alternative models? What makes the different models equivalent? Does this mean that you should choose a model that fits your hypothesized relationships?

E X E R C I S E 1 . 1

Logic of Path Modeling

This example uses real data collected from college students. In these particular models, the approach used is the one described in this chapter but also is path analysis. Each path (standardized regression) coefficient is "simple" (i.e., bivariate) and, therefore, in these cases path analysis reduces to analysis of simple correlations. No statistical procedures are needed to get the path coefficients.

Given the three variables Test Anxiety, Test Expectations, and Test Performance, examine the plausibility of the two models presented as follows for each of the four groups (think of them as four replications). No formal significance tests are necessary.

Correlation	Group 1	Group 2	Group 3	Group 4
Test Anxiety with Test Expectations	−.321	−.423	−.221	−.364
Test Anxiety with Test Performance	−.288	−.288	−.153	−.278
Test Expectations with Test Performance	.207	.311	.179	.306

NOTE: Figures are *r* values.

Model A: Test Anxiety → Test Expectations → Test Performance

This model hypothesizes test expectations as mediating the relationship between test anxiety and test outcomes. That is, students higher on test anxiety expect to do less well and therefore perform less well.

Is Model A plausible?

Model B: Test Expectations → Test Anxiety → Test Performance

This model, which cannot be true if Model A is true, hypothesizes that students with higher test expectations will be lower on test anxiety, which will cause them to do better. This latter model views test anxiety as less of an individual difference variable than personality theorists might view it.

Is Model B plausible?

Solution process. Each model is "tested" by multiplying two correlations together and comparing their product with the third correlation. If the model fits, then the product should equal the third correlation. The difference between the product and the third correlation is the part of the correlation that is unexplained by the model.

For Model A, the Test Anxiety–Test Performance correlation is compared to the product of the other two correlations.

For Model B, the Test Expectations–Test Performance correlation is compared to the product of the other two correlations.

(Neither model fits.)

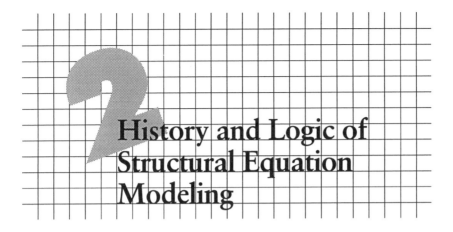

History and Logic of Structural Equation Modeling

Because the structural equation modeling (SEM) literature is spread across many fields and encompasses a number of traditions, readers new to SEM approaches often have a difficult time finding information that gives them a basic understanding of the context and purposes of SEM. The goal of this chapter is to provide a basic background and history, addressing questions such as the following. Who thought of these approaches? In what context were they developed? How have they been used? Who translated them or adapted them for other areas? What should one know about them to use them intelligently? In some instances, this explanation requires introducing terms that will be explained more fully in later chapters; in such instances, I attempt to provide enough context for readers to understand the point. The first section traces the history of SEM, and the second focuses on the broad class of research questions for which models can be useful.

History

Sewell Wright

As mentioned in Chapter 1, the roots of SEM go back to the 1920s, when Sewell Wright, a geneticist, attempted to solve simultaneous equations to disentangle genetic influences across generations. Wright faced a situation in which the causes (genes of the "parents") were known and the outcomes (the offspring's traits) were known, and causality went in a single direction without feedback or loops that circle back on themselves. In the SEM literature, his situation is called a **recursive** or unidirectional causal flow model.[2] It is the only kind of model that can properly be called **path analysis**. Wright wanted to estimate the sizes of the effects from each parent to the offspring. The solution could be determined by writing the system of equations, expressing the equations in terms of the correlations among the various variables, and solving for the unknowns (there were more knowns than unknowns, so the system was solvable). In describing his methodology, Wright (1921) stated,

> The present paper is an attempt to present a method of measuring the direct effect along each separate path in such a system and thus of finding the degree to which variation of a given effect is determined by each particular cause. The method depends upon the combination of knowledge of the degree of correlation among the variables in a system with such knowledge as may be possessed of the causal relations. In cases where causal relations are uncertain, the method can be used to find the logical consequences of any particular hypothesis in regard to them. (p. 557)

Note, in particular, the statement about finding **logical consequences** of any hypothesis. It is another way of saying, "If the model is true, then the relationships are . . ."

Later, Wright (1934) stated,

> The method of path coefficients is not intended to accomplish the impossible task of deducing causal relations from the values of correlation coefficients. It is intended to combine the quantitative information given by the correlations with such qualitative information as may be at hand on causal relations to give a quantitative interpretation. (p. 193)

---

2. The idea of "recursive" meaning the same as "unidirectional" always has been problematic, for it is inconsistent with other uses of recursion. Recently, Ed Rigdon provided an explanation for recursive on a structural equation listserve that makes sense to me: The models are recursive because they are made up of a set of equations, and those equations can be ordered such that one solves sequentially for each dependent variable/equation and then uses that information to return **recursively** to the system of equations to solve for later variables/equations.

In addition to introducing the methods of path analysis, Wright's statements clearly defined the purposes of the methodology, namely, to find the consequences of particular hypothesized structures. He also clearly stated limits of the approaches in terms of issues of causality.

Path Analysis in the Social Sciences

Perhaps surprisingly, work with the ideas of Wright in the social sciences was negligible until the 1960s, when Blalock (1964), Duncan (1966), and others introduced them to address social science issues. For path analysis, solution processes were relatively simple. Parameters were estimated by solving a system of equations using linear algebra (solving for a number of unknowns using a system containing an equal or a greater number of equations) or using multiple regression.

One of the prominent areas of early structural equation research was on what are called status attainment processes, namely, what determines the jobs and careers that we end up having. That research, done by Duncan and others, examined antecedents of success in attaining education and jobs. This research looked at variables such as social class of the family, past academic achievement, and social support as predictors of success. In such models, then, the primary dependent variables were educational attainment (e.g., years of education, degrees received) and job status. Because these models crossed large periods of time, they generally were unidirectional in their flow.

Unidirectional Flow Models

For models in which hypothesized causality goes in a single direction, the solution process was fairly straightforward and amenable to methodologies available from the time of Wright. Initially, algebra (simultaneous equations) and matrix algebra were used for estimation, solving one or more equations for some number of unknowns. Later, regression techniques were used as well. In some instances the two approaches yielded identical findings, but in others they could differ. In models that met the minimum condition necessary for uniquely solving for the unknown parameters to be estimated, namely, having the same number of equations as unknown parameters to estimate (called **just-identified models** in the path analysis and SEM literatures), regression and linear algebra approaches yielded identical results. That is, the same unique solution can be obtained either by solving for the equations using matrix algebra or by using regression approaches. (Readers could look ahead to Figure 3.2 to see a just-identified model. It has 10 paths to estimate and has enough information—10 correlations—to yield 10 equations.)

In models in which there were too many parameters to estimate for the number of observed measures, namely, having more unknowns than equations (called **under-identified models**), there would not be enough information available to uniquely estimate the parameters regardless of the approach used. The problem caused by not having enough information is that there are an infinite number of alternative solutions that are equally viable and no defensible way of choosing from among them. (Under-identification will be addressed in more detail in Chapter 5 as part of the discussion of non-recursive models.) Therefore, attempting to impose a single path analytic solution to interpret makes no sense. Once again, readers could look ahead at Figure 3.2. If we were to add any other possible path, for example, from X_4 back to X_3, then the model would have too many unknowns and not be uniquely solvable.

Finally, for models in which there are fewer unknowns than equations (called **over-identified models**), the equations hold enough information to produce more estimates than parameters. As a result, there will be more than one way of solving for at least some of the parameters, and the different ways will not necessarily (or usually) produce exactly the same estimates. Once again, readers can look ahead at Figure 3.2. If we were to drop any existing paths because we decided that theoretically they should be zero, then the model would become over-identified, for it would have more equations than parameters to solve. In such circumstances, regression, which produces only a single solution for interrelating a set of predictors to a particular criterion variable, has been shown to produce the best estimate (see Land, 1969). Furthermore, to anticipate later discussions of estimation using maximum likelihood approaches, in such circumstances least squares and maximum likelihood estimates are identical (e.g., Land, 1969). These estimates for a given parameter typically would be close to an average of the various ways of estimating that parameter through algebraic solutions.

Although it may seem difficult to believe from today's perspective, even as recently as during the 1960s a major constraint on the use of structural equation methods to solve broader classes of models was the relatively primitive state of computers and consequent unavailability of estimation techniques such as maximum likelihood. The hardware was not in place to allow general access to statistical analyses that could have addressed structural equation methods using relatively complex mathematical approaches. For example, one of the first papers to compare least squares, algebraic, and maximum likelihood estimates misestimated the maximum likelihood estimates and had to correct both the results and the interpretations in an addendum.

In summary, the approaches to SEM used during the "path analysis era" of the 1960s to solve for unidirectional causal flow models employed multiple regression techniques, often called ordinary least squares analysis. For **path analysis** models (which by definition have only single measures of each variable of interest), these techniques will yield results identical to those of the current approaches because, as already mentioned, least squares and maximum likelihood estimates are identical (e.g., Land, 1969). For variations on path analysis that employ measurement error or bidirectional causality/feedback loops (called nonrecursive models), variations on regression techniques such as indirect least squares, two-stage least squares, or three-stage least squares could be used.

To anticipate later parts of this book and direct the thinking of readers, it is important to note that a major advantage of the general linear model used in programs such as LISREL (e.g., Jöreskog & Sörbom, 1993), EQS (e.g., Bentler, 1989), and AMOS (e.g., Arbuckle, 1997) is that they can handle most types of models (recursive, nonrecursive, with and without random and nonrandom measurement error, and with observed and unobserved variables) and consequently do not require readers to learn an array of different techniques for different types of models. These programs, which give rise to the latent variable structural equation models, share the general linear model of regression models but differ insofar as they have unmeasured predictor variables (this point will be explained later). Lest the current point be lost, however, it is important to note that path analysis models are a class of multiple regression models. The shortcomings of regression approaches therefore are important to consider and are covered in Chapter 4 of this book.

■ Moving Beyond Path Analysis in Structural Equation Modeling Research

After a surge of interest in the least squares methods, the limitations, especially of path analysis techniques described in detail in Chapter 3, led the methods into disfavor. It was easy to criticize the approaches. For example, most theoretical variables are assessed inaccurately due to both imprecision in operationalizing them and inaccuracy in measuring the observed measures. These difficulties occur regardless of whether or not the conceptual model presented is viable. In other words, using path analysis techniques was a surefire way of inviting criticism for poor operationalization of the conceptual variables, and this made publication of SEM research difficult. In addition, if the hypothesized model contained feedback or causal loops, then that model could not be solved by ordinary regression techniques, which limited the applicability of the methods.

The next surge of enthusiasm was led by the works of Jöreskog (1969) and others including Bock, Wiley, Browne, and Keesling. These researchers developed a general linear modeling approach that allowed researchers to overcome many of the limitations of the least squares approaches by allowing for far better operationalization of theoretical variables. The approach (e.g., Wiley, 1973) has evolved over the past 20 years into the array of structural equation approaches and computer programs that are widely distributed today, among which LISREL, EQS, and AMOS are the most widely known. Discussion of the methods underlying those programs comprises the latter part of this book.

■ Why Use Structural Equation Modeling Techniques?

A fairly straightforward way of thinking about when to consider using structural equation approaches comes directly from multiple regression. Choosing regression as a starting point is logical because (a) the methodologies have evolved from regression techniques and build on the assumptions of regression and (b) the reasoning researchers use for selecting regression in many instances actually is better accomplished by using an SEM approach. This chapter builds primarily on the latter point.

There are two prominent reasons why researchers use multiple regression. The first focuses exclusively on explaining as much variance as possible in the dependent variable. For this type of use, the weights of the various predictor variables are much less important and sometimes even inconsequential or irrelevant. The goal is best prediction and in this book is called **regression for prediction**. One example of this approach might be a situation in which there is an array of information available, and a college wants to use that information to make "accurate" admissions decisions, namely, admitting students likely to stay and graduate. A second example could be an employer who wants to use available information to help determine which potential employees will be both effective and likely to stay with the company. A third could be the owner and coach/manager of a sports team trying to decide which athletes they want on their team. In each instance, the individuals involved in selecting may not care at all about the specific variables that contribute to the prediction. Rather, they are willing to use those variables in the aggregate (i.e., put them all in the equation as predictors) and try to maximize variance accounted for in predicting success or retention and minimize imprecision.

Regression for prediction does *not* provide logic consistent with SEM approaches. Rather, for this class of uses, SEM adds nothing important or even of value. Therefore, such problems fall at best at the periphery of the issues and problems covered in this book.

By contrast, the second set of uses of regression in which the particular predictors and their regression weights are of interest, called **regression for explanation** here, define why SEM techniques are so valuable. In such circumstances, the researchers want to know not only how well the predictors explain the criterion variable but also which specific predictors are most important in predicting. To illustrate, imagine a regression model in which the researchers have five predictor variables and a criterion variable. The five predictors likely will have been selected because they are thought to influence the criterion variable, and regression helps disentangle the relative influence of the various predictors.[3] In such a model, what is important is how the approach represents the hypothesized relationships. SEM techniques make use of all the information that is provided by regression techniques and allow the opportunity to consider additional information that helps disentangle possible impacts of various predictors.

Figure 2.1 presents a typical regression model in which the X's are the predictor variables, Y is the criterion variable, the b's are regression coefficients, the residual e is the unexplained variance, and the curved, double-headed arrows connecting the predictor variables represent their intercorrelations. Note that there are 10 intercorrelations that are given much less attention in regression than they deserve (for some statistic packages, even seeing them requires asking for optional output). If the predictor variables were orthogonal (i.e., independent of one another), then the situation would be a simple one and the (standardized) regression coefficients would be the correlations of the predictors with the criterion variable. Typically, however, the predictors are correlated, and the fact that different predictor variables are interrelated is much of what makes multiple regression interesting and leads investigators to want to disentangle the various influences. In such circumstances, the size of the regression coefficients reflects both the size of the correlation of the predictor with the criterion variable and the size of the intercorrelations among the predictor variables. In fact, of the problems in using regression approaches that are discussed later in this book, virtually all are tied to the size of the relationships among the predictor variables.

Consider, for example, an illustration that will be used throughout this book that is concerned about predictors of school achievement. There are many measures that correlate with student achievement including family social class, academic ability, measures of individual differences (e.g., self-concept, anxiety), peer relations, teacher evaluations, and expectations and aspirations of students. The challenge is to sort through the measures and identify those likely to

---

3. As an important aside, it also may be the case that more than one of the five predictors measures the same underlying construct. For example, if researchers believe that self-concept is an important predictor and are concerned that self-concept is difficult to assess accurately, then they might include two or more measures of self-concept as predictors. As will be explained in Chapter 4, such an approach may be self-defeating and misleading because it can underestimate the impact of self-concept.

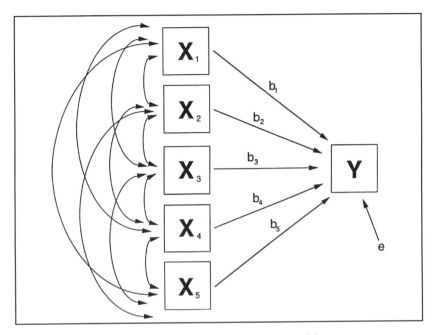

Figure 2.1. Regression Model With Five Predictor Variables

help shape achievement and separate them from ones that merely reflect achievement. What makes the challenge particularly difficult is that the measures tend to be related, which makes the sorting-out process more difficult both logically and methodologically.

As might be anticipated from the preceding example, problems in regression models are more likely to emerge in complex models because as the number of predictor variables increases, the number of intercorrelations increases much more rapidly. Their number can be calculated by using the equation

$$\text{Number of Correlations} = [p(p-1)]/2,$$

where p is the number of predictors. Whereas for two predictors there are twice as many regression coefficients as intercorrelations among predictor variables (2:1), for five variables there are only half as many regression coefficients as intercorrelations among predictor variables (5:10), and the ratio gets smaller as the number of predictors increases.

The point of major importance here is that because a user of regression techniques needs to understand the size and nature of the relationships among the predictor variables, those relationships should be made a visible part of the user's analyses. Doing so brings together regression and path analysis, for Figure 2.1 is a path model. Once regression models are viewed as path analysis models, however, the curved arrow relationships may be thought of somewhat differently. If the researchers who developed a model had ideas about how and why the predictor variables were causally interrelated, they could recast their model to represent some of the predictors as causing or being caused by other predictors. It is important that imposing an order among one's predictor variables *does not change* the *b*'s that appear in the model of Figure 2.1. It just necessitates adding other regression analyses to solve the equations for any predictor variables that are hypothesized as being influenced by other predictor variables.

In summary, then, the point of Figure 2.1 is that regression models in which the significance or nonsignificance of regression coefficients from specific predictors to the criterion variable is of primary importance can benefit by being specified as path models. Presenting them as path models should make researchers more aware of the kinds of problems that limit regression approaches while also encouraging them to formalize the intuitive ideas they may have about how and why their predictor variables are interrelated. Because path analysis models are solved using multiple regression, thinking of regression models as path analytic models should be noncontroversial. Furthermore, because path models and multiple regression provide the core information needed to understand the broad class of SEM, it is only a couple of more logical steps from regression to latent variable SEM.

Chapter 2 has briefly traced the history of SEM. It also has suggested that SEM approaches should be considered whenever researchers are interested in prediction that focuses beyond the variance accounted for (R^2) to the specific regression weights. In those instances, SEM approaches force researchers to articulate their thoughts about relationships of all variables with one another. Once those thoughts are articulated, their plausibility is subject to empirical examination.

Chapter Discussion Questions

1. In path analysis, do you always assume that the data set has been standardized?
2. Should multiple regression always be used to solve for path analysis models? Path analysis does not use any notation to signify partialing, but conceptually will path coefficients be the same as partial regression coefficients?
3. Does path analysis work with longitudinal data?
4. How do we gain a degree of freedom by taking out or leaving out a path? How does that help over-identification? What exactly do degrees of freedom permit researchers to do?
5. How can under-identified models be solved?
6. Do researchers still use path analysis?

Part 2

Basic Approaches to Modeling With Single Observed Measures of Theoretical Variables

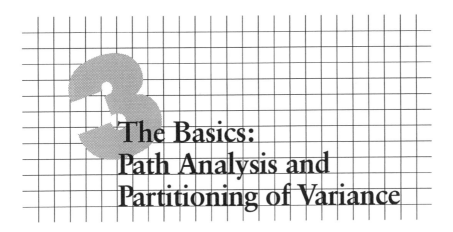

The Basics:
Path Analysis and
Partitioning of Variance

In this chapter, the basic building blocks of structural equation modeling (SEM) are presented. First, an intuitive basis for developing correlation coefficients/covariances is presented. Then notions about breaking those coefficients into "causal" and "noncausal" components are presented, followed by approaches for breaking apart components for a given model. Third, degrees of freedom for structural equation models are discussed. Finally, the formulas for three-variable partial correlation and partial regression are derived from path models to show the links between path models and common partialing techniques.

The discussion at this point focuses on **path analysis** models, which, when the term is used precisely (e.g., Duncan, 1975), are only those models (a) with unidirectional causal flow and (b) in which the measure of each conceptual variable is perfectly reliable. In assuming perfect reliability, path analysis assumes that each conceptual variable is assessed without error by a single measure. There can be no error in measuring each variable (called **measurement error**) or imprecision in operationalizing each variable (called **specification error**). That is, each measure is viewed as an exact manifestation of an underlying theoretical variable. Illustrations of the difficulty of eliminating both measurement error and specification error are provided later in this chapter.

Certainly, within the social sciences, assumptions about perfect reliability must be viewed as generally unrealistic. What social scientist ever has had models in which there is no measurement error and in which all measures perfectly operationalize the conceptual variables that are being assessed? This shortcoming helps explain why path analysis did not become particularly popular in social science research. Nonetheless, a path analysis framework is chosen because the modeling processes described hold true for all types of structural equation models and are most readily illustrated in the relatively simple and straightforward context of path analysis. Furthermore, these limiting assumptions of path analysis also apply to all regression approaches.

The limitations imposed by assumptions about measurement and specification error in path analysis are balanced by other features that make path analytic approaches very appealing. As was argued earlier, an important strength of path analytic models is that they force researchers to articulate the theoretical models that underlie their designs and their thinking. For the discussion in this chapter, however, it is a second and equally important strength of path models that is the focus, namely, the logic developed for attempting to take correlations or covariances and break them apart into causal and noncausal components (called **decomposition of effects**). All of the different structural equation approaches allow for decomposition of effects. The general approaches are presented here as they were developed along with path analysis.

Before discussing decomposition of effects, a basic review of the logic underlying correlations and covariances is presented. Readers comfortable with the logic of correlations/covariances should feel free to skip ahead to the subsequent section of this chapter.

▮ Logic of Correlations and Covariances

Imagine that you know nothing at all about correlational techniques and that you are trying to develop a method for assessing the association between two variables. One logical first step would be to think about what might happen if you multiply each individual's score for the first variable by the score for the second variable and divide the sum of the individual scores by the number of individuals or observations so that sample size does not affect the result. For variables that are associated, small numbers from one variable would be multiplied by small numbers from the other variable, whereas big numbers would be multiplied by other big numbers. For variables that are not associated, small numbers would be as likely to be multiplied by large numbers as by small ones. For variables negatively associated, small numbers on one variable would be more likely to be multiplied by large numbers on the other variable and vice versa. The size of this measure of association would increase from a negative association to no relationship to a positive association.

If one were to calculate such products, then the result, which in fact is called the **cross-product** of the two variables, could provide some information of value, particularly if a number of variables having the same scale are compared. At the same time, a major shortcoming becomes apparent when one attempts to compare cross-products of variables with markedly different means and standard deviations. At that point, it becomes clear that there is no easy intuitive basis for making sense of a cross-product from its size. A second shortcoming of the cross-product is that changes in means of the variables—adding/subtracting a constant to/from a variable's mean (which could in effect be what happens from one sample to another)—changes its cross-product with other variables. Certainly, different magnitude cross-products resulting from mean differences is a result that is not desirable when trying to draw inferences about associations or relationships for a single variable in different groups.

Problems caused by differences in means should not stymie us for long, however, for the solution is suggested by the nature of the problem. A second logical step is to remove the means from the calculations and then take cross-products once again. Removing the means results in the measures of association no longer providing any information about whether or not means differ or change. That consequence has little value insofar as comparisons of means typically are done through *t* tests and analyses of variance rather than through measures of association.[4] These new, "means-removed" cross-products would reflect only the variances around a mean of 0. Removing means

---

4. They also can be analyzed through SEM techniques but are complicated, requiring inputting an augmented moment matrix rather than a covariance or correlation matrix (e.g., Byrne, Shavelson, & Muthen, 1989; Sörbom, 1974, 1982), and will not be covered in any detail in this book.

works, for if we take the adjusted scores and multiply each individual's scores on the first variable by the scores on the second variable, sum those scores, and then divide by the number of individuals, we have the **covariance**. Because both variables have both positive and negative scores (both are centered around 0), the products can have both negative and positive signs. When the variables are unrelated, the sum of the products will approximate 0. For positively related variables, the overall product will be positive due to a preponderance of negative values on one variable being multiplied times negatives on the other and of positive values on one variable being multiplied times positives on the other. For negatively related variables, the overall product will be negative due to a preponderance of positive values on one variable being multiplied times negatives on the other and vice versa.

At this point, we have arrived at the basic building blocks for structural equation approaches. Covariances contain information about both the strength of the association between two measures and their variability for any given sample. At the same time, however, covariances are not ideal for comparing strength of associations between different pairs of variables, for after inspection of a number of covariances it becomes apparent that differences in variances make it difficult to make comparisons about strength of association across pairs of variables. To illustrate, look at a hypothetical covariance matrix that appears in Table 3.1. The goal of the table is to show measures with markedly different standard deviations. For purposes of illustration, imagine that Variable 1 is college grade point average (GPA), Variable 2 is intelligence test performance (IQ), Variable 3 is weight in kilograms (Weight), and Variable 4 is height in meters (Height). Hopefully, the respective standard deviations of 1.0, 15.0, 10.0, and 0.3, although "guesstimates," are reasonable. So, which pair of variables has the strongest relationship? In fact, if my calculations are correct, the variables all have the exact same magnitude standardized relationship, yet direct comparison of them is difficult.

To make relationships between different pairs of variables more readily comparable, a third step is possible and, for many purposes, is valuable. That step is to remove the differences in variances to facilitate direct comparison of different relationships by putting them all on a common scale. The differences in variances can be eliminated by giving all variables a common variance by rescaling them. Practi-

TABLE 3.1 Illustrative Covariance Matrix

	Grade Point Average	IQ Test Score	Weight (kilograms)	Height (meters)
	(1)	(2)	(3)	(4)
1. Grade Point Average	1.0			
2. IQ Test Score	7.5	225.0		
3. Weight (kilograms)	5.0	75.0	100.0	
4. Height (meters)	0.15	2.25	1.50	0.09
Standard deviation	1.0	15.0	10.0	0.3

NOTE: Grade Point Average assumes a range from 0 (F) to 4 (A). IQ Test Score has a normed mean of 100 and a standard deviation of 15.

cally, that is done by dividing each variance by some value that results in all the variances ending up with the same scale. To complete the rescaling, each covariance between two variables is divided by the product of the square roots of the values used for rescaling the variances of those two variables. Imposing a single common variance or scale makes relationships between different variables easy to compare; the ones with larger values have stronger relationships.

So long as a "common variance" is being arbitrarily selected for rescaling, one that maximizes simplicity and ease of interpretation should be selected. The best choice is to select the value 1 for the rescaled variance. Each variance is divided by itself, and each covariance is divided by the square root of the variance (the standard deviation). The result is that all relationships range between −1 (a perfect negative relationship) and +1 (a perfect positive relationship), and the square of the relationship represents the amount of variance that is shared between two variables. Said differently, choosing a rescaled variance of 1 expresses the relationships as **correlations** and optimizes comparison of relationships with one another. *To repeat, to change variances/covariances to correlations, divide each variance by itself and each covariance by the standard deviations (i.e., the square root of the variance) of the two variables that covary. To go the other way, from correlations to covariances, multiply the correlations times the product of the two appropriate standard deviations.*

EXERCISE

If the rescaling is imposed on the illustration in Table 3.1, then what is the common correlation between the pairs of variables? Do the calculations as described in the preceding paragraphs. (The correct answer appears at the end of the next paragraph.)

The final point of this section is that even though correlations are very appealing and were the building blocks for path analysis, they are not the ideal measure of association for many situations. As noted earlier in this chapter, covariances contain information both about the relationship between two variables and about the variability of each variable in the sample of interest, and this makes variance/ covariance matrices optimal for SEM. Despite the fact that correlations and covariances are just simple linear transformations of one another, they contain very different information. Correlations have given up the information from a sample about its variability. For comparisons of relationships across samples, across groups (e.g., comparing relationships between variables in a male sample with those in a female sample), or across time in a single longitudinal sample, correlations do not allow researchers to assess the extent to which the relationships reflect commonalities/differences in strength of association versus differences in variances. Because correlations do not allow for changes/differences in variances, only if variances are equal across samples/groups/times is it appropriate to compare correlations.[5] (The answer to the question in the exercise preceding this paragraph is $r = .50$.)

Although the difference between correlations and covariances often is a difficult one for readers to understand, one way in which to view it is to think about it in its extreme, namely, in situations where restriction of range in a variable attenuates its correlation with other variables. Imagine a sample in which there is almost no variability on a measure of interest. For example, think about trying to assess

---

5. Finally, although premature for the present discussion, it is important to note that for some of the estimation techniques described later in this book, the methods are worked out for covariances but not correlations and may produce problems if correlation matrices are analyzed (e.g., Cudeck, 1989).

relations of achievement scores with other variables for a sample selected because of the low achievement of its members. In such circumstances, correlations of achievement with other variables are greatly attenuated. In contrast to the correlation coefficient, the covariance, although still affected, should nevertheless capture the correspondence of that variable with other variables in raw score terms, that is, preserving the effects of the relationship of a raw score unit of change in one variable with some unit of change on the second.

A different instance can be illustrated by considering a case in which a researcher has given a sample a test that turned out to be so difficult or easy that virtually all the scores clustered together; there is little discrimination between many individuals who actually have differing levels of skill. In this instance, the covariance still is preferred, but it is limited by inappropriateness of the measure for assessing the underlying continuum of abilities of the particular sample of respondents.

▌ Decomposing Relationships Between Variables Into Causal and Noncausal Components

As suggested several times previously in this book, the principles underlying decomposition of effects are both the major strength of path analytic approaches and essential for understanding the class of approaches called structural equation modeling or SEM. The appeal of path analysis is its capacity to talk about indirect effects or noncausal relationships. For example, a strong association between two variables indicates nothing about the nature of the relationship. For a given model, however, one can talk about the amount of the association that is specified as causal and the amount that is specified as noncausal. The caveat, of course, is that unless the relationships between variables all are correctly specified and the measures perfectly assess the underlying theoretical variables, the division of variance into causal and noncausal will be imprecise and perhaps even wrong. In other words, for this section, **causal** should be read as if it is surrounded by quotation marks ("causal"), for causal means that *if* the model is true and *if* the theoretical variables are perfectly operationalized, *then* the relationships are as specified in the model. At the same time, however, it is important to remember that the consequences of models are assessed in part by the way in which they specify or hypothesize impacts of variables on other variables.

For any model, the relationships between variables can be decomposed into causal effects and noncausal relationships by using the logic introduced by path analysis. Furthermore, within causal and noncausal, the effects can be broken down even more. For causal effects, there are effects that go directly from one variable to a second variable (**direct effects**) and effects between two variables that are mediated by one or more intervening variables (**indirect effects**). For noncausal relationships, there are relationships between two variables that occur (a) because both are caused by a third variable (these are referred to as noncausal reflecting common causes or **noncausal due to shared antecedents**) and (b) because in models with more than one independent variable there can be relationships among them in which cause and effect are not theoretically articulated (often called **unanalyzed prior associations**). If all independent variables in a model are unrelated to one another, then there is no variability of this type. It is more common, however, to find models in which the independent variables are background types of variables where cause and effect among those variables cannot readily be specified. Relationships going through those associations are called **unanalyzed prior associations** because the model does not attempt to assign cause and effect (nature of relationship unanalyzed) and/or because the associations are due to processes that occur earlier than (prior to) the relationships on which the model focuses. Figure 3.1 illustrates the different types of associations.

Figure 3.2 provides a path analysis model that can be used to illustrate decomposition of effects. The model employs fairly standard path analytic notation. (A summary of general path notation appears in Appendix 3.1 at the end of this chapter.) Each variable is contained within a box. Straight lines with arrowheads at only one end indicate hypothesized causal influences between variables, from cause to effect. Each direct influence has a corresponding path coefficient, a "p" with two subscripts, the first for the variable affected (the effect) and the second for the determining or causal variable (the predictor). Curved, double-headed arrows indicate relationships whose causal dynamics are not of interest. Such arrows are used when relationships are not well understood, cannot be specified readily, occur prior to the processes in the model, or are unimportant to the

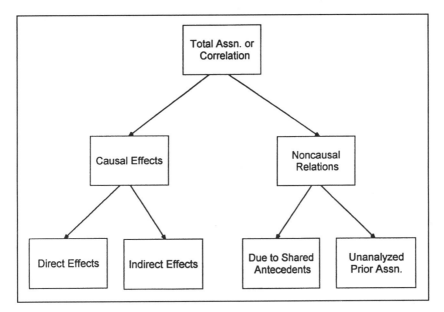

Figure 3.1. Decomposition of Effects

model. Straight-line arrows from "variables" with no boxes around them indicate residual influences, namely, all other influences not specified by the model. (For path analysis, which typically works with standardized coefficients, they are the traditional residual, $1 - R^2$, from regression analyses. More generally, they are total variance minus explained variance.) Note that only variables with arrowheads pointing to them have residuals. In the model, such variables are "dependent" (often called **endogenous variables**). X_3, X_4, and X_5 in Figure 3.2 are endogenous variables. Variables with no causal arrows pointing toward them (remember, the curved, double-headed arrows are not causal) are called independent or **exogenous variables**. X_1 and X_2 in Figure 3.2 are exogenous variables. If X_1 and X_2 were not related, then the double-headed curved arrow would be eliminated from the model; removing that path would not affect their status as exogenous variables. Keeping with traditional path modeling approaches, causality flows from left to right in the diagram. Because X_1 and X_2 are exogenous and have no causes, they do not need to have a residual specified; all of their variance is unexplained, and their residual is the same as their variance.

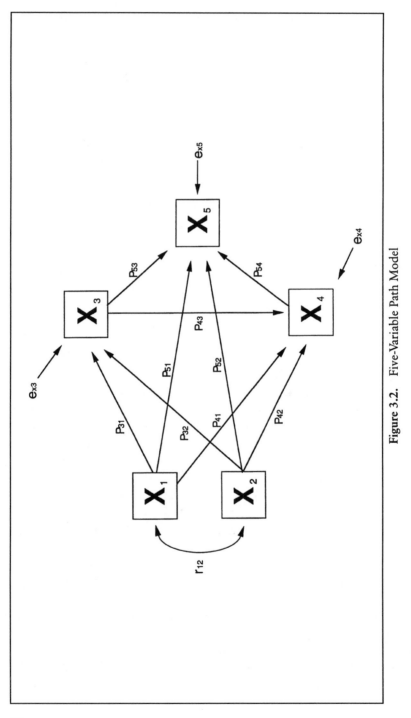

Figure 3.2. Five-Variable Path Model

▌ *Direct Causal Effects*

The model contains a number of relationships specified as direct causal effects (e.g., the path from X_1 to X_3). These paths go from one box to another and have arrowheads at only one end.

EXERCISE

Before going on, readers unsure about their level of under-standing should count the number of direct causal effects. How many are there? (The correct answer appears at the end of the next paragraph.)

In path models, the direct effects are estimated via least squares (sometimes called **ordinary least squares** or **OLS**) regression ap-proaches. Each of the endogenous variables needs to be thought of as having its own regression equation describing the structure of the relationships between variables, that is, **structural equations** (each regression equation is a structural equation). To solve for the direct paths, regress each endogenous or dependent variable *on the variables with direct paths to it.* For example, regress X_5 on X_1, X_2, X_3, and X_4 to solve for the direct effects to X_5. For models like the present one, which has exactly the same number of paths as pieces of information to use to estimate those paths and therefore is "just-identified," regression is one of a number of ways of getting to the same solution. In Chapter 2, identification was introduced. If there are more paths than pieces of information (i.e., underidentification), then no unique solution is possible. For models with the same amount of information as paths, all ways of solving the model (e.g., algebra, regression) provide the same solution. For overidentified path analysis models with more information than paths to estimate, regression provides optimal estimates. (**The answer to the question in the exercise pre-ceding this paragraph is 9, or all the arrows with *p*'s attached to them.**)

The regression equations for Figure 3.2, which provide the direct effects, are as follows:

$$X_3 = p_{31}X_1 + p_{32}X_2 + e_3 \qquad\qquad (3.1)$$
$$X_4 = p_{41}X_1 + p_{42}X_2 + p_{43}X_3 + e_4 \qquad\qquad (3.2)$$
$$X_5 = p_{51}X_1 + p_{52}X_2 + p_{53}X_3 + p_{54}X_4 + e_5 \qquad (3.3)$$

Note that there are nine paths: the nine direct effects.

▌ Indirect Causal Effects

Indirect causal effects occur in path models when one variable causes a second, which in turn causes a third. In such circumstances, the first variable exerts influence on the third via the second regardless of whether it has a path directly to the third variable. One might think of dominoes, where the first domino knocks down the second, which in turn knocks down the third. The first domino indirectly affects the third regardless of whether it directly comes in contact with the third domino.

Indirect effects do not add paths to path diagrams and do not "take up" degrees of freedom as do path coefficients. In path models, indirect effects are indicated by two or more direct effect arrows in combination linking two variables (see, e.g., Baron & Kenny [1986], for a discussion of mediation). Thus, X_1 and X_2 have indirect effects on both X_4 and X_5. Their indirect effects on X_4 occur through X_3, whereas their indirect effects on X_5 occur through X_3, through X_4, and through X_3 and X_4 combined.

Once one understands the logic of indirect effects, the remaining issue is the mechanics. That is, how does one calculate the magnitude of those effects? The answer is that for each indirect pathway linking two variables, the magnitude of that pathway is estimated by multiplying together the path coefficients along that pathway. Said differently, the paths combine multiplicatively to determine the magnitude of the indirect effects, or *each indirect effect is the product of the path coefficients that provide the pathway between the two variables that are causally related.* To determine the total indirect effect between two variables, the individual indirect effects from the various pathways are summed. That is, *the total indirect effect between two variables is the sum of the products taken in determining each individual indirect effect.*

To illustrate both individual indirect and total effects between two variables, return to Figure 3.2. In that model, X_1 causes X_5 indirectly through X_3, and the magnitude is the product of the paths from X_1 to

X_3 and from X_3 to X_5, namely, $p_{53} \times p_{31}$. Similarly, X_1 causes X_5 through X_4, and the magnitude of that relationship is $p_{54} \times p_{41}$; through both X_3 and X_4, the magnitude is $(p_{54} \times p_{43} \times p_{31})$. The total indirect effect of X_1 on X_5, according to the model, is the sum of the different indirect effects, namely, $(p_{53} \times p_{31}) + (p_{54} \times p_{41}) + (p_{54} \times p_{43} \times p_{31})$. In large models, indirect effects can include many intervening variables, and total indirect effects can consist of the sum of a large number of terms. Note finally that even without a direct effect, path p_{51}, X_1 still "causes" X_5 in the model. Thus, in contrast to multiple regression in which only the direct paths are examined, in path models the absence of a direct causal path does *not* mean that a variable is an unimportant predictor of a particular dependent variable.

Noncausal Relationships Due to Shared Antecedents

The focus now shifts to the relationships that can be called spurious. These relationships are the parts of the correlations/covariances that are, according to the model, not causal. Although two different types are described in this chapter, it is worth noting that most computer programs focus on the causal rather than the noncausal effects, with the result that noncausal effects are most commonly looked at as the difference between the total association (correlation or covariance) and the total causal effects. That is, they are total association minus total causal effects.

The first type of noncausal relationships to be discussed are relationships that reflect influences due to one or more causes that two endogenous variables share *in common*. Look again at Figure 3.2, focusing on Variables X_3 and X_4. Note that both X_3 and X_4 are caused by X_1 and also by X_2; they have two sources of noncausal relationships due to shared antecedent relationships. Part of the correlation between X_3 and X_4 occurs because they both are caused by X_1; another part occurs because they both are caused by X_2.

Although the relationship between X_4 and X_5 looks as though it might be similar to that between X_3 and X_4, the presence of an additional intervening variable (X_3) makes it much more complex. In the same figure, the X_4 with X_5 relationship reflects common causes X_1, X_2, and X_3, so there will be components paralleling the relationship between X_3 and X_4, namely, from X_5 to each of the variables X_1, X_2, X_3 to X_4, plus common causes from X_1 **through** X_3 (because X_1 causes both X_4 and X_5, one part of the relationship goes from X_5 back to X_1, then to X_3, and on to X_4, and a second part goes from X_4 back to X_1, then to X_3, and on to X_5) and X_2 **through** X_3 (similarly, one part of the relationship goes from X_5 back to X_2, then to X_3, and on to X_4, and a second part goes from X_4 back to X_2, then to X_3, and on to X_5). Readers should note that, in Figure 3.2, even though the X_5 to X_1 to X_4 relationship is the same as the X_4 to X_1 to X_5 relationship, the same cannot be said for the X_5 to X_1 to X_3 to X_4 relationship versus the X_4 to X_1 to X_3 to X_5 relationship. They are different because they involve different path coefficients. (For readers uncertain whether they understand these last points, tracing the paths for themselves from the figure is highly recommended.)

In the illustrations of shared antecedent or common cause relationships, the causal impact according to the model is attributed to the common cause and therefore cannot also be viewed as representing a causal relationship in which either of the endogenous variables is causally preponderant. In other words, the relationships between X_3 and X_4 that reflect their common causes X_1 and X_2 are attributed causally to X_1 and X_2 in the relationships of those variables with X_3 and X_4. In this instance, however, the relationship that is being examined is the one between X_3 and X_4, and the part of their relationship attributable to X_1 and X_2 does not reflect any causal relationship of one with the other. Note that this does not imply that they are causally unrelated, for the model specifies that X_3 causes X_4, and that path is a causal (direct) one. Rather, it signifies that their relationship, according to the model, can be divided into causal and noncausal components and that shared antecedent relationships are one type of noncausal relationship.

▌ Noncausal Unanalyzed Prior Association Relationships

This second type of noncausal relationship is used to describe relationships that pass through the double-headed curved arrows in models. Thus, if a model has uncorrelated exogenous variables or only a single exogenous variable, then there will be no variance component of this type. Because, in Figure 3.2, X_1 and X_2 are related and the causal nature of their relationship is unanalyzed (e.g., in a model of status attainment, we might decide that we cannot specify cause and effect between the **social class of the family** and the **ability**

of the child and thus make the relationship noncausal), variability that flows through their association cannot be viewed as causal because the model does not specify either variable as causally preponderant. Note that if two exogenous variables are highly correlated, this variance component gets relatively large, and this is not particularly desirable for decomposing effects. (There are more severe problems created by strong associations between predictor variables called multicollinearity; they will be discussed in Chapter 4.)

The curved arrow association between exogenous variables also results in unanalyzed prior association relationships between exogenous and endogenous variables and between pairs of endogenous variables. These again can be illustrated through Figure 3.2. First, all of the relationship between X_1 and X_2 is classified as noncausal, unanalyzed prior association. For all other relationships involving X_1 or X_2, a part of the association is of the same type. For example, X_1 is related to X_3 through its association with X_2 and X_2's effect on X_3. Similarly, part of the X_4-X_5 relationship comes because X_1 causes X_5, X_2 causes X_4, and X_1 and X_2 are related, and another part comes because X_1 causes X_4, X_2 causes X_5, and X_1 and X_2 are related. And we could go on and specify noncausal due to unanalyzed prior association parts of relationships between any other pair of variables in this model.

At this point, it is hoped that readers will feel as though they have some basic understanding of the various components of variance and which parts of various relationships fall under which categories. At the same time, because the previous section worked by example rather than by principles or methods that would allow the model to pull apart each of the relationships, no means have been provided for fully dividing a model into direct causal, indirect causal, and noncausal relationships. (Common questions might well include "How many causal components should I be finding?" and "How will I know if I have them all?") This shortcoming is addressed in the next section of this chapter.

One final point before turning to those approaches is that only for just-identified models and overidentified models that perfectly fit the observed data will the decomposition of effects perfectly divide the covariances/correlations into their components. For most instances in which there are degrees of freedom in the model, there will be discrepancies between the data and the values predicted by combining the causal and noncausal relationships predicted by the model.

In structural models, it is the size of the discrepancies (i.e., the mismatch between the relationships that actually are found and those predicted by the model) that allows models to be tested for adequacy. As noted in Chapter 1 (e.g., in Exercise 1.1, the "mismatch" there for each model is the difference between one correlation and the product of two others and is used to test the plausibility of the model), lack of fit allows models to be disconfirmed and rejected. Because the relationships predicted in any model include all the causal and noncausal variance components, the test of fit for a model is not one of how well the predictors explain the dependent or endogenous variables but rather of how well the entire model fits the data. Fit tests, called **fit indexes**, are a crucial part of structural equation approaches, and an entire chapter later in this book is devoted to them. The difference between model fit and prediction of dependent variables is an important distinction to make. A well-fitting model could do a poor job of predicting (accounting for variability in) the dependent variables in cases where the relationships between predictors and dependent variables are small. By contrast, a poorly fitting model could explain almost all the variability of each of the dependent variables. There is substantial diagreement among SEM researchers about how much one should focus on variability accounted for versus overall model fit.

▮ Approaches for Decomposing Effects

There are a number of different ways of fully decomposing effects. Some approaches yield only numerical values for total direct and indirect effects. Others allow calculation of each contributor to each effect and then require summing the various components to determine total effects. Some focus almost exclusively on causal effects. All provide direct effects because those are the path coefficients. Before presenting the approaches that I personally find most helpful and accessible, it is worth noting that many of the widely used structural equation programs provide indirect effects as either standard or optional output. They all should do so, for calculation of indirect effects is computationally simple for programs that work with matrices of parameter estimates. Because some programs provide indirect effects, it should be only a matter of time before they all include indirect effects.

I have chosen to begin with what are called the rules for tracing paths. The strength of this approach is that it provides logic that meshes well with what has been presented so far. The shortcoming is that, for complex models, it is easy to omit variance components and therefore to misestimate total effects. Although the rules have been presented in many alternative forms, I present them in a form that I find most intuitive.

First, select the pair of variables whose relationship in a model is to be decomposed. For each tracing, begin at one variable and go through paths and variables to the other.

1. If one causes the other, then always start with the one that is the effect. If they are not directly causally related, then the starting point is arbitrary. But once a start variable is selected, always start there.

2. Start against an arrow (go from effect to cause). Remember, the goal at this point is to go from the start variable to the other variable.

3. Each particular tracing of paths between the two variables can go through only one noncausal (curved, double-headed) path (relevant only when there are three or more exogenous variables and two or more curved, double-headed arrows).

4. For each particular tracing of paths, any intermediate variable can be included only once.

5. The tracing can go back against paths (from effect to cause) for as far as possible, but, regardless of how far back, once the tracing goes forward causally (i.e., with an arrow from cause to effect), it cannot turn back against an arrow.

Figure 3.2 can be used to illustrate the tracing rules. Take, for example, the relationship between X_3 and X_4. Always begin with X_4, for that is the effect (Rule 1). The paths are (a) X_4 to its cause X_3, or p_{43}; (b) X_4 to its cause X_1 and then (with an arrow) to X_3, or $(p_{41} \times p_{31})$; (c) X_4 to its cause X_2 and to X_3, or $(p_{42} \times p_{32})$; (d) X_4 to its cause X_1 through a noncausal path to X_2 and to X_3, or $(p_{41} \times r_{12} \times p_{32})$; and (e) X_4 to its cause X_2 through a noncausal path to X_1 and to X_3, or $(p_{42} \times r_{12} \times p_{31})$. Note that, first, as mentioned earlier, the effects are each the products of the various paths; second, each tracing goes through other variables only once (Rule 3); and, third, X_5 never is included in the decomposition because it is causally "downstream" and irrelevant. Attempting to include it violates Rule 5, for it would require going against a path (from effect to cause) after going with a path (from cause to effect). Note also that there are no indirect effects (X_3 does not cause X_4 through any intervening variable). Finally, as illustrated in Table 3.2, *Term (a) is the direct effect* and also total causal effect, *Terms (b) and (c) are noncausal due to shared antecedent* effects, and *Terms (d) and (e) are unanalyzed prior association* noncausal effects. The total noncausal effect is the sum of Terms (b), (c), (d), and (e). As mentioned earlier, the risk in the approach comes from missing one or more paths in complex models.

A second approach to decomposing effects, often called Duncan's rule (Duncan, 1966, 1975), employs the formula

$$r_{ij} = \Sigma_q\, p_{iq}\, r_{jq}, \tag{3.4}$$

where i and j are variables in the model ($i > j$) and q is an index over all variables with direct paths to i and j.

Looking at the relationship between X_3 (j) and X_4 (i) in Figure 3.2, plugging numbers into the formula gives the equation $r_{43} = (p_{41} \times r_{31})$ + $(p_{42} \times r_{32})$ + $(p_{43} \times r_{33})$. To make the equation look like the components from the tracing rules, we also need to solve for r_{31} and r_{32} ($r_{33} = 1.0$ and therefore disappears):

$$r_{31} = (p_{31} \times r_{11}) + (p_{32} \times r_{12}) = p_{31} + (p_{32} \times r_{12}) \text{ and}$$
$$r_{32} = (p_{31} \times r_{12}) + (p_{32} \times r_{22}) = (p_{31} \times r_{12}) + p_{32}.$$

Because r_{12} is a noncausal relationship between two exogenous variables, it cannot be decomposed. Through substitution,

$$\begin{aligned} r_{43} &= p_{41}\,(p^{31} + p_{32} \times r_{12}) + p_{42}\,(p_{31} \times r_{12} + p_{32}) + p_{43} \text{ or} \\ &= (p_{41} \times p_{31}) + (p_{41} \times r_{12} \times p_{32}) + (p_{42} \times r_{12} \times p_{31}) + \\ &\quad (p_{42} \times p_{32}) + p_{43}. \end{aligned} \tag{3.5}$$

Stated as the five variance components in the preceding and in Table 3.2, the terms are

$$r_{43} = (b) + (d) + (e) + (c) + (a).$$

As can be seen, the two approaches yield an identical result.

At this point, it may seem that there is not an easy way in which to decompose effects. If, however, one knows matrix algebra and can

TABLE 3.2 Decomposition of Effects for the Relation Between X_3 and X_4 for the Model in Figure 3.2

	Causal Effect	Noncausal Relationship	
	Direct	*Shared Antecedent*	*Unanalyzed Prior Association*
(a)	p_{43}		
(b)		$(p_{41} \times p_{31})$	
(c)		$(p_{42} \times p_{32})$	
(d)			$(p_{41} \times r_{12} \times p_{32})$
(e)			$(p_{42} \times r_{12} \times p_{31})$

do matrix multiplication, there is a method for disentangling causal effects (direct and indirect) that requires only setting up a matrix of path coefficients and then multiplying that matrix by itself. This approach is illustrated in Table 3.3. (Appendix 3.1 provides an introduction to matrix algebra.)

As can be seen from Table 3.3, for Matrix A, the path coefficients are set up so that the predictor variables define the columns and the dependent variables define the rows. The form is like the equations except that the variables are removed. Exogenous variables have only 0's in their rows. Endogenous variables have the coefficients of the paths to them, aligned according to predictor variables. Matrix $(A \times A)$ contains all first-order indirect effects, namely, effects with one intervening variable. Matrix $(A \times A \times A)$ contains all second-order indirect effects, namely, those with two intervening variables. Because there are only three endogenous variables in the model of Figure 3.2, no indirect effect can have more than two intervening variables, and Matrix $(A \times A \times A \times A)$ is null, as would be found if $(A \times A \times A)$ were multiplied by A. If the numerical values of the paths for a particular data set are put into Matrix A rather than the symbols for the paths, the resulting numbers will reflect the sum of the various coefficients. Total indirect effects for this model can be calculated by adding together the $(A \times A)$ and $(A \times A \times A)$ matrices; if their sum is added to A, which is the direct effects, then the result is the total causal effects for all relationships in the model. The difference between the total effects $(A + [A \times A] + [A \times A \times A])$ and the observed data matrix is the total of the noncausal effects.

TABLE 3.3 Illustration of Matrix Approach to Decomposing Effects

Variable	X_1	X_2	X_3	X_4	X_5
Matrix of path coefficients (A)					
X_1	0	0	0	0	0
X_2	0	0	0	0	0
X_3	p_{31}	p_{32}	0	0	0
X_4	p_{41}	p_{42}	p_{43}	0	0
X_5	p_{51}	p_{52}	p_{53}	p_{54}	0
Matrix of path coefficients multiplied by itself ($A \times A$)					
X_1	0	0	0	0	0
X_2	0	0	0	0	0
X_3	0	0	0	0	0
X_4	$(p_{43} \times p_{31})$	$(p_{43} \times p_{32})$	0	0	0
X_5	$[(p_{53} \times p_{31}) +$ $(p_{54} \times p_{41})]$	$[(p_{53} \times p_{32}) +$ $(p_{54} \times p_{42})]$	$(p_{54} \times p_{43})$	0	0
Matrix A multiplied by Matrix ($A \times A$) = ($A \times A \times A$)					
X_1	0	0	0	0	0
X_2	0	0	0	0	0
X_3	0	0	0	0	0
X_4	0	0	0	0	0
X_5	$[p_{54}(p_{43} \times p_{31})]$	$[p_{54}(p_{43} \times p_{32})]$	0	0	0

NOTE: The next order matrix product ($A \times A \times A \times A$) is a null matrix for Figure 3.2. The total effects are the sum of the three matrices A, ($A \times A$), and ($A \times A \times A$); the direct effects are A, and the indirect effects are the sum of the matrices ($A \times A$) and ($A \times A \times A$).

▌Determining Degrees of Freedom of Models

As noted in an earlier chapter, to estimate a solution to a model, all parameters to be estimated need to have unique estimates. For path analysis models (which deal with standardized relationships), the information used to estimate paths is the correlations of the variables with one another. Said differently, the correlations are the "knowns" in path analysis, whereas the path coefficients to be estimated are the "unknowns." Therefore, any path analysis model has as its maximum number of degrees of freedom its correlations. Of course, if a model had that maximum number of degrees of freedom, then it also would contain no paths between its variables. Thus, the number of degrees of freedom typically will be substantially less than the maximum possible, for there will be a number of paths of interest in most models.

The number of correlations of a given model can be calculated by using the formula

$$\text{Number of Correlations} = v(v - 1) / 2, \qquad (3.6)$$

where v is the number of variables in the model. For example, Figure 3.2, with its five variables, has $5 \times 4 / 2 = 10$ correlations. No model with five variables could have more than 10 degrees of freedom. The actual degrees of freedom of any model is determined by subtracting the number of coefficients to be estimated from the maximum number of degrees of freedom. For the current example (Figure 3.2), if one adds up the paths to be estimated between variables, then the total also is 10, which means that the model has no degrees of freedom $(10 - 10 = 0)$ or is just-identified. As noted earlier in this chapter, for just-identified models, solving using regression provides the same solution as does solving using possible alternatives (e.g., solving a system of simultaneous equations with 10 equations and 10 unknowns). If one or more paths from Figure 3.2 were dropped, then the model would be overidentified and have degrees of freedom; in such instances, different solutions may diverge, and regression approaches provide the "best" way of estimating the paths (e.g., Land, 1969). Finally, because all path analysis models can have no covariation among residuals and have a unidirectional causal flow, they always are identified.

Presenting Partial Regression and Partial Correlation as Path Models

Partial Regression

Figure 3.3 provides diagrams representing partial regression and partial correlation. Inspection of the partial regression model should help remind readers that path analysis employs partial regression approaches for its solutions; the partial regression model is just a basic path model. The path p_{31}, which also is $B_{31.2}$, is used to illustrate how the partial regression formula can be derived from the path model.

Using the tracing rules described earlier in this chapter, the relationship between X_1 and X_3 is

$$r_{31} = p_{31} + p_{32} \times r_{21}. \tag{3.7}$$

Because this equation provides us with only a single equation in two unknowns, a second equation is needed to solve for the path p_{31}. The relationship between X_2 and X_3 is used:

$$r_{32} = p_{31} \times r_{21} + p_{32}, \tag{3.8}$$

yielding two equations in two unknowns (the p's), which allows finding a solution. Now, if the second equation is expressed in terms of p_{32}, then it is

$$p_{32} = r_{32} - p_{31} \times r_{21}. \tag{3.9}$$

Then, substituting for p_{32} in Equation 3.7,

$$r_{31} = p_{31} + (r_{32} - p_{31} \times r_{21}) \times r_{21}.$$

Then, rearranging terms,

$$r_{31} = p_{31} + r_{32} \times r_{21} - p_{31} \times r_{21} \times r_{21},$$

and combining,

$$r_{31} = p_{31} (1 - r_{21}^2) + r_{32} \times r_{21}. \tag{3.10}$$

Finally, expressing the equation in terms of p_{31},

$$p_{31} (1 - r_{21}^2) = r_{31} - r_{32} \times r_{21} \text{ and}$$
$$p_{31} = (r_{31} - r_{32} \times r_{21}) / (1 - r_{21}^2), \tag{3.11}$$

which is the traditional formula for partial regression ($B_{31.2}$).

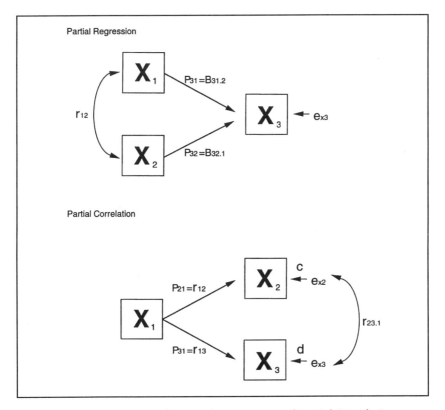

Figure 3.3. Path Diagrams for Partial Regression and Partial Correlation

Partial Correlation

The lower part of Figure 3.3 contains a diagram for partial correlation. In this instance, the relationship to solve for in terms of observed correlations is the one between the error terms e_{X2} and e_{X3}. To make the model fit basic path rules and the residual path a correlation (we are, after all, trying to solve for a partial correlation), the residuals are made standardized variables, and so paths need to be added between the errors and X_2 and X_3. Those paths, specified in the diagram as the coefficients c and d, are used to represent the relationship between the residuals and the endogenous variables. Those paths are not really unknowns to estimate, for they represent the unexplained variance (which, for any variable, is $1 - R^2$). Because the paths squared need to equal the unexplained variance, they are the square root of that variance; $c^2 = (1 - r_{12}^2)$, so $c = \mathrm{sqrt}(1 - r_{12}^2)$, and $d^2 = (1 - r_{13}^2)$, so $d = \mathrm{sqrt}(1 - r_{13}^2)$.

Using the rules for tracing paths (readers should note from this illustration that the tracing rules work for path models that are not path analysis models), the relationship between X_2 and X_3 is

$$r_{32} = p_{21} \times p_{31} + c \times r_{23.1} \times d. \tag{3.12}$$

Initially, this may seem like one equation with four unknowns. But we can substitute in the correlations where they are equal to paths. First, the two paths p_{21} and p_{31} are simple regression coefficients, which, in the standardized case, are correlations, namely, $r_{12} = p_{21}$ and $r_{13} = p_{31}$. Furthermore, as explained in the preceding section, $c = \mathrm{sqrt}(1 - r_{12}^2)$ and $d = \mathrm{sqrt}(1 - r_{13}^2)$. Thus, the equation becomes

$$r_{32} = r_{12} \times r_{13} + \mathrm{sqrt}(1 - r_{12}^2) \times r_{23.1} \times \mathrm{sqrt}(1 - r_{13}^2). \tag{3.13}$$

Solving for the partial correlation $(r_{23.1})$, the equation becomes

$$r_{23.1} \times \mathrm{sqrt}(1 - r_{12}^2) \times \mathrm{sqrt}(1 - r_{13}^2) = r_{32} - r_{12} \times r_{13},$$

which, specified differently, is

$$r_{23.1} = (r_{32} - r_{12} \times r_{13}) \, / \, \mathrm{sqrt}(1 - r_{12}^2) \times \mathrm{sqrt}(1 - r_{13}^2), \tag{3.14}$$

finally coming in Equation 3.14 to the traditional formula for partial correlation. The logic of the formula is fairly straightforward; it takes out the effects of a control variable from the relationship between the two variables whose partial is of interest $(r_{32} - r_{12} \times r_{13})$ and then adjusts the residual variables back to unit variance by dividing the resulting covariance by the standard deviations of the residuals ($\mathrm{sqrt}[1 - r_{12}^2]$ and $\mathrm{sqrt}[1 - r_{13}^2]$). One additional point related to generalizability of the formula is that higher order partials can be viewed as partials of partials; they can be extracted using the derived formula repeatedly to eliminate effects of various variables.

Finally, although it is not apparent from the examples because the same variables were not used for the two different types of partials, in fact the numerators of partial correlation and partial regression are identical. As will be illustrated in an exercise at the end of Chapter 4, however, partial correlation and partial regression coefficients usually are not the same, even when the same variables are partialed.

▌Peer Popularity and Academic Achievement: An Illustration

Throughout this book, I will try to employ a single data set using a variety of techniques ranging from path analysis, to panel analysis, to confirmatory factor analysis, to latent variable SEM. The data set I use addresses the issues presented in Figure 1.1, exploring the relationships between peer acceptance and achievement. The matrix used for the analyses appears later in Table 9.3. In practice, the sample size for the different analyses would likely vary from analysis to analysis because selecting different variables in different models would result in different sample sizes due to missing data. In these examples, however, a common matrix will be used for all analyses and a common sample size of 100. Because I am working from matrices that have precision well beyond the two or three digits that appear in the text, replication may not produce identical solutions to what I report.

The core question is the relation between acceptance by peers and academic achievement. That question will be looked at with single measures of each conceptual variable, both cross-sectionally (path analysis) and longitudinally (panel analysis). Then it will be addressed again using multiple measures of each conceptual variable (latent variable SEM). First, the relationships (correlations) among the latent variables will be examined through confirmatory factor analysis. Then, causal relationships among variables will be modeled. For all illustrations, the data will be analyzed using SEM programs, with other approaches used as well to show their equivalence.

For this chapter, the illustration focuses on path analysis.

Illustration 1:   Cross-Sectional Path Analysis

This model looks at the variables from Figure 9.2 but looks like Figure 3.2 with one exception, namely, that path p_{54} is set to 0 (i.e., omitted). The model is specified for path analysis; namely, it is recursive and has only a single measure of each theoretical variable. Prior information was used to select the "best" indicator of each theoretical variable for the path analysis, namely, the

Duncan SEI as the measure of Family Social Class (Duncan), the Peabody PVT as Academic Ability (Peabody), a semantic differential scale score of teacher's evaluation of each child (TchrEval), classroom seating choices by peer nominations for peer popularity (PeerPop), and performance on a standardized verbal achievement test as the measure of school achievement (VerbAch). Consistent with Figure 3.2, Duncan and Peabody are specified to be exogenous and are correlated, and each has direct paths to all three other variables. TchrEval has direct paths to PeerPop and VerbAch. Finally, PeerPop and VerbAch are not viewed as causally related, giving the model a degree of freedom, making it overidentified. The matrix is as follows:

Matrix to Be Analyzed

	Duncan	Peabody	TchrEval	PeerPop	VerbAch
Duncan	1.00				
Peabody	.01	1.00			
TchrEval	−.12	.24	1.00		
PeerPop	.04	.16	.17	1.00	
VerbAch	.09	.31	.30	.08	1.00

The problem can be solved by multiple regression, regressing each dependent variable on the variables with arrows to it. Readers interested in building their path analysis skills should try solving using regression. To make the illustration relevant to later SEM analyses, this illustration is set up to solve the problem using LISREL 8. (For any earlier version, drop the second to last line, "path diagram," and the problem can be solved. The output, however, will look somewhat different.) The control statements for LISREL appear in Appendix 3.2.

The output from the analyses, the regression coefficients with standard errors and *t* values, is as follows:

Regression Coefficients

	Independent Variables				
	Duncan	Peabody	TchrEval	PeerPop	VerbAch
Dependent variables					
TchrEval	−.12	.24	—	—	—
	(.10)	(.10)			
	−1.28	2.53			
PeerPop	.06	.13	.15	—	—
	(.10)	(.10)	(.10)		
	0.56	1.27	1.45		

Regression Coefficients (continued)

Independent Variables

	Duncan	Peabody	TchrEval	PeerPop	VerbAch
VerbAch	.12	.25	.25	—	—
	(.09)	(.09)	(.10)		
	1.27	2.66	2.60		

NOTE: Standard errors are in parentheses. *t* values are in rows below standard errors.

As noted earlier, the model has 1 degree of freedom (there is no path between PeerPop and VerbAch). The fit statistic from LISREL is as follows:

```
GOODNESS OF FIT STATISTICS
CHI-SQUARE WITH 1 DEGREE OF FREEDOM = 0.0070 P=1.00)
THE FIT IS PERFECT.
```

The slight optimism in LISREL about overall fit should be noted but ignored. Note that if this method is appropriate and the model depicts reality accurately, then the following interpretations can be made:

1. Social class is unimportant for this model.
2. Academic ability is related to both teacher ratings and student achievement.
3. None of the variables predicts acceptance by peers in the pre-desegregation classroom (choices from students from similar ethnic backgrounds).
4. Teacher ratings also are related to student achievement.
5. Given the modest sizes of the paths, there is much unexplained variance in each of the variables.
6. Even though no relation between peer acceptance and achievement is hypothesized, the good overall fit shows that no relationship exists between the two variables (assuming the model is appropriate).

Chapter Discussion Questions

1. Does the input matrix for path analysis come from regressions? If not, then where does it come from?

2. What is the difference in logic between partial correlation and partial regression? Is there a reason why one would use partial correlation over partial regression?

3. Are there ever reasons to use matrices of partial correlations for path analysis, or is the correlation matrix always used?

4. Are the signs and values of nonstandardized regression coefficients really meaningful?

5. Is stepwise regression not cheating? Does it not just let the data self-select without theoretical basis?

6. Will other SEM techniques be separating relationships between variables into the same categories (direct, indirect, common causes, and unanalyzed)?

7. Can the matrix form of decomposition be used for models that are not just identified (i.e., the degrees of freedom are more than the number of paths)?

8. Are analyses of variance ever used in path analysis, or will regression always be used?

E X E R C I S E   3 . 1

Another Path Analysis Illustration

Look at the model that appears in Figure 3.4. That diagram was constructed using the program AMOS, which is very easy to use to produce high-quality diagrams.

A. Use information contained in the following regression equations to solve for the path coefficients.

B. Use the regression equations to decompose effects into direct, indirect, and noncausal (including spurious) regression equations.

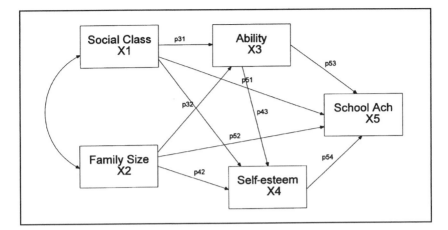

Figure 3.4. Path Analysis Illustration

Regression Equations

DV	IV	WT	DV	IV	WT	DV	IV	WT
X_5	X_1	.38	X_4	X_1	.06	X_5	X_1	.19
	X_2	−.15		X_2	−.07		X_2	−.02
				X_3	.14		X_3	.58
							X_4	.08
X_4	X_1	.11	X_5	X_1	.19			
	X_2	−.11		X_2	−.02			
				X_3	.59			
X_3	X_1	.32						
	X_2	−.23						

NOTE: DV = dependent variable; IV = independent variable; WT = regression weight.

Correlations

	X_1	X_2	X_3	X_4	X_5
X_1	1.00				
X_2	−.33	1.00			
X_3	.39	−.33	1.00		
X_4	.14	−.14	.19	1.00	
X_5	.43	−.28	.67	.22	1.00

A P P E N D I X   3 . 1

Path Modeling Notations

BOXES are used to describe observed measures. Observed measures are sometimes called *indicators*.

CIRCLES are used to describe theoretical variables. Other terms that are used are *latent variables, unmeasured variables,* and *constructs*.

This ARROW, whether between two boxes or two circles, represents a causal relationship from a causal variable to an effect.

This ARROW, which also can connect two boxes or two circles, represents a noncausal relationship between two variables.

This ARROW, which does not originate from a box or circle, represents a residual to a measure or variable.

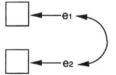

This ARROW represents a covariance between two residuals.

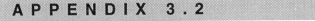

A P P E N D I X   3 . 2

LISREL 8 Setup for Figure 3.4

Readers should refer to a LISREL program manual to understand each of the symbols. Bracketed statements are not part of the program, but they provide description.

Mexican American data for peer acceptance, class illustration

```
DA NI=5 NO=100 MA=KM
KM SY FO FI=a:MAcsecmt.rx
(8F10.7)
```

[This assumes that the matrix that appears above is on the A drive and is called MAcsecmt.rx and that each element covers a 10-column field. The mysterious name is my idiosyncratic attempt at abbreviation of Mexican American cross-sectional matrix.]

```
MO NY=5 NE=5 LY=id BE=fu,fi PS=sy,fi TE=di,fi
FR BE 3 1 BE 3 2 BE 4 1 BE 4 2 BE 4 3 BE 5 1 BE 5 2
   BE 5 3 C
PS 2 1 PS 3 3 PS 4 4 PS 5 5
st 1.0 PS 1 1 PS 2 2
path diagram
OU PT SE TV AD=OFF
```

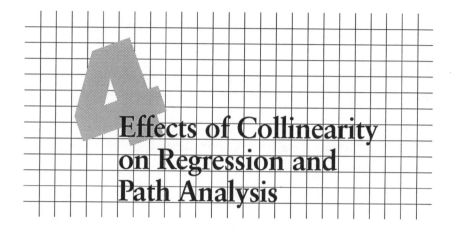

Effects of Collinearity on Regression and Path Analysis

$\mathbf{A}$s stated earlier in Chapter 2, interrelationships among predictor variables in regression models are both the things that make multiple regression and structural equation modeling (SEM) in general so interesting and the source of a number of problems. In the simplest case, if one has an array of predictor variables that are unrelated to one another, then the coefficients from multiple regression are reduced to simple bivariate regression coefficients and interpretation of those coefficients is straightforward. By contrast, if predictors are interrelated, then issues of partitioning of variance become important and interesting—and the mathematics becomes more than inspection of a correlation or covariance matrix. As is discussed in more detail later in this chapter, the partial regression coefficients have to spread the common variance among predictor variables across the set of predictors. Finally, if the correlations among predictors become too large, then the solution from regression analyses potentially becomes unstable and individual coefficients can change dramatically and go from strongly significant to nonsignificant across even nearly identical samples.

This chapter focuses on problems that can occur when the predictor variables in multiple regression are strongly related. Those problems usually are called problems of **multicollinearity**. Regression and other structural equation approaches cannot be used appropriately and effectively unless collinearity effects are well understood. It is important that structural equation approaches can help deal with some cases where the correlations among predictors are large. For example, having to label conceptual variables and operationalize them in path diagrams should prevent researchers from including two variables that measure the same conceptual variable as predictors. In path models, they might be combined or one would be dropped; in latent variable models described later in this book, the two variables would together define a single conceptual variable. Although the latent variable approach is preferable, in either case their high relationship and redundant relationships with other variables would be removed from the regression equation. Although latent variable approaches help in most instances by removing measurement and specification error from variables, they ironically may make high collinearity appear in cases where it previously has not been a problem. Problems seem most likely to emerge for variables that change a lot when they are included in latent variable models, for example, those assessed by measures with low reliability, that are difficult to assess or have been poorly operationalized (the result is that the variable actually measured is not what is intended to be measured), or that have been imprecisely conceptualized and are not conceptually distinct from other variables in the model.

Issues of collinearity or multicollinearity and of biased estimation (often called ridge regression or reduced variance regression [e.g., Darlington, 1978]) to address collinearity are discussed in this chapter. Ridge estimation is discussed briefly because it is an option in some of the structural equation programs (e.g., LISREL). Matrix algebra concepts are used. (Appendix 3.1 provides an introduction to matrix algebra.) They greatly facilitate explanation of collinearity issues and will be useful at various points throughout the book to explain concepts and approaches. Readers who have taken regression courses that cover collinearity issues and matrix algebra should have been exposed to the issues addressed here and may choose to skip this chapter. For additional information on regression, see, for example, Darlington (1990).

■ Regression and Collinearity

As suggested in the preceding section, in virtually all instances where regression approaches are used, the variables collected will be inter-correlated with one another. Uncorrelated predictor variables can be found primarily in experimental research when experimenters, by ensuring that the cell sizes for the various conditions are equal, produce orthogonal or uncorrelated effects. In such circumstances, if regression approaches are used to analyze the data (which is done in general linear model approaches to statistics), then the analyses are straightforward and simple to explain. Each effect is independent of all other effects; the independence extends as well to interactions between predictor variables. (Multiplying together two standardized variables that are independent of one another yields a third variable that is uncorrelated with the other two.) Therefore, total variance accounted for in any dependent variable is the sum of the independent effects, and the multiple regression coefficients are the simple regres-sion coefficients, which, in the standardized case, are the correlations.

By contrast, if in experimental research it turns out that cell sizes are unequal, then one has to make a new decision in selecting the analyses used because the independent variables no longer are inde-pendent of one another. Even though the total variance accounted for in the dependent variable does not change, different ways of ordering the extraction of effects lead to different interpretations of the sizes of individual effects, the same problem encountered by researchers conducting nonexperimental research and using regres-sion approaches.

Correlated independent variables are the typical case for nonex-perimental research and for multiple regression techniques. Thus, the challenge for regression approaches is to partition common vari-ance among the various predictor variables. Although regression approaches partition variance in logical ways, the techniques cannot perform magic such as uniquely assigning variance to particular predictor variables, let alone identifying "true causes" (see, e.g., Goldberger, 1964). What the approaches can do is spread common variance across correlated predictor variables. Problems emerge pri-marily when the correlations get substantial. (For a listing of sugges-tions about when the correlations are "too big" [i.e., when collinearity may be a problem], see Table 4.1. Unfortunately, there is no simple rule to define when one should worry about collinearity.)[6] In the extreme case where two variables are identical, there is no mathematical solution to a multiple regression problem because variance cannot be partitioned. In more moderate cases, as is illustrated in this chapter, a mathematical solution is possible, but it can be unstable, sometimes defying interpretation—collinearity has given rise to the term **bouncing betas** to describe coefficients that change signs or "bounce" through the zero point—and yielding solutions that cannot be trusted. (For a discussion of stability of regression coefficients, see, e.g., Green, 1977.)

An illustration of why collinearity causes problems in regression can be illustrated from the general matrix form of the regression equation, namely, $Y = XA + E$. Readers unfamiliar with matrix notation may want to look back at Appendix 3.1. For the illustration, standardization of variables is assumed, so the metric will be one of correlations rather than covariances.

To illustrate solving for regression models, Figure 3.2 is used once again. For this illustration, the equation for X_4 is used, and we are trying to solve for the regression coefficients for X_4, namely, p_{41}, p_{42}, and p_{43}. The equation is

$$X_4 = X_1 p_{41} + X_2 p_{42} + X_3 p_{43} + e_4. \tag{4.1}$$

Equation 4.1 does not provide enough information to solve for the unknown regression weights, for the equation has three coefficients to estimate. Additional information can be brought to bear by multiplying the equation by X_1, then by X_2, and then by X_3, producing three

---

6. For researchers analyzing their experimental data using multivariate analysis of variance (MANOVA) approaches, the same type of problem can occur if the various dependent variables in the MANOVA are highly intercorrelated; their collinearity can lead to an overall significance level that is misleading. For example, a colleague and I found a nonsignificant MANOVA effect in a study where each of the nine dependent variables' univariate ANOVA effects was significant (Maruyama & Miller, 1980). Because the nine measures all contained the same information (i.e., were unidimensional), the canonical correlation solution produced by the MANOVA program was nonsignificant. We solved our problem by taking a single linear composite for our dependent variable. Its effect was highly significant.

TABLE 4.1 Ways of Detecting Multicollinearity

1. When the variance (standard errors) in beta weights is large.
2. When signs on beta weights are inappropriate.
3. When regression weights change radically due to the inclusion or exclusion of single variables.
4. When the determinant of the correlation matrix of the predictor variables approaches zero.
5. When a factor analysis of the predictor variables yields a very large "condition number," where the condition number is defined as the square root of the ratio of the largest eigenvalue to the smallest eigenvalue. (An eigenvalue is the amount of variance explained by each factor, expressed in a correlational metric so that an eigenvalue of 1 means that a factor accounts for as much variability as one variable.) There is not perfect agreement on rules of thumb for condition number; both 30 and 100 have been suggested.
6. When one or more eigenvalues approach zero.
7. When the "variance inflation factors" (VIFs), defined as the diagonal elements of the inverse of the correlation matrix, get large. Those elements are $1 / (1 - R^2)$, where R^2 is the amount of variance in each predictor variable that can be explained by the other predictor variables. A suggested rule here for VIFs is that none should be greater than 6 or 7.
8. When simple correlations are greater than .80 or .90.
9. When simple correlations between two predictor variables are greater than the R^2 of all the predictor variables with the dependent variable.

NOTE: These suggestions come from a variety of sources, so some are more liberal than others.

equations in three unknowns in terms of the correlations. The resulting equations are

$$(X_1X_4) = (X_1X_1)\, p_{41} + (X_1X_2)\, p_{42} + (X_1X_2)\, p_{43} + (X_1e_4) \quad (4.2)$$
$$(X_2X_4) = (X_2X_1)\, p_{41} + (X_2X_2)\, p_{42} + (X_2X_3)\, p_{43} + (X_2e_4) \quad (4.3)$$
$$(X_3X_4) = (X_3X_1)\, p_{41} + (X_3X_2)\, p_{42} + (X_3X_3)\, p_{43} + (X_3e_4). \quad (4.4)$$

Taking expected values, the terms in parentheses can be expressed as correlations. Because the correlation of the errors with variables is zero, the final term drops out in each equation, yielding

$$r_{14} = (r_{11})p_{41} + (r_{12})p_{42} + (r_{13})p_{43} \quad (4.5)$$
$$r_{24} = (r_{21})p_{41} + (r_{22})p_{42} + (r_{23})p_{43} \quad (4.6)$$
$$r_{34} = (r_{31})p_{41} + (r_{32})p_{42} + (r_{33})p_{43} \quad (4.7)$$

In matrix form, the equations are

$$|r_{14}| = |(r_{11})p_{41} + (r_{12})p_{42} + (r_{13})p_{43}|$$
$$|r_{24}| = |(r_{21})p_{41} + (r_{22})p_{42} + (r_{23})p_{43}|$$
$$|r_{34}| = |(r_{31})p_{41} + (r_{32})p_{42} + (r_{33})p_{43}|,$$

which is the same as

$$|r_{14}| = |(r_{11})(r_{12})(r_{13})| \; |p_{41}|$$
$$|r_{24}| = |(r_{21})(r_{22})(r_{23})| \; |p_{42}|$$
$$|r_{34}| = |(r_{31})(r_{32})(r_{33})| \; |p_{43}|.$$

When the elements of the matrices are expressed in terms of the X and Y variables and the regression weights (A), they are equivalent to

$$X'Y = X'XA. \tag{4.8}$$

In other words, in matrix terms, what the previous operations did was premultiply the equation presented at the start of this section, $Y = XA + E$, by the transpose of X. As just noted, there would be an $X'E$ matrix/vector, but it drops out because by definition it contains only zeros. The expected value of $X'Y$ is the correlations of the X's with the dependent variable Y (in this case r_{41}, r_{42}, and r_{43}), whereas the expected value of $X'X$ is the intercorrelations among the X's (r_{11} to r_{33}) and A is the regression weights (p_{41}, p_{42}, and p_{43}).

To solve for A, $X'X$ needs to be eliminated from the right side of the equation. That is accomplished by doing the matrix equivalent of dividing both sides by $X'X$, namely, multiplying $X'X$ by its inverse. The notation for the inverse of $X'X$ is $(X'X)^{-1}$. Because each side has to be multiplied by the same quantity, the resulting equation is

$$(X'X)^{-1}(X'Y) = (X'X)^{-1}(X'X)A = A. \tag{4.9}$$

The quantity $(X'X)^{-1}(X'X)$ is an **identity matrix** and drops out. It is the matrix equivalent of the scalar number 1; when an identity matrix is multiplied by any other matrix, the result is that other matrix.

In effect, then, the regression coefficients are estimated by multiplying the correlation or covariance matrix containing the relations of the independent variables with the dependent variables ($X'Y$) by the inverse of the correlation/covariance matrix containing the relations among the independent variables ($[X'X]^{-1}$). The first important point is that if one or more of the X's are perfect linear combinations of other X's, then $X'X$ is singular, which means that it can have no inverse, so there can be no solution for the regression weights. The other extreme is where the independent variables are uncorrelated; then the matrix $X'X$ is an identity matrix with 1's on the diagonal (the diagonals would be variances if we were working with covariances) and all other elements are 0, and it is the same as its inverse. In such a case, $X'Y = A$, which means that the regression coefficients are the correlations.

Of most importance, however, is not the limiting conditions of independence or perfect collinearity but rather those between the extremes. Regression coefficients are a function of the correlations of the X's not only with the dependent variables but also with each other, and those relationships with each other are the causes of collinearity problems.

Fortunately, there are fairly straightforward ways of examining extent of collinearity. The easiest require inspecting the inverse of the correlation matrix of predictor variables. The diagonal elements provide information about collinearity of each predictor variable with the rest of the predictors; for a correlation matrix, they are ($1 / [1 - R^2]$). Thus, when the squared multiple correlation of a predictor with the others gets large, the diagonal element of the inverse also gets large. In Table 4.1, Point 7 for detecting multicollinearity, the inverse is called the variance inflation factor, and a rule of thumb for large diagonal elements is given. Inverses can be obtained from most factor analysis programs, which invert the correlation matrix as a starting point for iterative principal factors solutions. (The appropriate correlation matrix to examine includes only the predictors.)

Although there are many ways of illustrating the impact of the correlations among predictor variables, I try by example. The following example draws heavily from Robert A. Gordon's illustrations in his 1968 *American Journal of Sociology* article, "Issues in Multiple Regression."

▮ Illustrating Effects of Collinearity

This section is built around a hypothetical correlation matrix of 10 variables. Of these variables, 4 measure one construct, 3 measure a second, 2 measure a third, and a single variable measures the fourth construct. Interpretation of the results would be the same if the first 4 variables measured one set of highly related constructs, 3 measured a second set of related constructs, and so forth.

Following the logic of Gordon (1968), all the within-construct correlations are .7, the cross-construct correlations are .2, and all the correlations with the dependent measure are .5. They appear in Table 4.2.

The questions of interest center around interpretation of results from multiple regression. Inspection of the correlation matrix should suggest a number of conclusions, namely, that the constructs seem well defined (based on the within-construct correlations), that each is related moderately to the dependent variable (the .5 correlations), and that the predictor constructs are not very highly interrelated. The primary issue here is what happens if all 10 variables are entered into the regression equation rather than using composite variables or latent variable approaches that employ multiple measures of each construct.

Imagine, for example, that researchers are collecting survey data from a large sample and that they are searching for "new" predictor variables that account for variance that has not been accounted for previously by other predictors. They decide to operationalize the constructs underlying the new predictors in several ways; after all, if the variable is elusive (and it must be given that others have not been able to either identify or define it in ways that have allowed it to add to prediction), then they want to measure it effectively. Furthermore, they may want to show that the various measures converge to define a single construct. Finally, because they are concerned about construct validity, they want to show that that construct is related to other constructs in predicted ways. Thus, they include (smaller numbers of) "more traditional" variables that have previously been reported to predict the dependent variable. If they do a regression analysis and enter all the predictor variables to see which variables "come through" and predict the dependent variable, then a situation such as the one illustrated will have been created because there will be multiple measures of the constructs of "greatest interest" and fewer measures of traditional or well-established predictors.

A second circumstance might occur if researchers differentially sampled from different sets of domains, choosing four variables of one type, three of a second, and so forth. Differentially sampling

TABLE 4.2 Artificial Correlation Matrix

	A_1	A_2	A_3	A_4	B_1	B_2	B_3	C_1	C_2	D_1	Y
A_1	1.0										
A_2	.7	1.0									
A_3	.7	.7	1.0								
A_4	.7	.7	.7	1.0							
B_1	.2	.2	.2	.2	1.0						
B_2	.2	.2	.2	.2	.7	1.0					
B_3	.2	.2	.2	.2	.7	.7	1.0				
C_1	.2	.2	.2	.2	.2	.2	.2	1.0			
C_2	.2	.2	.2	.2	.2	.2	.2	.7	1.0		
D_1	.2	.2	.2	.2	.2	.2	.2	.2	.2	1.0	
Y	.5	.5	.5	.5	.5	.5	.5	.5	.5	.5	1.0

might result if one were to "throw in" a variable or two on a whim or as a last-minute addition. One might imagine, for example, including a variable such as "birth order" because it seems intuitively interesting. If there is only a single indicator of birth order and many indicators of other variables, then the situation could readily occur.

Table 4.3 shows what happens when the various indicators are entered into multiple regression equations. In the illustration, the variables assessed by three or four different measures all are nonsignificant, whereas the ones with fewer measures contribute significantly to prediction. The lower parts of the table show what happens when each subset is excluded from the group of predictor variables; in this illustration, however, the changes are not major. Ironically, what comes through consistently in the illustration is that what makes a measure a significant predictor is *not having* other measures that assess the same underlying variable that it does. Gordon (1968) called the problem caused by differences in number of indicators **repetitiveness**.

A second issue discussed by Gordon (1968) is what happens when the correlations of the predictor variables with the criterion variable are not uniform but instead vary. Again, as an illustration following the spirit of his article, in Table 4.4 one of the correlations with the criterion variable is changed slightly and the solutions are reestimated. The full 10-variable array of predictors is included in this

TABLE 4.3 Regression Analyses Based on Table 4.2

	A_1	A_2	A_3	A_4	B_1	B_2	B_3	C_1	C_2	D_1
Regression analyses using all 10 predictor variables										
Y	.097	.097	.097	.097	.124	.124	.124	.172	.172	.279
Standard error	.090	.090	.090	.090	.086	.086	.086	.079	.079	.059
t value	1.081	1.081	1.081	1.081	1.441	1.441	1.441	2.178	2.178	4.747
Residual variance = .308										
Squared multiple correlation = .692										
Regression analyses omitting the single indicator variable (D_1)										
Y	.109	.109	.109	.109	.140	.140	.140	.193	.193	
Standard error	.100	.100	.100	.100	.095	.095	.095	.087	.087	
t value	1.098	1.098	1.098	1.098	1.465	1.465	1.465	2.216	2.216	
Residual variance = .379										
Squared multiple correlation = .621										
Regression analyses omitting the two indicator variables (C_1, C_2)										
Y	.113	.113	.113	.113	.144	.144	.144			.324
Standard error	.102	.102	.102	.102	.098	.098	.098			.066
t value	1.104	1.104	1.104	1.104	1.473	1.473	1.473			4.898
Residual variance = .397										
Squared multiple correlation = .603										
Regression analyses omitting the three indicator variables (B_1, B_2, B_3)										
Y	.114	.114	.114	.114				.202	.202	.328
Standard error	.103	.103	.103	.103				.090	.090	.067
t values	1.107	1.107	1.107	1.107				2.235	2.235	4.915
Residual variance = .406										
Squared multiple correlation = .594										
Regression analyses omitting the four indicator variables (A_1, A_2, A_3, A_4)										
Y					.147	.147	.147	.203	.203	.331
Standard error					.099	.099	.099	.091	.091	.067
t value					1.479	1.479	1.479	2.238	2.238	4.925
Residual variance = .411										
Squared multiple correlation = .589										

regression illustration. In each of the four variations illustrated, one correlation is increased; different illustrations vary correlations in different constructs. The magnitude of the increase is only from .50

to .55, well within the confidence interval for a correlation for most sample sizes. (A discussion of confidence intervals for correlations appears later in this chapter.) Note that when a correlation is increased in either the three- or four-indicator construct, that indicator becomes significant along with indicators from the two- and one-indicator constructs.

Most important for this book, inspection of the correlations shows that modest changes in the magnitude of correlations—of a magnitude that would occur due to sampling fluctuations—can markedly change the interpretation of regression coefficients. (For more illustrations of the effects of issues such as the ones covered in this chapter, readers can refer to Gordon [1968]. Gordon also illustrates what happens as the correlations within constructs increase, a situation he labels as **redundancy**, for the predictors then contain more redundant information.)

These illustrations are important for this book for two reasons. The first and obvious one is that they point out weaknesses inherent in multiple regression. "Bad" decisions in the selection of predictors for inclusion in regression equations can produce misleading (or at least difficult to replicate) results, as can sampling fluctuations in the size of correlations. Second, and of greater importance, is that multiple indicators and latent variable approaches minimize the problems described in the preceding by eliminating differential repetitiveness (each conceptual variable appears only once in a regression equation) and by adjusting for differential reliability of measures.

▮ Confidence Intervals for Correlations

Relatively few researchers seem to have much experience in estimating confidence intervals for correlations. The lack of experience in such estimation may result because significance of correlations typically is determined by computer programs that correlate variables and because there are tables in many statistics books that provide significance information on correlations. It also may occur because estimating confidence intervals is fairly complex. Finally, the resulting confidence intervals are nonsymmetric, which makes them more difficult to explain or understand. Regardless of the cause, the shortcoming is ironic given that confidence intervals provide the best information on expected fluctuations in correlations across samples. A recent

TABLE 4.4 Variation on the Regression Analyses From Table 4.3, Increasing a Single Relationship With the Criterion Variable From .50 to .55

	A_1	A_2	A_3	A_4	B_1	B_2	B_3	C_1	C_2	D_1
Increasing a correlation in the first set of predictors										
Y	.227	.060	.060	.060	.123	.123	.123	.170	.170	.277
Standard error	.087	.087	.087	.087	.084	.084	.084	.077	.077	.057
t value	2.592	0.686	0.686	0.686	1.468	1.468	1.468	2.218	2.218	4.834

Residual variance = .292
Squared multiple correlation = .708

	A_1	A_2	A_3	A_4	B_1	B_2	B_3	C_1	C_2	D_1
Increasing a correlation in the second set of predictors										
Y	.096	.096	.096	.096	.243	.076	.076	.170	.170	.276
Standard error	.087	.087	.087	.087	.083	.083	.083	.077	.077	.057
t value	1.102	1.102	1.102	1.102	2.911	0.915	0.915	2.220	2.220	4.841

Residual variance = .290
Squared multiple correlation = .710

	A_1	A_2	A_3	A_4	B_1	B_2	B_3	C_1	C_2	D_1
Increasing a correlation in the third set of predictors										
Y	.096	.096	.096	.096	.122	.122	.122	.272	.105	.275
Standard error	.087	.087	.087	.087	.083	.083	.083	.076	.076	.057
t value	1.105	1.105	1.105	1.105	1.473	1.473	1.473	3.575	1.382	4.852

Residual variance = .286
Squared multiple correlation = .714

	A_1	A_2	A_3	A_4	B_1	B_2	B_3	C_1	C_2	D_1
Increasing the correlation in the fourth set of predictors										
Y	.095	.095	.095	.095	.121	.121	.121	.167	.167	.335
Standard error	.085	.085	.085	.085	.082	.082	.082	.075	.075	.056
t value	1.110	1.110	1.110	1.110	1.481	1.481	1.481	2.237	2.237	5.998

Residual variance = .278
Squared multiple correlation = .722

article by Olkin and Finn (1995) provides expressions for confidence intervals for simple, partial, and multiple correlations.

Calculating confidence intervals requires converting correlations to Fisher's z (which, for those who care to know, is the hyperbolic arctangent of the correlation), calculating confidence intervals for the z, and converting the z's for the upper and lower limits of the confidence interval back to r's. One formula for converting a correlation to Fisher's z is

$$z = \tfrac{1}{2}[\log_e(1 + r) - \log_e(1 - r)]. \qquad (4.10)$$

Many statistics books contain tables with r to Fisher z conversions. It turns out that for small correlations (less than .25), the z approximates the correlation; however, as the correlation increases beyond .25, the two diverge, with the z increasing more rapidly. The standard error for correlations is calculated from the sample size using the formula

$$\text{Standard Error} = 1 / \text{sqrt}(N - 3), \qquad (4.11)$$

where N is the sample size. Then multiplying the standard error times the z score value for the probability level gives the confidence interval.

　　To illustrate, imagine that we want to determine the confidence interval around a correlation of .50 for sample sizes of 100 and 500. The Fisher z for $r = .50$ is .549, and the respective standard errors are $(1 / \text{sqrt}[97]) = .1015$ and $(1 / \text{sqrt}[497]) = .0449$. Choosing a probability level of .05 (two-tailed), the appropriate z score is 1.96, and the confidence intervals for Fisher's z become .549 ± (1.96)(.1015), or .549 ± .199, and .549 ± (1.96)(.0449), or .549 ± .088. For the sample size of 100, the confidence interval z scores range from .350 to .748, equivalent r's being .336 and .634; for a sample of 500, the z score interval is from .461 to .637, equivalent r's being .430 and .560. The example illustrates the importance of having large samples; with a sample of 100, correlations should be expected to fluctuate markedly across samples. The lack of symmetry in the confidence interval expressed in correlations should be apparent from the illustration. Most important for the collinearity example illustrated in Table 4.4, a fluctuation in a correlation from .50 in one sample to .55 falls within the bounds of sampling error, even for a sample of size 500. Thus, *the differences among the first three solutions presented in Table 4.4 may result from modest fluctuations in correlations across samples, yet the interpretations about important predictor variables would change markedly.* In other words, drawing meaning from significant predictors in regression analyses is risky business.

　　So what is one to do if faced with collinearity problems? Are there ways of stabilizing solutions across samples? There are techniques, such as jackknifing, in which values for a set of predictors are reestimated repeatedly, each time dropping one predictor until all have been omitted. Substantial changes in the regression weights by omission of single variables point to collinearity. In addition, there are ways of addressing collinearity that still use basic regression approaches, including eliminating some of the variables from the regression equation, combining variables that represent single constructs (i.e., using composite variables), and increasing sample size to increase one's confidence in the sample estimates.

Furthermore, as a general principle, in large samples one should randomly split the sample and cross-validate the findings (i.e., estimate a solution on half of the sample and see whether it can be replicated in the other half) (see, e.g., Cudeck & Browne, 1983). Although cross-validation is valuable for many reasons (e.g., to allow some post hoc model changes), consistency across the two samples argues against sampling fluctuations producing misleading results. Finally, one could abandon traditional regression and its reliance on unbiased estimates and instead use a set of methods known as ridge regression, reduced variance regression, or ridge estimation. These are discussed because some structural equation programs (e.g., LISREL) include ridge estimation.

Ridge or Reduced Variance Regression

Ridge estimation techniques (e.g., Darlington, 1978) provide a means of stabilizing the solution for a collinear prediction model. In those approaches, a more stable solution is attained by adding a small constant to the elements of the diagonal of the correlation matrix. The first challenge for ridge approaches is to introduce as small a constant as possible to keep the matrix yielding the ridge solution as close to the original matrix as possible. Thus, a typical ridge program slowly increases the constant that is added to the diagonal (often beginning with a constant as small as .001) and successively reestimates the regression coefficients. At some point in the process of increasing the constant, all the regression estimates become stable (i.e., change very modestly across successive solutions) and begin to slowly move toward zero. At that point, the ridge solution has been obtained. The different approaches for estimating the ridge constant are not presented here, for the goal is not to teach the methodology but rather to simply introduce the logic and generally describe the methodology. Price (1977), among others, provides suggestions about selecting ridge constants.

Estimates from a ridge solution should cross-validate well across samples, for they should be stable despite instability in the actual data due to collinearity affecting the $(X'X)^{-1}$ matrix. On the other hand, the costs of attaining stabilization of the solution are that (a) the estimates are biased, (b) they will not have standard errors (and so significance of individual predictors cannot be established), and (c) the variance accounted for will be decreased somewhat.

Lack of significance testing and bias may be small prices to pay for circumstances in which perfect collinearity occurs, particularly if such collinearity seems unavoidable (some econometric models are particularly likely to face such problems), for no solution would be possible without an approach like ridge estimation. In those circumstances, the choices are to select a biased solution or to get no information from one's data set. Although there are arguments for both positions, my preference is the pragmatic one, namely, to use ridge techniques to get estimates and to use the information both about what could have caused the collinearity problems and about what the estimates suggest in planning the follow-up study.

For circumstances in which collinearity is high but a solution can be estimated without ridge techniques, the introduction of bias that results during ridge estimation has led to some disagreement among social scientists about whether or not ridge techniques should be used. One question is whether we want to draw inferences from biased coefficients. The answer to that question has to be weighed against trying to interpret the values from ordinary least squares estimation when those coefficients can defy logic. For example, standardized regression coefficients can greatly exceed 1 and have signs opposite their zero-order correlation.

A nice illustration of ridge estimation is reported by Price (1977), who describes results from analyses of a highly collinear five-predictor data set assessing employee satisfaction. In his example, the five collinear predictors, which basically seem to define a single factor, have correlations with the dependent variable ranging from .158 to .827. Despite the fact that all correlations in the matrix are positive, the reported standardized regression coefficients range from −3.69 to 2.11 and include a 1.85 and a 1.25. Only the 2.11 is significant, which should say a lot about the size of the standard errors. (In regression with standardized variables, large standard errors, which mean large variances for the estimates, are a good indicator of collinearity problems.) Finally, the −3.69 is a classic example of a bouncing beta, where a strong correlation yields a regression coefficient with a puzzling (backward) sign.

In Price's (1977) data, the collinearity is apparent from inspection of the correlation matrix (it includes correlations between predictors of .91, .87, and .82) as well as from inspection of the diagonal elements from the inverse of the matrix of predictors (variance inflation factors include 493 and 129). In other instances, effects of collinearity may be more subtle. Nevertheless, the illustration is a nice one because it shows the impact on the regression coefficients, has bouncing betas, and has a solution that changes quickly as a ridge constant is introduced and increased.

In summary, this chapter has presented and illustrated how collinearity can produce problems for basic regression approaches. Collinearity problems (a) point out issues that are fundamental to understanding the entire range of structural equation approaches and (b) highlight an advantage of latent variable approaches to SEM techniques, namely, that many problems related to collinearity *within constructs* are eliminated when a set of collinear predictors is replaced by a single composite predictor. The problems cannot be solved when one or more measures are exact linear composites of other measures (in which case no approach will yield a viable solution) and when measures are so close to being composites that they make the solution process unstable. Latent variable approaches also do not help when the very high correlations among predictors are of predictors from different conceptual variables. In those instances, it makes sense first to address issues of convergent/discriminant validity to assure oneself that the conceptual variables are in fact different. Matrix form was used to illustrate the underlying nature of collinearity problems, followed by an example derived from Gordon (1968) to show how small fluctuations in the size of correlations could affect regression coefficients dramatically. The high likelihood of those types of fluctuations was illustrated through a discussion of confidence intervals for correlations. Finally, one approach for dealing with collinearity, ridge regression, was discussed briefly.

E X E R C I S E   4 . 1

Partial Correlation and Regression

Given the variables

$$X_1 = \text{Social Class}$$
$$X_2 = \text{Family Size}$$
$$X_3 = \text{Ability}$$
$$X_4 = \text{Self-Esteem}$$
$$X_5 = \text{School Achievement}$$

as well as their correlations

	X_1	X_2	X_3	X_4	X_5
X_1	1.00				
X_2	−.33	1.00			
X_3	.39	−.33	1.00		
X_4	.14	−.14	.19	1.00	
X_5	.43	−.28	.67	.22	1.00

and the following findings from regression equations predicting X_3, X_4, and X_5 as dependent variables, the following coefficients are standardized regression coefficients:

DV	IV	WT	DV	IV	WT	DV	IV	WT
X_5	X_1	.38	X_4	X_1	.06	X_5	X_1	.19
	X_2	−.15		X_2	−.07		X_2	−.02
				X_3	.14		X_3	.58
X_4	X_1	.11	X_5	X_1	.19		X_4	.08
	X_2	−.11						
				X_2	−.02			
X_3	X_1	.32		X_3	.59			
	X_2	−.23						

NOTE: DV = dependent variable; IV = independent variable; WT = regression weight.

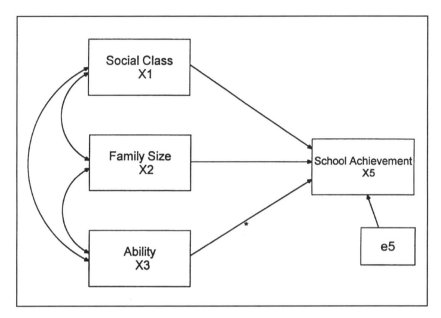

Figure 4.1. Partial Regression Illustration

A. *Partial regression.* Using the preceding variables and analyses, what is the regression weight or path coefficient from Ability to School Achievement for the diagram in Figure 4.1? (The goal here is simply to determine the appropriate equation and find the regression coefficient.)

B. *Partial correlation.* Again using the preceding correlation matrix, what is the partial correlation between Social Class and School Achievement for the model in Figure 4.2? (By contrast, this requires work.)

Solution suggestion. Solving requires estimating second-order partialing, which can be done by partialing variables one at a time and using the formula presented earlier in this book. Successively partial X_2 *and* X_3 from *all* remaining relations, leaving only a residual relation between X_1 and X_5. As you do

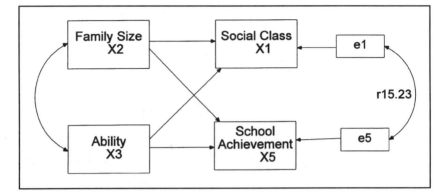

Figure 4.2. Partial Correlation Illustration

this, think about how difficult it would be to estimate fifth-, sixth-, or even higher order partials by this approach (and *thank* whoever invented computers!).

C. What is the value of the partial regression coefficient from Part A relating Social Class to School Achievement (p_{51})?

How does the partial correlation between X_1 and X_5 controlling for X_2 and X_3 compare with the partial regression coefficient from X_1 to X_5 controlling for X_2 and X_3? Are they the same or different?

What is the logic of each approach?

Effects of Random and Nonrandom Error on Path Models

As has been mentioned throughout this book, the term *path analysis* refers only to a restricted subset of path models. In this chapter, extensions from the subset of models that can be called path analysis are considered. First, models that contain measurement error are introduced, followed by models in which both multiple traits and methods are included in the data. In moving beyond path analysis models, one faces the possibility that the models developed cannot be uniquely solved, that is, are not identified. Discussion of identification issues will be covered in the next chapter along with another variation on path analysis, models with bidirectional or even multidirectional causality.

Measurement Error

Background

Inability to allow for measurement error has been the primary downfall of path analysis models. There are few places in the social sciences where a case can be made that the variables of interest can be measured without appreciable error. Particularly in areas such as assessment of attitudes, it simply is implausible to assume that the conceptual variables are measured anywhere near perfectly. Inability to make that assumption in effect rules out use of path analysis. As is illustrated later in this chapter, when measurement error is present, path coefficients become biased and the solution cannot be trusted to accurately reflect the processes involved.

Before beginning to discuss specifics, a general background for thinking about measures is provided. This perspective draws from reliability theory (e.g., Mehrens & Lehmann, 1984), which partitions the variance of measures into true and error variance. Consistent with factor analysis logic (e.g., Gorsuch, 1983), however, it further partitions true score variance into variance related to the dimension of interest and variance that is reliable but taps something other than the dimension of interest. For this discussion, reliability should be thought of in terms of internal consistency reliability.

The three variance components of a measure are as follows. First, true score variance related to the theoretical construct(s) of interest to researchers is the part that researchers want to isolate and keep. This component is part of the reliable variance of the measure. In most instances, however, it is less than the total reliability of the measure because not all of the reliable variance is related to the construct(s) of interest. This first variance component can be called **true score common variance**. A second variance component is the difference between the reliability of the measure and its relation to the construct(s) of interest. This variance component is not error and will consistently appear each time the measure is used. This component can be called **true score unique variance**. A third variance component is traditional **error variance**, the unreliable variance that is part of a measure. Of course, if a measure is assessed without error, then this component is zero. This component stays the same regardless of the theoretical variable that is being assessed.

For example, if we were to try to assess self-concept, we would choose one or more measures that purportedly assess the theoretical variable of self-concept. But those measures would likely tap more than just self-concept. In addition to measurement error, they could contain method variance, have measure-specific variance, or even assess a second theoretical variable. As a consequence, their estimate of internal consistency reliability would be greater than their relationship with the pure conceptual variable of self-concept. It is assessing only parts of measures that provides the greatest challenge for researchers using structural modeling. They need to be able to extract from their measures the part of the variability that assesses the theoretical variable of interest. One might think of work in fields such as chemistry, where impurities frequently need to be extracted to work with solutions whose properties are perfectly understood. The challenge for social scientists is parallel: to remove parts of measures with unwanted properties so that the actual effects of theoretical variables can be clearly observed.

As will be argued later in this book when factor analysis logic is introduced, the ideal situation for operationalizing a theoretical variable is one in which there are available multiple measures of it. Only with multiple measures can various variance components be teased apart using principles of convergent and discriminant validity and can the variance related to the construct of interest be isolated.

As a second example, imagine that I have a measure of family size. If I use that measure to assess a theoretical variable also called family size, then the measure is likely to be made up almost entirely of true score common variance and error variance. The true score unique variance should effectively be zero. If instead I use family size to assess a different theoretical variable, one called family social class, then the proportions of true score common variance and true score unique variance change markedly. For any measure, the relative sizes of the first two components depend on what the researcher is trying to assess.

Specifying Relationships Between Theoretical Variables and Measures

Although there are different ways of thinking about the relationships between the measure and its underlying construct, in the structural equation field those relationships typically are viewed as reflecting influence of the construct on the measure. Thus, the arrows from path modeling will go from the underlying construct to the measure unless the case can be made that the measure causes the theoretical variable (for a discussion of causal indicators, see Bollen & Lennox, 1991; MacCallum & Browne, 1993; Tanaka, Panter, Winbourne, & Huba, 1990). A common diagram representing the relationship between a measure and its underlying construct appears in Figure 5.1.

Consistent with the logic presented in the preceding discussion and with factor analysis, the unmeasured construct "causes" the measure because the measure assesses variability from that construct. The residual includes measurement error as well as true score unique

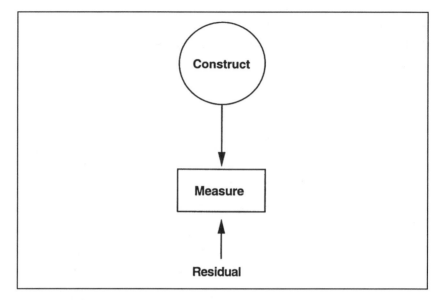

Figure 5.1. Expressing Measures in Terms of Constructs

variance. In other words, the measure is viewed as being made up of variability from the construct of interest plus other variability. Because the figure is a path model and follows that logic, by definition the residual is made up of all causes of a measure that are not included in the model. That is, the residual is all of the variance other than the construct of interest. If, however, other variables were to be included in the model as causes of the measure, then part of the unique variance in Figure 5.1 would become common variance in the modified model and would be represented by arrows from the additional causes to the measure. The residual then would be smaller.

To return to the point made earlier about a measure of family size, the construct of **social class** can be used to illustrate the three types of variance components. Social class supposedly assesses one's socioeconomic status. It reflects a combination of prestige, of access to resources including knowledge/expertise, of economic advantage, and of values consistent with prestige and attainment.

Social class typically is operationalized (imperfectly) as some combination of measures of income, occupational status, and educational attainment. Even though measures of income, status, and attainment each could be used to make the point about variance partitioning, it can be made along with a second point by focusing on family size, which has been used to assess social class in instances where measures of one or more of the three domains are missing.

Family size has been used as a measure of social class because in our culture more advantaged people tend to have smaller families. One could, of course, argue that family size is a questionable measure of social class, which undoubtedly is true. Yet, a researcher with a data set having only a flawed measure of a potentially important construct such as social class needs to balance the competing arguments in deciding whether to exclude a potentially important construct or to assess it imperfectly. Assume that in this case the decision is that social class is too important to omit from the model, and so it is included even though the only measure that taps social class is family size. Family size can be measured with a high degree of reliability, in fact almost perfectly so. Unreliability may be limited to coding errors by investigators or families that are in flux due to marriages, separations, divorces, or other instabilities. In other words, the measurement error component is very small. Yet, family size in no way is close to a perfect measure of social class, for it contains variance due to many other variables. Other variables influencing family size include cultural values (e.g., some groups in our culture value large families more than do others), religious practices (e.g., Roman Catholics have different beliefs about use of birth control than do many other religious groups), and fertility differences and understanding of effective birth control practices. Those other sources of variability not related to social class do not diminish the reliability of the "family size" measure; they are components of true score variance of family size and are reliable. Yet, they are not part of the underlying dimension of social class. They are portions of variance not shared with other measures of social class (i.e., not common variance); instead, they are true score unique variance. True score unique variance diminishes the reliability of family size *with respect to* the underlying construct of social class. Furthermore, if these variance components were hypothesized to be related to the same criterion variables that social class should predict, then they will lead to problems of interpretation. In Figure 5.1, these latter sources of variability ideally would be part of the residual, which would mean that they are not related to the dependent variables with which social class is related.

To summarize, for variables in the social sciences, there almost always are discrepancies between the conceptual variables and the measures that operationalize them. These discrepancies make it critical to accurately partition reliable variance into true score common variance and true score unique variance. For path models, it would be ideal to partition variance in a way that leaves only the true score common variance as reliable and lumps together the true score unique variance with measurement error.

Unfortunately, such partitioning cannot be done until multiple measures of constructs are introduced and the logic of factor analysis is used, yielding latent variable structural equation modeling (SEM) techniques described in Chapter 8. The closest approximations of those approaches in single-indicator, manifest variable path modeling use composite measures in path models. The composite measures ideally combine common true score variance in an additive fashion, whereas random errors and unique true score variance components combine in true random fashion, not increasing (e.g., Mehrens & Lehmann, 1984). Unfortunately, all too often the composite measures contain common method or other shared variance, with the result that errors combine additively as well.

For the measurement error models described in this chapter, true score common variance and true score unique variance typically will be combined as reliable variance. In such models, only measurement error appears as error.

Random Measurement Error

Random measurement error is error that actually meets the desired properties of error variance, namely, that is unrelated to predictor variables, criterion variables, and errors of other measures. Because it is unrelated to any variables, it exists independently of other measures. That is, it does not contribute to the relationships of the measures having random errors with any other measures. Because it is not related to any other measures, its presence reduces the relationship of the measure it affects with other measures. In path models, it results in misestimation of the strength of various relationships from the model. In the bivariate case, the strength of the relationship always is underestimated. In the multivariate case, unfortunately, such a simple and straightforward conclusion is not possible. If there is only one variable with less than perfect reliability, then its relationships with other variables appear weaker than they should. At the same time, reducing the relationship of one predictor variable with a dependent variable below what it should be may allow relationships of other predictor variables to become stronger than they would have been if error had not been involved. In other words, some coefficients get bigger than they should, whereas others get smaller.

In sum, in multivariate instances, random error produces neither an ideal case nor a predictable one. It may increase as well as decrease relationships. Furthermore, unreliability has different effects on the dependent variable in a regression equation than it does on an independent variable.

For **dependent variables**, error gets absorbed into the residual. Error reduces the variance accounted for and the standardized regression coefficients. On the other hand, slopes, the unstandardized coefficients, remain unaffected, and this is a persuasive reason for working with covariances (nonstandardized data) if there is concern about error in one's dependent variables (e.g., Kenny, 1979). On balance, then, measurement error in the dependent variable does not create terrible problems, for it gets absorbed into the error term, with predictable results.

Using a typical regression model, it is easy to illustrate what happens when random error exists in the dependent variable. In such an instance, the equation desired is $Y_t = XA + e$, where Y_t is the true score Y. Yet, the observed Y is not the same as Y_t, for it is made up of reliable variance plus error. That is, $Y = Y_t + v$, where v is the error in Y. Because $Y_t = Y - v$, the actual equation becomes $Y_t = Y - v = XA + e$, and so, expressed in terms of the observed variables, $Y = XA + e + v$. Because the error on Y is random, v is unrelated to X, and so the nonstandardized regression weight is not affected, but the error term for Y becomes $e + v$ rather than e. Because the error term has become larger, the R^2 is reduced and the standardized regression coefficients are reduced.

For **independent variables**, the effects of error are more problematic. Because the regression coefficient is estimated for all of the variance in the independent variable, the new error term biases the regression weight and therefore cannot readily be dismissed. To illustrate, begin with the desired equation, $Y = X_t A + e$. When X is measured with error, however, $X = X_t + u$ and, therefore, $X_t = X - u$, where u is the error in X. Thus, $Y = (X - u)A + e$, or $Y = XA + (e - uA)$. Note that the value of the regression weight A is affected by the residual u, clearly an unwanted effect that biases the regression coefficient. Furthermore, the error term is not independent of the regression weight (A). In the bivariate case, because u is unrelated to Y, whereas X presumably is related to Y, the relationship between X and Y is underestimated. In the multivariate case, underestimating relationships of imperfectly assessed variables with the dependent variable affects other relationships in unpredictable ways. On balance, then, if one were to have error in a single measure, then it would be preferable to have it in the dependent variable, where its effects are easier to address.

Because random error creates such a problem for multiple regression, it might seem as though someone would have determined ways of getting rid of the error. For example, could unreliability not be removed by correcting correlations for attenuation, that is, by adjusting them to what they would have been if unreliability had not been involved? In principle, yes, but in practice it is not so easy. The biggest problem is determining exactly what the reliability of the measure should be for the sample at hand. Should preestablished reliability for a well-established measure be used, or should sample reliability be used? Should reliability be defined in terms of the construct that is assessed rather than in terms of error in assessing the measure (remember the illustration of family size)? That is, is the measure the critical predictor whose reliability needs to be used for correction, or should correction for unreliability adjust with respect to the underlying construct?

Unfortunately, there are no right answers to how to "perfectly" correct for unreliability. What is clear, however, is that if reliability is judged to be higher than it really is, then the correction will not fully remove the unreliability and the relationships of the "corrected" variable with others still will be underestimated. In such a circumstance, the impacts of the measure are likely to be understated. In the opposite circumstance, if reliability is judged to be lower than it really is, then the correction will be too great and the relationships of the "corrected" measure with other variables will be stronger than they should be. In such a circumstance, the impacts of the measure are likely to appear stronger than they actually are, or collinearity problems may be exaggerated or may appear when in fact collinearity should not be problematic.

Neither overestimation nor underestimation is desirable, for one important underlying purpose of structural equation methodologies is to identify causal processes that can be used to target interventions. It would be undesirable to have variables dropped from an equation or viewed as unimportant because of poor reliability or to select as the target for an intervention a variable that actually has much weaker effects than it appeared to have because one has overcorrected for its unreliability. Thus, the bottom line with respect to correcting a matrix for unreliability is as follows: Even though superficially attractive, correcting for unreliability is risky and can be potentially problematic.

At the same time, however, the logic of reliability correction is the heart of multiple-indicator, latent variable SEM. Those techniques provide a means to overcome the types of problems that have just been described. They produce a generally effective way in which to address problems of random error by estimating reliability in terms of the specified model.

Nonrandom Error

Nonrandom error is error variance that is related in some systematic way to a variable or other error term. In other words, nonrandom error can result both from error variance that is shared across measures and from extra sources of reliable variance shared across measures. The most common types of nonrandom error are those that result from two measures having more than one underlying dimension (construct) in common; the extra dimensions may be substantive, but they also could be purely method variance. For example, if all measures in a path model were drawn from a single paper-and-pencil survey, then there potentially could be common method variance that would exaggerate the relationships of the different variables. If so, the method could be considered a type of nonrandom error.

A diagram illustrating nonrandom error appears in Figure 5.2. Note that the relationship between X and Y occurs not only due to the relationship between the constructs that they measure but also due to the relationship between their residuals. As suggested in the preceding discussion, that relationship could represent another variable that causes both X and Y, or common method variance. If the nonrandom error (i.e., the arrow between e_x and e_y) were ignored, then the relationship between X_t and Y_t would be estimated inaccurately.

Models containing nonrandom errors cannot be solved by using traditional regression techniques. In some instances, the nonrandom errors may be estimated by calculating partial correlations (e.g., the partial correlation model in Chapter 3), in others they may be solvable through matrix algebra, and in still others they may be estimated

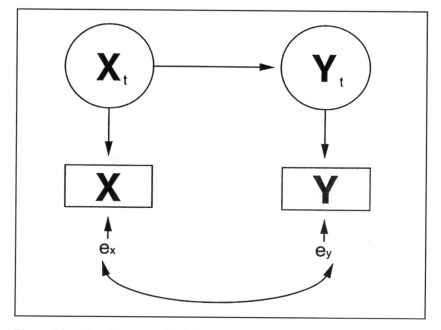

Figure 5.2.   Two-Construct Model

through multistage least squares techniques. Rather than attempting to show how they can be solved in various ways, I will leave them for the discussion of latent variable structural equation models. Using those techniques, they can be dealt with either as residual covariances, as methods factors, or even as unmeasured variables. Regardless of how they are specified, in latent variable models they require no special methods but are estimated as part of the general model in which they are included.

Method Variance and Multitrait-Multimethod Models

The remainder of this chapter focuses on issues related to method variance. It discusses method variance and describes the multitrait-multimethod (MTMM) approach. In the language of MTMM approaches, what we thus far have called constructs or theoretical variables are termed **traits**. Any additional systematic variability that reflects the ways in which data were collected is collectively referred to as **methods**.

Method Variance

The notion of method variance should not be a new one for readers; it has been mentioned throughout this chapter. Method variance is a prominent and common type of nonrandom error. It can occur in a number of different ways when the method used intrudes to introduce additional common variance. A frequent example of common method variance occurs when two measures are administered as part of a single instrument, particularly if their items are interspersed.

Potentially having measures with common method variance should not be seen as necessarily bad, for method variance may be a needed byproduct of a researcher's efforts to tap substantive dimensions of interest. For example, if one or more of the measures to be collected are likely to be reactive (i.e., respondents will know what they are responding to and may choose to answer in ways that differ from what would be their true responses), then those measures potentially could be made less obtrusive if mixed in with items tapping different content areas. This logic has been used to measure racial prejudice against African Americans in the United States (e.g., Crandall, 1994; McConahay, 1986). In contrast to administering sequentially a series of items about attitudes toward African Americans, these prejudice measures embed the items within a much larger series of items assessing differing attitudes. The expectation is that by "hiding" items, respondents will be less aware that their racial attitudes are being assessed and, consequently, will respond more truthfully rather than in more socially desirable or other reactive ways. A potential cost of these approaches is that the mixing of items potentially leads to shared method variance across the different attitudes, inflating their actual relationships.

A second source of common method variance can be broader in scale, for example, resulting from collection of a number of different measures via a single method such as a paper-and-pencil survey, particularly if all items share a common response format. All responses collected by a single approach may be related due to the way in which the measures are collected. Yet a third potential source of common method variance is interviewer bias, reflecting ways in which interviewers shape and interpret information provided to them by respondents.

In most instances, method variance is relatively easy to include in path models so long as researchers are aware of its effects. If method variance is shared by two measures or indicators, then their residuals can be connected by a path that signifies their second source of common variance (as was illustrated in Figure 5.2). In Figure 5.2, imagine that X and Y are assessed using a common method and that they are viewed as sharing method variance over and above their other relationship. Their relationship can be estimated based on the tracing rules for path analysis. Their method variance relationship is modeled through the residuals; the relationship through the con- structs (X_t and Y_t) is modeled through their respective relationships with those constructs and the relationship between the constructs X_t and Y_t. By the tracing rule, both the trait and method relationships are the products of three paths.

Figure 5.2 cannot be solved, for there are identification problems in trying to separate trait variance from method variance. Problems would occur even if X and Y measured a single trait, for it would be impossible to disentangle trait variance from method variance. As will be discussed in more detail later in this chapter as well as in the chapter on factor analysis (Chapter 7), only with more measures and using a factor model could the model be solved. An illustration of a model that is identified appears in Figure 5.3, where both X and Y have two measures. In Figure 5.3, only X_1 and Y_1 share a common method. As will be explained later in this book, building models with latent variables and multiple indicators allows many instances of nonrandom error to be modeled successfully.

If common method variance is shared across more than two measures, then an alternative is to model method as an additional latent (unmeasured) variable rather than to view method variance as nonrandom error. If it were specified as nonrandom error, then the residuals between all pairs of variables would be connected by arrows. But from the perspective of factor analysis, which tries to identify sources of common variance, specifying shared method variance as a latent variable makes better sense than does specifying multiple residual covariances, for method is a source of common variance.

The logic of modeling method as a theoretical variable (or, in the language of factor analysis, as a common factor) is somewhat different from just allowing the residuals to covary among each pair of vari-

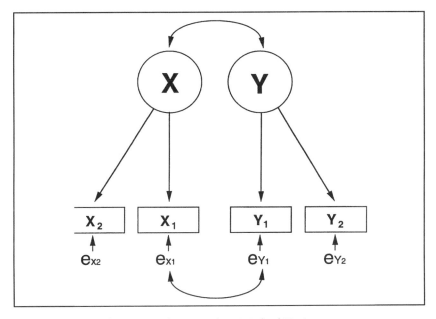

Figure 5.3. An Illustration of Nonrandom Method Variance

ables. Modeling method as a single latent variable requires greater consistency in relationships. For example, imagine a case in which there are three indicators sharing a common method. Modeling pairs of residuals could yield 0, 1, 2, or 3 significant residual covariances. Consider the case in which two are significant and the third is not. In such an instance, it is difficult to envision the method variance as defining a single method factor. A single method factor could have an appreciable effect on none or one of the measures (in which case there would be no **common** method factor) or on two or three measures (in which case there would be a common method factor). If method affected only two measures, then two of the indicators should share appreciable method variance, resulting in one significant residual covariance. If method affected all three measures, then all three residuals should be significant. By contrast, two significant residual covariances would mean that two of the pairs of indicators share a second appreciable source of common variance, whereas the third pair has only a single source of common variance. Such findings are not consistent with a single factor model but rather would suggest *two* additional sources of common variance.

In other words, if one believes that method variance is an appreciable source of extraneous variance across three or more indicators sharing a common method, then the best way in which to model that variance is by specifying a common method factor rather than by allowing all pairs of residual covariances. Allowing pairs could yield patterns of findings not consistent with the presence of a single method factor.

At this point, a caveat is in order. I have seen many instances in which my students have tried to extract both method and trait variance from a set of indicators that supposedly measure a single factor via a single method. This is *not possible*; with only a single method, it is impossible to separate method variance from trait variance. The two sources of common variance are confounded. Adding additional indicators that assess the same trait by the same method does not help; the problem exists whether there are 3 indicators or 30 indicators. Only when an additional indicator measuring either the trait or the method but not both is available is extraction of both trait and method factors possible. In the language of construct validity, that additional indicator provides information about discriminant validity that is needed to tease apart method and trait effects.

To the extent that method variance crosscuts the theoretical variables of interest, effects of method can be separated from effects of other sources of common variance. One way in which to design a study so that method effects are separable from other sources of common variance, which here are called trait factors even though not all of them may be traits in a traditional sense, is to cross methods and traits. Such an approach, analogous to an experimental study in which the factors are crossed, can sample all traits with all methods. Such an approach has been called an MTMM matrix approach (Campbell & Fiske, 1959). Logic for this approach, which was worked out well in advance of availability of appropriate structural equation methods, is presented next.

Additive Multitrait-Multimethod Models

Campbell and Fiske (1959) presented a model for interpreting traits across methods. Although, as is discussed later, there are non-obvious problems in using path modeling approaches to solve for MTMM data, the logic of method variance is of central importance to structural equation methods. The general goal of the MTMM approach is to be able to address issues of validity without those issues being confused by the presence of common variance caused by common methods.

Campbell and Fiske (1959) argued that without measuring multiple methods as well as multiple traits, the relative contributions of trait and method variance cannot be determined. They presented MTMM data, defined different types of elements of the correlation matrix depending on their trait-method combination, and developed rules of thumb for determining validity of trait variables.

First, Campbell and Fiske (1959) put their efforts into a framework of convergent and discriminant validity. They reminded readers that "validation is typically *convergent*, a confirmation by independent measurement procedures" (p. 81, emphasis in original). In other words, a variable assessed by one method should be strongly related to that same variable measured by a different method; if the relationships across methods are small, then the variable fails the test of convergent validity. The flip side of convergent validity is **discriminant validity**, which means that to be a valid measure, that measure needs to be less substantially related to measures of different variables. If correlations of measures across variables are too high, then one may wonder whether the measures are assessing what they purport to be measuring. Thus, different traits assessed by a common method should not in general be very highly correlated. Exceptions may occur if the different traits are expected to be substantially correlated or if the traits being assessed are elusive ones, readily overpowered by method variance.

The idea of "elusive traits" is not one mentioned by Campbell and Fiske (1959) but is one that has intrigued me. There are variables that inherently are difficult to assess because responses that tap those variables also tend to trigger other variables and method variance. They may be overlooked or ignored because of the difficulty in measuring them. Sometimes the variables can be "aggregate" types of variables, such as family support or social climate, which seemingly have to include many aspects/components. Others could include personality variables that people talk about but have difficulty operationalizing, such as empathy and ambition. Ambition seems particularly prone to demand characteristics and social desirability, and questions about ambition potentially seem to tap ability and achievement as well as ambition.

Another good illustration is provided by a variable mentioned earlier in this chapter: prejudice. Despite the many ways and times researchers have tried to measure prejudice, there exists no widely accepted way in which to measure it. Insofar as variables such as prejudice are likely to prove to be important if they ever can be effectively assessed, it seems natural to attempt to use approaches that might disentangle those variables from methods and other sources of extraneous variance. Only then will researchers be able to identify them and their relationships with other, more reliably assessed variables.

Campbell and Fiske (1959) took as their departure point for MTMM matrices the need for multiple traits and multiple methods. They suggested moving the point to its logical end, namely, measuring each trait assessed by all methods used. The result is a fully crossed trait × method correlation matrix. Readers should try to think broadly about what is a trait and what is a method, for there are opportunities to use traits and methods creatively. For example, McGarvey, Miller, and Maruyama (1977) used an MTMM model to compare different ways of scoring field dependence using the Witkin rod and frame apparatus.

Table 5.1 presents the prototype MTMM matrix, a 3 trait × 3 method matrix. Campbell and Fiske (1959) divided the matrix up into four different types of correlations based on same/different method and trait combinations. First, the underlined elements, the main diagonal, are the **monotrait-monomethod** correlations. Campbell and Fiske put the reliabilities on that diagonal to define the maximum possible relationship that exists between each measure and any other measure. Second, the three sets of three correlations that form triangles next to the reliability diagonal (e.g., r_{21}, r_{31}, and r_{32}) are called the **heterotrait-monomethod** correlations. These share common method variance but assess different traits. Third, bold print is used to identify the three sets of three correlations along the subdiagonals within the heteromethod blocks. These are **monotrait-heteromethod** correlations, which Campbell and Fiske called the **validity diagonals**. They are called validity diagonals because ideally they tap common trait variance independent of method variance. Finally, fourth are the correlations within blocks on either side of the validity diagonals. These are the **heterotrait-heteromethod** correlations, those that share neither common trait variance nor common method variance.

TABLE 5.1 Illustrative 3×3 Multitrait-Multimethod Matrix

	Method 1			Method 2			Method 3		
	Trait A_1	Trait B_1	Trait C_1	Trait A_2	Trait B_2	Trait C_2	Trait A_3	Trait B_3	Trait C_3
Method 1									
Trait A_1	r_{11}								
Trait B_1	$\mid r_{21}$	r_{22}							
Trait C_1	$\mid r_{31}$	r_{32}	r_{33}						
Method 2									
Trait A_2	r_{41}	r_{42}	r_{43}	r_{44}					
Trait B_2	r_{51}	r_{52}	r_{53}	$\mid r_{54}$	r_{55}				
Trait C_2	r_{61}	r_{62}	r_{63}	$\mid r_{64}$	r_{65}	r_{66}			
Method 3									
Trait A_3	r_{71}	r_{72}	r_{73}	r_{74}	r_{75}	r_{76}	r_{77}		
Trait B_3	r_{81}	r_{82}	r_{83}	r_{84}	r_{85}	r_{86}	$\mid r_{87}$	r_{88}	
Trait C_3	r_{91}	r_{92}	r_{93}	r_{94}	r_{95}	r_{96}	$\mid r_{97}$	r_{98}	r_{99}

Campbell and Fiske (1959) suggested four conditions that would need to be met to establish validity.

1. Entries in the validity diagonals "should be significantly different from zero and sufficiently large to encourage further examination of validity" (p. 82). That is, traits measured by differing methods still should be highly correlated.

This first condition is the test of convergent validity. The remaining three conditions test discriminant validity.

2. The value of each element in the validity diagonals should be higher than the values lying in its column and row in the heterotrait-heteromethod triangles. This almost always should be found, for it requires only that the correlation of a single variable assessed by different methods be greater than different variables assessed by those same different methods. To illustrate, the correlation r_{82} should be larger than either r_{81}, r_{83}, r_{72}, or r_{92}.

3. For each measure, common trait variance should be greater than common method variance. In the words of Campbell and Fiske, "A variable [should] correlate higher with an independent effort to measure the same trait than with measures designed to get at different traits which happen to employ the same method" (p. 83). Practically, elements of the validity diagonal need to be greater than their corresponding elements

in the heterotrait-monomethod triangles. The comparison is between a measure's correlations with other measures of the same trait by different methods and the measure's correlations with measures of different traits by the same method. To illustrate, to test for Trait A by Method 1, r_{41} and r_{71} should be larger than r_{21} and r_{31}; to test for Trait B by Method 2, r_{52} and r_{85} should be greater than r_{54} and r_{65}.

4. The relative size (or at least rank) of the elements within each heterotrait block should be maintained across blocks. In Campbell and Fiske's words, "The same pattern of trait interrelationships [should] be shown in all of the heterotrait triangles of both the monomethod and heteromethod blocks" (p. 83). Again, to illustrate, if $r_{21} > r_{31} > r_{32}$, then we also should find that $r_{54} > r_{64} > r_{65}$ and that $r_{42} > r_{43} > r_{53}$, and so forth, for all heterotrait blocks.

These rules were important ones when analysis of MTMM matrices needed to be done by inspection. With the development of more sophisticated methodologies capable of teasing apart various variance components in matrices (e.g., Kenny & Kashy, 1992), they became less important even though their logic is basically sound.

From my perspective, the first two conditions are straightforward and fairly obvious. The third is really unneeded, for there is no real reason why trait variance has to be stronger than method variance so long as they can be separated; it is this difference in perspective from Campbell and Fiske (1959) that has generated my interest in elusive traits. Finally, barring extra sources of common variance (which of course could be modeled as residual covariation if they were anticipated), Condition 4 also seems reasonable and quite possible to attain.

Presenting MTMM matrices in path model form requires a basic understanding of the logic of factor analysis. As a result, MTMM matrices will be discussed more fully in the later chapter on factor analysis (Chapter 7). At this point, only one more point is covered in this chapter: that the discussion about MTMM matrices has assumed that traits and methods combine additively. Alternatively, they have been hypothesized as combining multiplicatively (Campbell and O'Connell, 1967), which yields very different approaches.

Nonadditive Multitrait-Multimethod Models

Despite the intuitive appeal of an additive MTMM model, several researchers have argued that, in many instances, traits and methods combine in a multiplicative fashion. The first to suggest this pattern were Campbell and O'Connell (1967). They suggested as alternatives (a) an inverse relationship between traits and methods in which the stronger the trait relationship between two variables, the less the impact of common method on their relationship, and (b) a multiplicative relationship in which the stronger the relationship between traits, the more it is augmented by common method variance. Their analyses of several MTMM data sets were in general more consistent with a multiplicative relationship between traits and methods than with either an additive or an inverse relationship. On the basis of their analyses, they questioned whether an additive effects model from factor analysis is appropriate for MTMM matrices.

The position of Campbell and O'Connell (1967) has been refined by Browne (1984) and others. Cudeck (1988) provided an illustration contrasting additive and multiplicative models as well as presenting approaches for assessing whether or not effects combine in multiplicative fashion. Because those approaches fall outside the set of structural equation methods described in this text, they are not discussed here. SEM researchers should, however, consider these other approaches as important alternative methodologies for MTMM data.

Summary

This chapter has presented how mesurement error produces types of path models that go beyond path analysis. First, the consequences of random and nonrandom error were discussed. Random error in dependent variables reduces the R^2 but does not bias unstandardized path coefficients. Random error in independent variables reduces relationships in the bivariate case but has more complex and unpredictable effects in the multivariate case. Nonrandom error leads to fundamental problems in estimation when "normal" regression approaches are used. Alternative approaches are needed. Second, method variance, specifically as it co-occurs along with trait variance, was discussed, and the logic of MTMM analysis was presented. For SEM approaches, traits and methods are assumed to combine additively.

Chapter Discussion Questions

1. What again is the rationale for focusing on covariance rather than correlation matrices? Are there trade-offs?

2. What are some of the basic tests that you would need to do to check out the violations of assumptions such as "too much nonrandom error"?

3. Standardized B's are understood to be b/SE. In the measurement error example, "standardized" seemed to be used in a different sense. Is that so?

4. Would it be advantageous for methods to correlate?

5. MTMM was first used in the 1950s. Is it not used any longer?

E X E R C I S E   5 . 1

Elusive Constructs

Individually and, if possible, then in groups, brainstorm about constructs that have been difficult to assess but that might be interpretable once method variance is taken out and other trait dimensions are separately extracted.

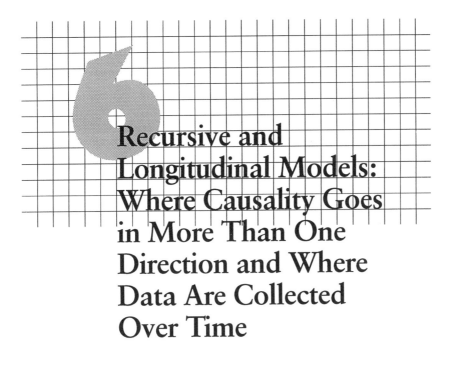

6 Recursive and Longitudinal Models: Where Causality Goes in More Than One Direction and Where Data Are Collected Over Time

Up to this point, there has been little discussion of ways of analyzing structural model data where the arrows in models do not go in a single direction and where there is repeated assessment of particular measures across time. This chapter focuses on the analysis of such data because they contribute a unique piece to the understanding of structural equation approaches. In both cases, data cannot be analyzed satisfactorily using the path analysis/ordinary least squares techniques described thus far. Models with feedback loops cannot be analyzed by ordinary regression analysis because the assumption of independence of errors is violated. Data collected repeatedly from a single sample over time introduce a new set of problems (e.g., growth over time, identification), concerns, and opportunities. Finally, as is elaborated in detail in this chapter, the two approaches are linked because, to the extent that the multidirectional processes occur across time, modeling processes across time can allow multidirectional causal influence within a unidirectional flow model.

▌ Models With Multidirectional Paths

In the structural equation literature, models in which the causal arrows flow in more than one direction are called **nonrecursive models**. In contrast to path analysis models, nonrecursive models may not be uniquely solvable, even in instances in which the degrees of freedom suggest overidentification. The first part of this chapter discusses nonrecursive models and then covers tests that can be used to assess whether or not nonrecursive models can be uniquely solved.

Up to this point, all the models that have been introduced have had causality flowing only in a single direction. In other words, there always is a "downstream" flow to the models. By contrast, in nonrecursive models causation does not follow such a straightforward path. The models may include feedback loops ($A \rightarrow B \rightarrow C \rightarrow A$) through which causality turns back on itself, reciprocal causal relationships (see Figure 6.1) in which two or more variables cause each other simultaneously, or even both. Because the notion of simultaneous causation is both difficult to envision and somewhat controversial, an alternative way in which to think about simultaneous causation models is as illustrated in the lagged model of Figure 6.1, which represents situations in which two or more variables continuously cause each other over some time period.

▌ *Logic of Nonrecursive Models*

Although nonrecursive models have been used quite frequently in the social sciences, researchers should be sure that in fact their nonrecursive models really are nonrecursive. In many instances, it seems that researchers develop models based on the limitations of their data rather than on the underlying theory, for example, testing a nonrecursive model because the data that they have available are cross-sectional rather than longitudinal.

One critical principle to consider during model development is the principle of **finite causal lag**. This principle states that any cause produces an effect on a second variable after some (finite amount of) time has passed; thus, there is a lag from cause to effect. The lag can be very short, as, for example, an eyeblink response to a puff of air (cause: air puff; result: eye blink), but nonetheless there is a lag. As a consequence, the variable that is caused becomes different across the

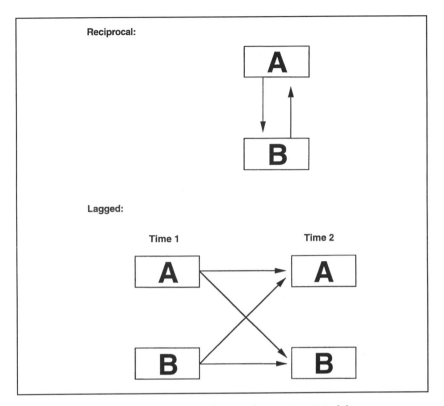

Figure 6.1. Reciprocal Causation and Lagged Causation Models

lag time interval, so if it also causes the variable that has caused it and the two causes (i.e., measures) are assessed at the same time, then it actually is affecting a later version of that variable rather than the causal version. In other words, the variable that is being caused is different from the variable that is the cause, for time has to pass for a cause to produce an effect. Note that it is not possible to justify a model of reciprocal causality by arguing that the variables in the bidirectional relationship do not change, for then there can be no causal effect.

In many instances, an alternative that may be more accurate than reciprocal causation is a lagged, cross-causal model often called a cross-lag panel model (the topic of the next section of this chapter). The two alternatives are presented in Figure 6.1.

If the logic presented in the preceding is at all persuasive, then readers may be wondering whether there really are nonrecursive models or whether models always should attempt to cross time. Here one gets into disciplinary as well as individual differences in perspectives. Some researchers will take the preceding arguments as defining fact and argue that there never are reciprocal causation models because bidirectional causation really is the lagged model of Figure 6.1. Others take equally strong positions in support of reciprocal causation models, for example, arguing that a variable measured at a single point in time is the aggregation of an array of influences from across time and, consequently, that it can be caused by a variable that it causes. For processes of continuous bidirectional causation and fairly high stability of the variables involved, little, if anything, is likely to be lost by modeling the process as nonrecursive. In fact, if the causal processes are continuously ongoing, then it might produce exactly the same outcome as would a unidirectional lagged model but without having to collect longitudinal data. Another argument is that the reciprocal causation model can be used to "test" competing models of causation, with the expectation that the model will separate cause from effect and typically leave a recursive model once the primary cause is identified.

For an illustration of nonrecursive models, I return again to the example of the relationship between acceptance by peers and school achievement. Both peer relationships and student achievement develop over time. From my perspective, the best way in which to model such relationships probably is longitudinally, for example, through measures collected at the beginning and again at the end of a school year. Alternatively, however, one could argue that at any point in time each of them is an aggregation of a series of influences that have occurred across time and that modeling them as reciprocally related would pick up the ongoing processes of change and influence (e.g., Maruyama & McGarvey, 1980).

Regardless of one's views about nonrecursive models, they are an important part of structural equation modeling (SEM) because (a) causal processes cannot be restricted to one-directional causation and (b) thinking about alternative ways of modeling bidirectional causation is integral to accurate model development. Without the logic of feedback and reciprocal relationships, path models become much weaker methodological approaches. Finally, if only cross-sectional data are available, then the only way in which to represent bidirectional relationships is to use reciprocal causation models.

■ Estimation of Nonrecursive Models

Estimation of path coefficients in nonrecursive models differs from path analysis in two important ways. First, basic (i.e., ordinary least squares) regression approaches do not work. Second, model identification becomes a critical issue. For example, in the top part of Figure 6.1, there is a single relationship between two variables, but there are two paths to estimate, making that model underidentified. Furthermore, even if the number of relationships (correlations or covariances) were to be made greater than the number of paths by adding other variables, the assumption of independence of residuals is violated. Specifically, if *A* causes *B* and if *B* causes *A* as in Figure 6.1, then *A*'s residual is not independent of *B*'s residual.

Once identification is established (an approach for assessing identification is addressed in the latter part of this section), to solve for path models using regression approaches one needs to use multistage least squares techniques. Such approaches are not treated in detail here for two reasons (but interested readers can see, e.g., Kenny [1979]). First, nonrecursive models can be handled routinely within the general framework for latent variable SEM. Second, there is little carryover from regression approaches for estimating parameters in nonrecursive models to latent variable structural equation approaches to those models. In other words, once one understands how to do latent variable SEM, which will be addressed later in this book, there is no need to learn a multistage regression approach for solving nonrecursive models. For readers interested in understanding how to solve for such models using regression approaches, a brief description follows. (Some readers may be interested in knowing that SEM computer programs [e.g., LISREL] may generate the initial estimates of parameters to be estimated by using a variation of multistage least squares techniques.)

In regression approaches, the reciprocally related variables first are each separately regressed on the full array of predictor variables. Predicted scores for them are calculated. Those predicted scores are then included in place of the original endogenous variable in the regression equations for predicting the other endogenous variable(s). Thus, the regression analyses have been done in two stages: first, regressing each endogenous variable in a reciprocal relationship on *all* exogenous variables and, second, solving for the structural paths by including the predicted score for the endogenous variable in a regression analysis with all predictors that have direct paths to the endogenous variable. Note that if all of the exogenous variables are included in the equation, then a solution would not be possible because the predicted score variables are perfect linear combinations of the full set of exogenous variables. Such a model also would be underidentified. Furthermore, if the variables excluded from the equation (called instrumental variables) are unrelated to the predicted score variable, then the same collinearity problems appear.

At this point, readers may be wondering what happens to any covariation between the reciprocally related variables that is not shared with the exogenous variables. It certainly is not desirable to assume that their relationship is tied totally to exogenous variables. The way in which that issue is resolved in stage estimation is that the residuals between reciprocally related variables typically are specified as covarying. Residual covariation picks up relationships that exist over and above relationships with exogenous variables.

The multistage least squares approaches need to be put into a broader context. Whether or not one follows the logic about two-stage least squares approaches is relatively unimportant, for nonrecursive models can be solved using the general linear model that is used in latent variable SEM. The latent variable SEM approach handles nonrecursive models in the same way as it does recursive ones. Furthermore, because the solution is a full information one, specifying covariation between residuals of reciprocally related variables is not necessary. Residuals should be specified as covarying only if there is a substantive reason for believing that there is an additional source of common variance between the two variables beyond their reciprocal causal relationship.

Finally, as one thinks about nonrecursive models from the framework of path modeling, it is important to remember that decomposition of effects works differently in nonrecursive models. For example, the matrix approach for solving for indirect effects will not work because the matrix used (see Chapter 3) never goes to zero. An alternative that works for nonreciprocal relations is to use a modified tracing rule approach (see Kenny, 1979) in which the result from the tracing rule is divided by the quantity $(1 - ab$, where a and b are the paths between the two feedback variables). Because the current versions of structural equation programs compute indirect effects for models, it seems sufficient for readers to understand the logic underlying decomposition of effects. Therefore, the mechanics of decomposition for nonrecursive models are not explained further (but interested readers can see Kenny [1979]).

Model Identification

Unlike recursive path models without measurement error that always will be identified, there is no guarantee that a unique solution can be obtained for nonrecursive models. Some nonrecursive models can be underidentified and therefore not solvable. To ensure identification, certain conditions need to be met. Those conditions can be met when some of the predictor variables do *not* have direct paths to certain endogenous variables. The term frequently used to describe such variables is **instrumental variable** or **instrument**. A predictor variable serves as an instrument for an endogenous variable and helps to identify its equation, provided that variable has a direct path to other endogenous variables but *not* to the variable of interest. For a model to be identified, each equation needs to have as many instruments (variables without direct paths) as there are variables in reciprocal relationships. Furthermore, as is explained in the next section of this chapter when the rank condition for identification is described, the instruments have to be distributed in particular ways for each dependent variable to have a solvable equation.

Consider the illustration in Figure 6.2. How could we tell whether or not it is identified? Consider first estimating the model including the dashed line path. There are five variables (therefore, $5 \times 4 / 2 = 10$ degrees of freedom) and exactly 10 paths, suggesting that the model might be identified. Furthermore, X_3 is an instrument for the Y_1 equation. But notice also that all three of the exogenous variables have arrows directly to Y_2, which means that the endogenous variable has no instruments, and therefore its equation is not identified. Once the dashed line path is dropped, however, X_1 becomes an instrument for the equation of Y_2 and the model becomes identified.

There are two conditions that must be met to ensure identification. Before presenting these two conditions, however, it should be noted that, particularly for complex models, ensuring identification may be very difficult. In principle, however, the computer programs that analyze structural equation models should provide tests for model identification. If the proposed model is underidentified, then

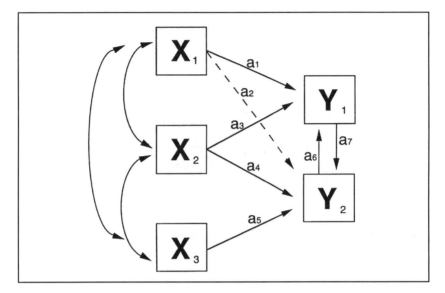

Figure 6.2. Nonrecursive Path Model to Illustrate Model Identification

the program should not be able to generate a complete solution. Specifically, calculation of confidence intervals requires inverting the matrix of estimates. A matrix called the information matrix (see, e.g., Jöreskog & Sörbom, 1988), which is based on the matrix of estimates, should be singular and noninvertible for an underidentified model, with the result that confidence intervals cannot be produced for the estimated parameters. Although this should provide a surefire test of model identification, there is waffling about identification because exceptions seem to have been found. Therefore, readers concerned about complex models are referred to the works of Bollen (e.g., 1989) and his colleagues as well as Rigdon (1995).

The treatment of identification issues for manifest variable models that I find most understandable is the one presented by Namboodiri, Carter, and Blalock (1975, pp. 502-505). I will try to model my description after theirs. The first condition, which they called the **order condition,** is a necessary but not a sufficient condition for identification. It requires that for any system of N endogenous variables (which therefore means that there will be N equations, one for each endogenous variable), a particular equation will be identified only if at least $N - 1$ variables are left out of that equation (i.e., their regression weights are set to 0). For the Y variables in Figure 6.2, with two endogenous variables the two equations are

$$Y_1 = a_1{}^*X_1 + a_3{}^*X_2 + 0{}^*X_3 + a_6{}^*Y_2 + e_1 \qquad (6.1)$$
$$Y_2 = a_2{}^*X_1 + a_4{}^*X_2 + a_5{}^*X_3 + a_7{}^*Y_1 + e_2. \qquad (6.2)$$

The residuals can be ignored because they go to the left side of the equation, whereas the dependent variables join the other variables on the right side of the equation (the signs on the coefficients also are inconsequential and can be ignored), yielding

$$-e_1 = a_1{}^*X_1 + a_3{}^*X_2 + 0{}^*X_3 - 1{}^*Y_1 + a_6{}^*Y_2$$
$$-e_2 = a_2{}^*X_1 + a_4{}^*X_2 + a_5{}^*X_3 + a_7{}^*Y_1 - 1{}^*Y_2.$$

In terms of the **order condition**, each equation needs to have $(2 - 1)$ variables omitted from the equation. The first equation is fine because X_3 is omitted, whereas the second equation fails to meet the order condition. Once the a_2 coefficient is set to zero, that equation also meets the order condition for identification.

The second condition, more restrictive than the first and both a necessary and a sufficient condition for identification, is called the **rank condition**. Given a system of N dependent variables, for the rank condition to be satisfied for a particular equation, it must be possible to form at least one nonzero determinant of rank $N - 1$ from the coefficients of the variables omitted from that equation. Using the last set of the preceding equations, with the residuals isolated from all other variables, follow these three steps.

1. Form a matrix from the coefficients (signs again can be ignored). For the example, it would be as follows:

	X_1	X_2	X_3	Y_1	Y_2
Y_1	a_1	a_3	0	1	a_6
Y_2	0	a_4	a_5	a_7	1

2. To test for identification of a particular equation, delete from the matrix (a) the row of that equation and (b) all columns that do not have a zero in the row of the equation of interest.
3. Find a nonzero determinant of rank $N - 1$ from the remaining values.

Concretely, for Y_1 the entire first row (the Y_1 row) is deleted, as are the first (X_1), second (X_2), fourth (Y_1), and fifth (Y_2) columns, leaving $[a_5]$, which happens to be a 1×1 matrix with a nonzero determinant unless a_5 happens to be exactly 0. For Y_2, the entire second row is deleted, as are the second through fifth columns, leaving $[a_1]$, another 1×1 matrix with a nonzero determinant unless a_1 is exactly 0. Because both a_5 and a_1 are being estimated, they are expected to be nonzero. If so, the modified Figure 6.2, with the dashed path from X_1 to Y_2 omitted, is an identified model. As suggested earlier, X_1 serves as an instrument for Y_2 and X_3 as an instrument for Y_1.

A few final points about identification are in order. First, if the X variables are highly intercorrelated, then it may make little sense to argue that one X can readily be dropped from each equation given that they share much common variance and are not easily distinguishable one from another. Ideally, instruments are basically independent of other exogenous variables. An important point is that although instruments are essential for attaining model identification, in some instances it may be very difficult to find variables that meet the requirements of good instruments. Second, what if the two endogenous variables "shared" the same instrument, for example, if in Figure 6.2 we were to put a_2 back into the model and remove a_5. The answer is that the rank condition no longer could be satisfied because the 1×1 matrices would be 0. The important point here is that each endogenous variable in a reciprocal relationship needs its own separate instruments.

▌Longitudinal Models

The remainder of this chapter focuses on stability and change of variables and relationships between variables across time. The focus is *not* on changes in scores of individuals. That type of change is modeled differently (e.g., Willett & Sayer, 1994). Readers who are trying to look at both stability of relationships and changes in mean levels should see, for example, McArdle and Aber (1990).

The data discussed in this chapter most typically are called **longitudinal data**. They also have been described as **panel data** or even **cross-lag panel data**. Although the terms sometimes are used almost interchangeably, one distinction that can be made between them is that the former refers to any set of data in which measures are collected at different points in time even if no measure is collected more than once, whereas the latter two typically are reserved for instances in which some of the same measures are collected at two or more different points in time. It is the instances when measures are collected more than once that warrant special description, so the term "panel data" is used in this chapter to describe those instances.

The first part of this section focuses on the logic underlying longitudinal approaches. It builds on the discussion from the preceding section on nonrecursive models. It includes an introduction to the terminology for analysis of panel data, a discussion of identification issues for panel models, and a review of the unique nature of longitudinal data. Then, in the second part of this section, manifest variable panel analysis approaches are discussed.

Logic Underlying Longitudinal Models

Of most importance to users or prospective users of structural equation methodologies is the logic underlying structural equation analysis of panel data. This logic provides a perspective that refines and extends the logic of path analysis by explicitly introducing notions of stability and change. Without those notions, resulting models for panel data are unlikely to accurately explain causal processes.

Longitudinal models are important for users of structural equation methodologies because (a) they add into structural modeling notions of stability and change, (b) they provide the best way of modeling reciprocal causation to researchers who are persuaded by the concept of finite causal lag, (c) they provide an additional perspective for thinking about model identification, and (d) the language used is explicit in separating particular types of relationships and types of residual covariation from other types. This last point, which is covered next, is particularly useful to researchers when they attempt to explain their models to others.

In contrast to the importance of the logic, most of the methodologies that were developed to analyze longitudinal data have major shortcomings that make them less than appealing (e.g., Rogosa, 1980). The methods include both analysis of panel correlations (e.g., Calsyn & Kenny, 1977) and path regression approaches (e.g., Shingles, 1976). They are variants of two-variable, two-wave models. All have problems and shortcomings due to assumptions of nonrandom error and of causes not specified in the models. Once again, an appropriate and flexible way in which to model such data is to use latent variable SEM, for it can allow researchers to design models that make realistic assumptions.

▌ Terminology of Panel Models

Consider Figure 6.3, which is used to illustrate the terminology of longitudinal analyses. The model in Figure 6.3 is a two-variable, two-wave, longitudinal panel (path) model. Variables X and Y both are measured at two points in time. For the moment, ignore the directions of the paths and the fact that Figure 6.3 is a variant of a regression model. Focus instead on the different types of zero-order relationships, or correlations, between variables. In the language of cross-lag panel analysis, the relationships between the two exogenous variables (X_1 and Y_1) and between the two endogenous variables (X_2 and Y_2) both are called **synchronous** correlations; they represent relationships between two different variables at a single point in time. In purely cross-sectional models, all correlations are synchronous. The X_1-X_2 and Y_1-Y_2 relationships are called **autocorrelations**, or **stabilities**, reflecting the amount of change in a single variable across time. The X_1-Y_2 and Y_1-X_2 relationships are the lagged or **cross-lagged** (because they cross between variables) correlations. Finally, the paths between the residuals (e's), which typically are not included as part of a panel analysis model, are **residual covariances**, or autocorrelated residuals, sometimes generically called correlated errors. This last type of path reflects the fact that when a measure is administered at different times, there is the likelihood of substantial variance being shared across the different administrations of that measure due not to the underlying construct that is assessed but rather to particulars of the measure that is administered (i.e., measure-specific variance).

EXERCISE

Given that you should now be familiar with identification, is Figure 6.3 identified?

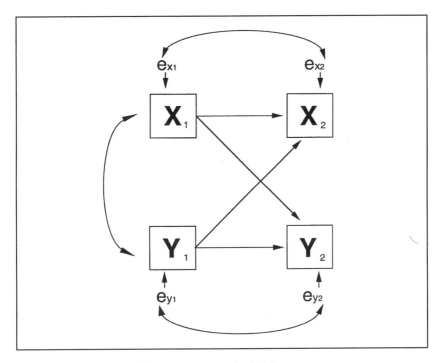

Figure 6.3. Two-Variable, Two-Wave Panel Model

Identification

Issues of identification tie back into the exercise just presented. The answer to that question is *no*, for there are only six correlations but seven paths to solve. The important point here is that some panel models, despite being recursive, still may not be identified. The reason why identification becomes an issue is that repeated assessment of the same measure produces two sources of common variance, one due to the underlying construct and the second due to measure-specific variance. This latter source of common variance usually would be part of the unique variance of the measure; however, because the same measure is collected twice, that variance becomes part of the common variance of the measure. The model would be identified if a researcher were willing to allow the two sources of common variance within the measure to be lumped together, but combining the two yields an inaccurate assessment of the stability of the underlying variable. To build models that are closer to the processes that occur, it is necessary for researchers to consider whether or not autocorrelation exists across time between the residuals when administering measures repeatedly. If it is likely to exist, then multiple-indicator models are needed. They would be identified even if measure-specific variance were included.

▌ Stability

Without detracting from the importance of terminology or identification issues, the most important concept added by panel models is **stability** of a variable. To illustrate, imagine that some variable called Z is perfectly stable. By definition, then, Z measured at Time 1 (Z_1) will have no causes other than itself, for it is perfectly determined by itself from an earlier point in time, here called Time 0 (Z_0). Yet, if Z_1 is modeled in a cross-sectional model as an endogenous variable, as it is with respect to Z_0 (remember that cross-sectional models would have data collected at only one point in time, so the earlier time point version of that variable, Z_0, cannot be a predictor because it would not have been assessed), then other variables either correlated with Z_0, causing Z_0, or caused by Z_0 all could appear to be causes of Z_1. All that needs to happen for the possibility of incorrect inferences to occur is that some other variables that are related to Z need to be placed in a model causally prior to Z_1, that is, with arrows pointing directly to it. Even though placing them causally prior to Z would result in a model that is misspecified, that misspecification could easily go undetected. Such misspecification could occur, for example, when there are arguments for bidirectional causation and the other variables are collected temporally prior to Z_1.

As an example of issues of stability, consider a hypothetical situation in which antecedents of school achievement are sought. The importance of identifying variables that could improve achievement is sufficiently motivating to lead researchers to look widely for predictors of achievement. To illustrate, would it not be wonderful to find ways of markedly improving the achievement of children who are struggling in school? In thinking about this situation, remember that an intervention that improves the achievement of all children but preserves their relative achievement levels in comparison to one another would neither affect stability nor appear to be a cause in a structural model for the intervention sample. The means would change, but the covariances would be unaffected. Only in a multisample study in which treatment is a dummy variable would the effect be apparent. Said differently, the processes being examined look at relationships, not mean (level) shifts. For SEM models to identify changes, the relative achievements of students would have to change, for example, as an intervention raised the achievement of children who are lowest in achievement. If everyone is affected by an intervention, then dramatic changes in means could be invisible in structural models.

To search broadly for possible predictors while building a model that seems realistic, researchers should sample an array of possible predictors. Such predictors might include personality measures, peer relations, teacher and parent ratings, and demographics (see, e.g., Maruyama [1977] for such a study). The researchers should frame their work by recognizing that, at an aggregate level, achievement is likely to be highly stable, for children who do relatively well in one year by and large do relatively well in subsequent years as well. Yet, if the data examined to explore antecedents of achievement were cross-sectional and failed to include past achievement as a variable, then the omission of past achievement might result in the emergence of a number of "promising" predictors. Those promising predictors are most likely to be variables strongly related to past achievement. In effect, those promising predictors may just be correlated with or caused by past achievement (which, in the preceding discussion, is the Z_0 variable).

For researchers attempting to be sensitive to issues of stability within the limitations of a cross-sectional design, there always is the option of trying to collect longitudinal data at a single point in time through retrospective reporting. For example, in a study of academic performance, students may be asked about their cumulative grade point averages prior to the present year; in a study of attitudes, participants may be asked about how they thought they used to think about some issue; and in a social status study, participants may be asked about their past earnings or their families' social status. Such data may allow a more realistic model to be tested for viability. They are not, however, the same as multiwave longitudinal sampling, which provides current data at each time period. Particularly for research in areas like attitude assessment but also for areas like reporting of past achievement, retrospective reporting gets distorted by current perspectives. Other things being equal, it likely leads to greater consistency across time than would be found if data were collected at two or more different points in time.

The goal of this discussion is not to dissuade one from ever attempting to collect retrospective data. Such data can be very valuable if collected thoughtfully. Rather, it is to warn researchers about limits of relying on retrospective reports to replace longitudinal sampling.

A second potential type of problem or shortcoming can occur when collecting retrospective or file data to supplement the current time data. To the extent that the retrospective or file information provides imperfect data about the underlying variable, the resulting measures are unreliable. If, in the preceding achievement illustration, the measure of past achievement is less than perfectly reliable, then the Z_0 variable will not perfectly determine Z_1. As a result, other predictors could appear to be important when in fact they are not. This problem is not unique to retrospective data collection. It also can occur in panel data and is the same unreliability problem as was discussed in Chapter 5.

Finally, the "flip side" or converse of stability is change or variability. Low stabilities suggest that a variable is changing rapidly or at least appreciably within the time interval studied. Although such change might be viewed as an opportunity for research in that it could allow many variables to exert causal influence, it may have other meanings. One possible explanation to consider as causing low stability across time is poor reliability. If the measures have low reliability, then the variable can be problematic for any structural modeling.

A very different alternative explanation is that, due to some process such as developmental changes in subjects, the variable as assessed during the early time may not be the same variable as is collected at the later time point. An example of the latter possibility may be provided by assessment of mathematics skills among young children. If one were to sample certain skills at two points in time, then at the earlier time point a cluster of skills may be poorly differentiated or even undeveloped, and might be unidimensional aspects of general ability. By the later time, however, the cluster of skills may be much more developed and differentiated, with the consequence that the skills tap more than a single dimension. In such circumstances, the stability of the construct should be relatively poor.

In conclusion, the idea of stability is an important one for structural equation models. If stability of a variable across time is not assessed accurately, then misinterpretations of causal impact can readily occur. Variables that do not change can appear to be affected by other variables. Variables that are measured unreliably will, when modeled as causes, likely appear to have less of an impact than they actually do and, when modeled as effects, likely appear to be influenced by more variables than actually influence them.

The need to effectively model stability of constructs provides an important reason to use panel designs. Because accurate modeling of stability and reliability issues is almost impossible without using multiple indicators, latent variable approaches are preferable. Those approaches can effectively partition measures into variance components. Finally, and a point that I return to later in this chapter, longitudinal data provide a reason why models should work with covariance rather than with correlation matrices, namely, to allow for changes in variability across time.

▌ Temporal Lags in Panel Models

The concept of finite causal lag introduced in the nonrecursive model section has important implications for the understanding of panel models. First, from one perspective, it is finite lag that leads to the development of longitudinal models to examine reciprocal causation. Second, and of much greater importance for the current discussion, if influence occurs over a finite interval, then it is critically important to have an a priori understanding about how long the causal lag actually is. In the ideal world, two reciprocally related variables cause each other at the same rate, so the only issue is to estimate the length of a single lag interval. That is, the time that it takes for one to cause the second is the same as the time it takes for the second to cause the first. In such circumstances, all that is needed is to assess the two variables across a time interval the same as (or slightly greater than) the time lag. Figure 6.4 provides an illustration of causal processes in which two variables influence each other across a time interval of 1 unit: 1 causes 2, 2 causes 3, and so forth. In such an instance, we would want to ensure that the time lag selected is at least as long at 1 unit.

Accepting "slightly greater" is recommended based on a consideration of the consequences of overestimating the causal interval versus underestimating the causal interval. If the interval is overestimated, then data will be collected too far apart. The cost here is that

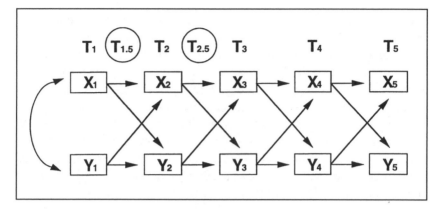

Figure 6.4.   Multiwave Panel Model

the causal relationships will have "decayed" somewhat from their maximums. By contrast, if the interval is too short, then the processes will not yet have occurred and no effect should be apparent.

Consider as an illustration of selecting appropriate causal lags the diagram in Figure 6.4. In Figure 6.4, overestimating could occur if we were to collect data at Time 1 and halfway between Times 2 and 3 (Time 2.5). We would be able to assess any influences that occurred with a causal lag of one time interval, but those influences would be reduced by any changes in the measures from Time 2 to Time 2.5.

The cost of selecting too long an interval depends on how fast the variable changes; it may range from trivially underestimating to missing virtually all of the effect. The latter possibility should be relatively unlikely unless the processes occurred only once and did not continue to repeat themselves across time. (The issue of stability of causal processes is discussed in more detail later in this chapter.) That is, in Figure 6.4, collecting measures at Times 1 and 4 would underestimate the effect dramatically only if the stability of X and Y were low across intervals and the processes occurred only from Time 1 to Time 2.

On the other hand, what if the interval selected were too short? Looking again at Figure 6.4, imagine that we were to assess the variables at Time 1 and halfway between Times 1 and 2 (Time 1.5). The consequence would be that not enough time would have passed for the causal processes to occur, so no causal impact would be apparent or detectable. In other words, the cross-lagged paths would effectively be zero, a definitely unappealing result for instances in which causal impact occurs.

Further complicating longitudinal models is that, in many instances, it is not possible to assume that the causal lags between variables are the same. If they are not, then two different time lags need to be estimated. If data were to be collected at only two points in time, then selection of different length time lags tied to one of the relationships could markedly change the inferences drawn either by underestimating the effects of one predictor by selecting too long a lag for that relationship or by missing the effects of the other predictor by selecting too short a lag for that relationship. The potential for incorrect inferences is particularly great when the goal is to talk about preponderant influence of one variable on another. The one with the stronger impact could change depending on the interval selected.

Even though differing lags complicate longitudinal research, there are ways of building accurate models despite them. For example, if the lags differed substantially, then three-wave data could be collected tied to the different intervals to tap both causal processes.

In summary, collection of longitudinal data introduces new types of problems and complexities that require careful thought before collecting data, for in cross-sectional sampling researchers never have to worry about what the temporal lag should be. At the same time, however, as important as it is to make researchers articulate the length of predicted causal lags, that articulation should not deter individuals from longitudinal research; rather, it should only make them explicitly state something that shaped their thinking and model development. If it is new thinking, then their work was incompletely developed and the model was not well thought out. In other words, a normal part of thinking about relationships between any two variables is to ask the following question: If the relationship is causal, then how long does it take for one variable to affect the other? If both variables affect each other, then the question has to be asked twice.

▌ *Growth Across Time in Panel Models*

Yet another important issue when developing panel models is the issue of growth or change. This issue was mentioned earlier in this chapter when the illustration of increasing complexity of mathematics achievement in children was presented. When the same measures are collected repeatedly, there are dangers in using standardization because it removes differences in variability across time/occasions. In other words, the methodology that allows for growth is SEM using covariances, which focus on raw score relationships. By contrast, correlations focus on standard deviation unit relationships, and changes in the size of the standard deviations can result in apparent strengthening or weakening of standardized relationships.

Said differently, for longitudinal models, there is only one occasion in which use of standardized relationships makes logical sense, namely, the occasion in which there is no change in variability of any of the variables across time. In such a situation, analysis of correlations provides results identical to analysis of covariances, which is why analysis of correlations is acceptable for that situation. Given the small likelihood of all the variances remaining unchanged across time (and the temptation to decide that small, nonsignificant differences between variances are "small enough" to be considered as equivalent or unchanged), it seems advisable to ignore this "special case" altogether and to always model longitudinal data using covariance matrices. Furthermore, Cudeck (1989) pointed out that SEM approaches are worked out for covariances, not correlations.

▌ Stability of Causal Processes

As mentioned earlier in this chapter, stability of any causal processes is an additional issue of importance for panel models. This type of stability differs from stability of measures across time that was discussed earlier in this chapter, for it refers to causal dynamics across time rather than single variables across time. Stability of causal processes means that the way in which some variable, X, affects a second variable, Y, across one time interval is the same as its impact on Y across a second time interval of the same length. Unless causal processes are basically stable, longitudinal models can be misleading and at best will tap processes specific to the particular intervals sampled.

As an illustration, look back to Figure 6.4 and assume that the figure accurately represents causal processes between X and Y. In that figure, so long as the different coefficients from X to Y are of similar magnitude as the different coefficients from Y to X, the processes stay the same regardless of the starting point selected or of the particular interval crossed. Panel data from Time 1 to Time 2 would yield the same findings as would data from Time 4 to Time 5.

By contrast, if the pattern of true causal relationships (arrows) were to differ across time periods, then the processes would be unstable. The relationships identified by the analyses would differ depending on the starting point selected. Because different processes are occurring at differing time points, general statements about causal dynamics are impossible. It is particularly undesirable for circumstances in which one wants to speak generally about causal dynamics. On the other hand, modeling unstable processes may be very attractive if the dynamics are predicted to vary across different intervals, as might be predicted for developmental data or where an intervention was implemented between two intervals. In such circumstances, however, the time points selected for data collection are critical and warrant clear justification.

▌ *Effects of Excluded Variables*

One final point important for analysis of panel models is a point that is true for all structural models but one that is made particularly salient by repeated sampling of variables across time. That point is that structural models **assume a closed system**, namely, that all variables that are important are included in the model. A second way in which to say the same thing is that no omitted variable should by its inclusion change any of the paths in the model. Clearly, this assumption is widely violated, for it assumes that researchers are able to start at the end of a process of identifying important variables. That is, if models had to be correctly specified before the first study was conducted, then there would be little research. By contrast, for any set of possible relationships, we come to understand causal processes over time and through the accumulation of research. That research often includes elements of trial and error.[7]

The important point for longitudinal models is that, due to repeated sampling across time, the number of variables in a model

---

7. The iterative process of model refinement makes salient the tension between use of SEM techniques for model confirmation versus for model development. There are clear disagreements about how much models can be changed within a single data set to improve the match between the data and the model. Discussion of these issues will be left for a later chapter, when techniques that guide model refinement are presented.

increases rapidly. Resulting models potentially can be very complex
and difficult both to estimate and to interpret. In such cases, there is
the temptation to exclude variables to keep the model manageable.
If, however, critical variables are omitted in the model simplification
process, then some of the paths that are estimated may well be
"wrong." The wrong paths are any that would be different if the
omitted variable had been included. Researchers need to carefully
trade off between models that are large and complex (which may be
difficult to estimate even if they are well thought out and articulated)
and simpler models (which may misrepresent causal processes).

■ Correlation and Regression Approaches for Analyzing Panel Data

Now that a number of basic issues underlying use of panel models
have been presented, manifest variable/observed measure approaches
to model estimation for panel data are discussed. These include both
correlational and regression techniques. All begin from two-variable,
two-wave models.

One of the unique features of panel analysis is that the methods
seem to have been developed independently by two groups of researchers from different fields (see, e.g., Pelz & Andrews, 1964;
Rozelle & Campbell, 1969). Both sets of researchers attempted to
find ways of using cross-time and cross-variable correlations to assess
the relative causal influences of two variables on each other.

Although the logic underlying the approaches was similar (i.e., to
find a way in which to compare the magnitude of the cross-lag
correlations), the methods chosen were not. The approach of Rozelle
and Campbell (1969), in general, compared magnitudes of the cross-
lag correlations after adjusting for differences. It was made more
sophisticated through a range of adjustments for potential confound-
ing factors such as differential reliability. Pelz and Andrews (1964),
by contrast, employed partial correlations to examine plausibility of
causal impact.

There is little value in discussing either of the two approaches any
further or in going into detail about how their methods actually can
be used. As suggested earlier, data analysis methods in this field have
been flawed and therefore limited in what they are capable of

accomplishing. They have not been able to take advantage of the sophistication of the thinking underlying panel models.

For readers who nevertheless think that they might be interested in using panel analysis or need to understand the different approaches so that they can effectively convince colleagues that using cross-lag panel methods would be a waste of their time, Shingles (1976) provided a comprehensive review and critique of the potential uses of various approaches. A second source is Rogosa (1980), who also provides a critique of cross-lag panel methods.

If cross-lag panel methods per se have any role among various social science methods, then that role may be to help suggest possible inferences about causal preponderance in situations where only correlations are available and there are not enough variables available to build a multiple-indicator structural model. In such circumstances (e.g., when archival data sets are available but have limited measures), cross-lag panel methods might be valuable in providing guidance about "more likely" causal impacts.

Although the shortcomings in panel methods in large part have reflected the lack of effective techniques for analyzing data, they also have a second, and perhaps even more critical, shortcoming. That shortcoming would have been avoided had panel models been viewed as a class of path models (Rozelle and Campbell [1969] were more guilty of this than were Pelz and Andrews [1964]). As can be seen from Figure 6.3, considering cross-lag panel models as path models would make issues of identification and model specification immediately apparent.

With respect to identification, two-variable, two-wave panel models really are underidentified path models. They can most readily be made identified by dropping the residual covariances, in effect allowing any measure-specific variance to be merged with stability of the construct. If such an assumption is made, then the model is solvable as an overidentified, albeit misspecified, path model using ordinary least squares regression.

Even if one can estimate values for the relationships between the variables, there are basic questions about the adequacy of model specification. That issue primarily is whether or not the closed system assumption of panel models is tenable. In most instances, the two-wave, two-variable models that have been articulated in cross-lag panel approaches suffer terminally from the closed system assumption; there are few, if any, situations in which it is safe to assume that two variables cause each other without any other variables being important.

▮ Summary

This chapter began with a discussion of nonrecursive models, namely, models with reciprocal causal relations or with feedback loops. Because nonrecursive models can lead to problems of model identification, necessary and sufficient conditions for model identification were described. Longitudinal models provided the second topic of this chapter. Those models share commonalities with nonrecursive models but bring a somewhat different logical perspective to data analyses.

For users of structural equation techniques, there is much to learn from early work on nonrecursive models and panel analysis. What needs to be learned is not the manifest variable methods of two-stage least squares estimation or cross-lag panel analysis, for those are inferior and flawed. Instead, what is most important is an understanding of how principles of finite causal lag and stability of variables across time can be used to develop more realistic SEM models. Said differently, the understandings developed from this chapter should be straightforward. They are not cumbersome methods specific to panel designs but rather are principles that can guide one's thinking as models are constructed. Furthermore, they illustrate in another way the value of employing multiple measures to operationalize the theoretical variables of interest in a structural equation model.

E X E R C I S E   6 . 1

Testing Model Identification

Which of the diagrams in Figure 6.5 is (are) identified? What needs to be done to identify the one(s) that is (are) not identified? (Analysis of identification of the models in Figure 6.5 appears in Table 6.1.)

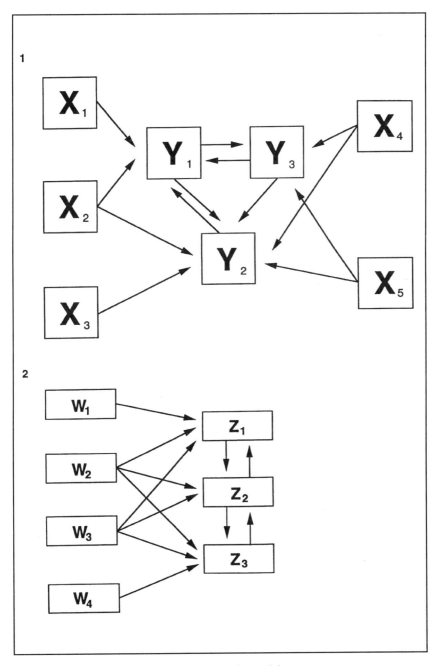

Figure 6.5. Examples of Nonrecursive Path Models

TABLE 6.1 Identification Tests for Models in Figure 6.5 (a) Figure in Top Panel ($N = 3$; thus, $N - 1 = 2$)

	X_1	X_2	X_3	X_4	X_5	Y_1	Y_2	Y_3	Condition Met?
Order condition (requires two or more zeros, each row)									
Y_1	γ_{11}	γ_{12}	0	0	0	1	β_{12}	β_{13}	Yes
Y_2	0	γ_{22}	γ_{23}	γ_{24}	γ_{25}	β_{21}	1	β_{23}	No
Y_3	0	0	0	γ_{34}	γ_{35}	β_{31}	0	1	Yes

Rank condition (requires a 2 × 2 non-zero determinant matrix)

				Condition Met?
Y_1	$\begin{vmatrix} \gamma_{23} & \gamma_{24} & \gamma_{25} \\ 0 & \gamma_{34} & \gamma_{35} \end{vmatrix}$			Yes
Y_2	$\begin{vmatrix} \gamma_{11} \\ 0 \end{vmatrix}$			No
Y_3	$\begin{vmatrix} \gamma_{11} & \gamma_{12} & 0 & \beta_{12} \\ 0 & \gamma_{22} & \gamma_{23} & 1 \end{vmatrix}$			Yes
For Y_2, if $\gamma_{24} = 0$	$\begin{vmatrix} \gamma_{11} & 0 \\ 0 & \gamma_{34} \end{vmatrix}$; if $\gamma_{25} = 0$	$\begin{vmatrix} \gamma_{11} & 0 \\ 0 & \gamma_{35} \end{vmatrix}$		Yes (both)

(b) Figure in Bottom Panel ($N = 3$; thus, $N - 1 = 2$)

	W_1	W_2	W_3	W_4	Z_1	Z_2	Z_3	Condition Met?
Order condition (requires two or more zeros, each row)								
Z_1	γ_{11}	γ_{12}	γ_{13}	0	1	β_{12}	0	Yes
Z_2	0	γ_{22}	γ_{23}	0	β_{21}	1	β_{23}	Yes
Z_3	0	γ_{32}	γ_{33}	γ_{34}	0	β_{32}	1	Yes
Rank condition (requires a 2 × 2 non-zero determinant matrix)								
Z_1	$\begin{vmatrix} 0 & \beta_{23} \\ \gamma_{34} & 1 \end{vmatrix}$							Yes
Z_2	$\begin{vmatrix} \gamma_{11} & 0 \\ 0 & \gamma_{34} \end{vmatrix}$							Yes
Z_3	$\begin{vmatrix} \gamma_{11} & 1 \\ 0 & \beta_{21} \end{vmatrix}$							Yes

Illustration 2: Peer Popularity and Academic Achievement—Panel Analysis of Observed Variables

Because the data set described initially in Chapter 3 is longitudinal, the model presented there can be extended across time. This illustration takes the same measures and relationships as in that earlier example but adds second and third time periods with the peer acceptance and achievement variables. Because schools were desegregated between the first and second time periods and the issue of interest was how acceptance by mainstream peers shaped achievement in desegregated classes, the acceptance measure used was choices by white peers.

Methodologically, longitudinal sampling provides additional information but requires allowing variability to change across time in paneled variables. In other words, as explained in the text, a covariance matrix needs to be analyzed. In this case, I chose to scale the matrix to a correlation-like metric (e.g., Meredith, 1964), standardizing each measure the first time it appeared and expressing later times in terms of the variance at the first point in time (i.e., a ratio of the variance at each later point to the variance at the first point). Because the model is a manifest variable (single-indicator) model, the results from regression analysis are identical to those from SEM programs and from maximum likelihood estimation. I illustrate how to estimate the model using the SEM program LISREL.

The first five variables are the same as in the previous example. The additional variables in this model are seating popularity with white peers at Time 2 (SeatPop2) and Time 3 (SeatPop3) and achievement test performance at Time 2 (VerbAch2) and Time 3 (VerbAch3). The input matrix (a rescaled covariance matrix) is as follows:

Covariance Matrix to Be Analyzed (called MAMATRIX.LG)

	Fam SocClass	Peabody	Tchr Eval	Seat Pop1	Verb Ach1	Seat Pop2	Verb Ach2	Seat Pop3	Verb Ach3
FamSocClass	1.00								
Peabody	.01	1.00							
TchrEval	−.12	.24	1.00						
SeatPop1	.04	.16	.17	1.00					
VerbAch1	.09	.31	.30	.08	1.00				
SeatPop2	.04	.01	.11	.12	.10	1.00			
VerbAch2	.08	.28	.42	.12	.33	−.05	.81		
SeatPop3	−.03	−.03	.01	.00	.00	.19	−.05	1.05	
VerbAch3	.02	.22	.68	.23	.43	.19	.52	−.01	1.24

Note that the Times 2 and 3 standardized test scores have variances other than 1.0, as does peer acceptance at Time 3. Those are variables that appear at more than one point in time. (Because the peer choices variable changed from Time 1 [before desegregation] to Time 2, the measures were not scaled against one another.)

Once again, the solution could be obtained from regression analysis, but the nonstandardized paths would be the ones that should be interpreted. Because this solution was produced from a scaled matrix, it should be replicable only from a program that will analyze a covariance matrix that the user supplies. Otherwise, the coefficients would be either standardized (not appropriate) or nonstandardized from a true covariance matrix. Appendix 6.1 provides the LISREL command statements that could be used to analyze the matrix.

The estimates from the LISREL solution appear in the following. For each dependent measure and path coefficient, there is the estimated path, its standard error, and its t value. For example, the path from Peabody to TchrEval is .24, with a standard error of .10 and a t value (the coefficient divided by the standard error) of 2.53, which is significant.

Independent Variables

	Fam SocClass	Peabody	Tchr Eval	Seat Pop1	Verb Ach1	Seat Pop2	Verb Ach2	Seat Pop3	Verb Ach3
Dependent Variables									
TchrEval	−.12	.24	—	—	—	—	—	—	—
	(.10)	(.10)							
	−1.28	2.53							
SeatPop1	.06	.13	.15	—	—	—	—	—	—
	(.10)	(.10)	(.10)						
	0.56	1.27	1.45						
VerbAch1	.12	.25	.25	—	—	—	—	—	—
	(.09)	(.09)	(.10)						
	1.27	2.66	2.60						
SeatPop2	—	—	—	.12	.09	—	—	—	—
				(.10)	(.10)				
				1.16	0.91				
VerbAch2				.10	.32	—	—	—	—
				(.08)	(.08)				
				1.14	3.84				
SeatPop3						.19	−.05	—	—
						(.10)	(.11)		
						1.88	−0.45		
VerbAch3						.22	.66	—	—
						(.09)	(.10)		
						2.36	6.36		

NOTE: Standard errors are in parentheses. t values are in rows below standard errors.

Overall, the fit of the model is much worse than was found for the cross-sectional model: chi-square with 21 degrees of freedom = 54.81 ($p = .000075$). The same conclusions about relationships between variables that were stated for the cross-sectional model hold for the longitudinal one, for "downstream" variables do not alter the relationships that precede them. In terms of the longitudinal elements of the model, achievement was not very stable through the desegregation experience but was much more stable (although still changing substantially) within desegregated classrooms. Peer relations were not significantly stable through desegregation and were only marginally stable within the desegregated classrooms. The only significant cross-lag path was from peer acceptance Time 2 to achievement Time 3. In other words, if this model accurately depicts what happened, then desegregation markedly disrupted the peer relations and achievement of Mexican American students, and achievement did not seem to influence peer relations, but peer relations in the desegregated classrooms did seem to be related to later achievement. In other words, there is some support for a peer acceptance to achievement relationship.

A P P E N D I X   6 . 1

LISREL Commands for Panel Illustration

One setup that works for LISREL 8 is as follows:

Mexican American data, for choices of whites, class illustration

```
DA NI=9 NO=100 MA=CM
KM SY FO FI=a:MAMATRIX.LG
```

[Note that the matrix is on the A drive.]

```
(8F10.7)
SD FO
(11F7.5)
1.0 1.0 1.0 1.0 1.0 1.0 .901 1.025 1.114
MO NY=9 NE=9 LY=id BE=FU,FI PS=sy,fi TE=di,fi
FR BE 3 1 BE 3 2 BE 4 1 BE 4 2 BE 4 3 BE 5 1 BE 5 2
   BE 5 3 C
BE 6 5 BE 6 4 BE 7 5 BE 7 4 BE 8 7 BE 8 6 BE 9 7 BE
   9 6 c
PS 2 1 PS 3 3 PS 4 4 PS 5 5 PS 6 6 PS 7 7 PS 8 8 PS
   9 9
ST 1.0 PS 1 1 PS 2 2
path diagram
OU PT SE TV AD=OFF
```

For any earlier version of LISREL, remove the "path diagram" line.

Fit indexes from the output

According to the LISREL program, the measures of model fit are as follows:

```
GOODNESS OF FIT STATISTICS
CHI-SQUARE WITH 21 DEGREES OF FREEDOM = 54.81 (P =
   0.000075)
ROOT MEAN SQUARE ERROR OF APPROXIMATION (RMSEA) = 0.13
90 PERCENT CONFIDENCE INTERVAL FOR RMSEA = (0.087 ;
   0.17)
P-VALUE FOR TEST OF CLOSE FIT (RMSEA < 0.05) = 0.0019
CHI-SQUARE FOR INDEPENDENCE MODEL WITH 36 DEGREES OF
   FREEDOM = 143.55
ROOT MEAN SQUARE RESIDUAL (RMR) = 0.11
STANDARDIZED RMR = 0.11
GOODNESS OF FIT INDEX (GFI) = 0.91
ADJUSTED GOODNESS OF FIT INDEX (AGFI) = 0.82
PARSIMONY GOODNESS OF FIT INDEX (PGFI) = 0.43
NORMED FIT INDEX (NFI) = 0.62
NON-NORMED FIT INDEX (NNFI) = 0.46
PARSIMONY NORMED FIT INDEX (PNFI) = 0.36
COMPARATIVE FIT INDEX (CFI) = 0.69
INCREMENTAL FIT INDEX (IFI) = 0.72
RELATIVE FIT INDEX (RFI) = 0.35
```

Because I have not yet talked about fit statistics, readers should wait and look back at the various statistics when they finish Chapter 10.

Chapter Discussion Questions

1. What does "lag" refer to? Is it the same as "variable" or "time lag"?
2. Stability was used in a sense that proportional increments in x and y were the same. Can y then be "stable" in some sense without x, or is stability tied to collinearity?

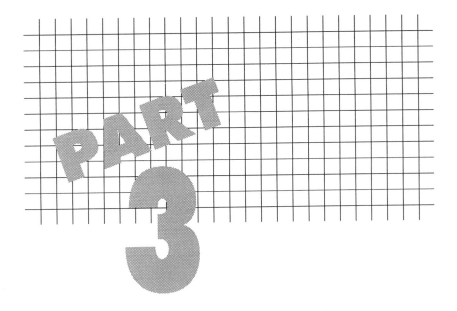

FACTOR ANALYSIS AND
PATH MODELING

Introducing the Logic of Factor Analysis and Multiple Indicators to Path Modeling

This chapter introduces and explains two related perspectives that provide methods for ideas presented earlier in the text. The first, factor analysis, articulates principles underlying the use of unmeasured variables in path models. Throughout this text, there has been discussion of constructs, or unmeasured theoretical variables, operationalized by some measure or set of measures. There are marked advantages in having available multiple measures of constructs. In fact, *in most instances the only defensible way in which to create viable models is to use multiple measures of each construct assessed.* Up to this point, however, there has been no attempt to explain the mechanics of how to go about actually using unmeasured variables in models. (To refresh their memories, readers may want to review the beginning of Chapter 5; in that chapter, ideas about unmeasured variables initially are introduced.) By introducing perspectives developed in the factor analysis literature, notions about unmeasured variables can be developed more fully. As part of the description of factor analysis, this chapter introduces **confirmatory factor analysis** or **CFA,** namely, techniques in which the items defining each factor and the relationships among factors are specified a priori rather than letting the factor analytic methods define factors. CFA is one type of latent variable structural equation model. As part of the discussion of confirmatory factor models, different levels of constraint that can be imposed on the relations of measures to factors are discussed, and the multitrait-multimethod (MTMM) model presented earlier is reintroduced. The reintroduction of MTMM issues is important insofar as dealing effectively with issues of method variance is an important part of structural equation models and methods.

The second perspective, developed by Costner and his colleagues (e.g., Costner, 1969; Costner & Schoenberg, 1973) and articulated nicely by Kenny (1979), applies perspectives of factor analysis to path models. That perspective uses simple algebraic calculations to demonstrate how having multiple measures of a construct can help separate common variance from unique true score variance as well as from error variance and covariance. The approach explained allows preliminary data screening "by hand" before attempting to run structural equation computer programs. The preliminary screening can be particularly helpful for complex models or when there has been little empirical work to guide model development.

▌ Factor Analysis

▌ Logic of Factor Analysis

Factor analysis is designed to link observed measures to a smaller number of underlying conceptual variables (for a fuller description, see, e.g., Gorsuch, 1983; Mulaik, 1972). Factor analysis represents the observed measures in terms of (unobserved) common factors plus unique variance; the relationships between unobserved factors and observed measures are defined in terms of weights (e.g., regression weights) linking factors to measures. In other words, factor analysis provides a vehicle for moving from a "single measure for each construct" path model to a multiple measure of each construct or multiple-indicator path model. One still can examine the same underlying theoretical variables that were of interest in path analysis. Those variables now are thought of as factors, and several measures are collected of each theoretical variable to take advantage of improved measurement properties that come from multiple measures.

As with most other extensions of path analysis, when logic of factor analysis is integrated with path modeling, the resulting models cannot be solved by ordinary least squares regression techniques.

To illustrate, consider once again a model linking peer relationships and academic achievement, focusing on the academic achievement construct. In earlier path model illustrations, a measure of verbal achievement based on a standardized test was used. Alternatively, we also might have chosen as a measure of achievement teacher ratings of their students' performance, student grades, standardized test performance on a domain other than verbal skills, or performance of students in meeting some types of standards. Because regression analyses limit us to a single measure of each construct, we had to pick a measure of achievement that we thought was close to the theoretical variable of interest and hope that what it assesses is what we want. If a range of measures were available, our best choice *for path analysis* usually would be to create a composite measure of the different choices.[8] In principle (see the Chapter 5 discussion of measurement error), that measure should display the best reliability even though it still contains some error from the summed measures.

By contrast, rather than attempting to select a "best" measure, in a factor analytic approach a number of different measures of achievement (as many as are available) could be selected to assess achievement. The construct of achievement (one factor) is defined by what those measures have in common. The achievement factor is what is interrelated with other theoretical variables, each also a factor defined by a set of measures. In a path model with single-headed arrows linking factors, the correlations (covariances) among factors are turned into path coefficients in the same way that regression analysis turns correlations or covariances into path coefficients.

One of the classic areas of focus for factor analysis has been the assessment of abilities, for example, defining primary mental abilities and addressing whether or not there is a general ability that underlies other abilities (e.g., Thurstone, 1938). In this illustration, a primary ability such as verbal comprehension is defined through factor analysis by attempting to extract a single source of common variability from a number of measures that ostensibly tap that ability. Furthermore,

---

8. In the illustration, that was not done so readers could see how specific measures performed when included in regression as compared to being an indicator in a multiple indicator model.

when measures of different primary abilities (e.g., verbal comprehension, numerical ability) are included in a single factor analysis, measures of verbal comprehension should define one factor, whereas measures of numerical ability should define a second. Because the factors are thought to be related, the different abilities are expected to correlate with one another. If a researcher had measures of a number of primary abilities, then their correlations could be used in a second, "higher level" factoring (described in Chapter 11) to see whether underlying them is a single construct that could be called general ability.

For readers unfamiliar with factor analysis but who have followed all that has been covered thus far in this book, factor analysis can be seen as being very much like regression in that it shares the general linear model (e.g., Gorsuch, 1983). It can be viewed as a variant of regression, the most prominent difference being that in factor analysis not all of the variables in the regression model are measured. It also is generally the case that in factor analysis the matrix being analyzed is a correlation matrix; thus, the analogous regression solution would focus on the standardized (beta) coefficients.

The basic regression equation in matrix form is $Y = BX + E$, whereas the basic factor analysis equation in similar form is $Y = Pf + U$. In the latter equation, only the Y's actually are measured. Those Y's are defined in terms of a vector of f factors representing the unmeasured factors; a weight matrix, P, that is the matrix of coefficients relating factors to the observed measures Y; and a vector of residuals, U. The elements of P are essentially partial regression coefficients but usually are described by terminology of factor analysis as being elements of the factor pattern matrix. The elements of U, the residuals after the common factors are extracted, are called uniquenesses in factor analysis. The factor analysis equation is parallel in form to the regression equation.

Although the parallel to regression can be reassuring for some readers, it also can create confusion because it is difficult to think about using unmeasured variables to predict other variables. For example, how can one know what the predictors are when there are no scores on them? Can they be anything? Can they not change from measure to measure? In fact, the most complex and controversial part of exploratory factor analysis (EFA) is determining what the factors are. (How many factors are there? What should the factors be called? What do those factors actually represent?) There is, for example, the risk of inaccurate labeling of factors, which Cliff (1983) called the nominalistic fallacy; naming factors does not make them what they are labeled.

At the same time, the idea of unmeasured variables as causes should not seem altogether unfamiliar to readers. In the reliability model presented in Chapter 5, the true scores, which parallel the factors in factor analysis, are unmeasured and are causes rather than effects. As mentioned in the discussion of reliability, measures are viewed as caused by the common dimensions that they tap as well as by their unique variance and error. For example, subjects' scores on a measure of ability can be seen as caused by three components: (a) the underlying ability dimension that the measure is supposed to assess, (b) any unique dimensions that the measure consistently may tap, and (c) error.

An additional reason why unmeasured variables should not pose too great a problem is that, in principle, researchers should have a pretty good idea about what the factors are when they collect their measures. That is, measures should be selected to tap particular underlying dimensions, and issues about the number of factors and what they are should have been well thought out in advance. When researchers have organized their measures around an a priori set of underlying dimensions, factor analysis is used much more for confirmation or model testing than for exploration. In practice, however, determining the nature of the unmeasured variables is not always straightforward given that factor analysis techniques also have been used as exploratory techniques. Using factor analysis to define dimensionality of measures that have been assembled atheoretically or been combined somewhat haphazardly can lead to problems in interpreting unmeasured factors.

A second issue relevant to path modeling is whether or not predictors, because they are unmeasured, can be made the same as some of the observed measures. After all, would that not give pretty good (i.e., perfect) prediction of those observed measures as dependent variables and help one to know what the predictor variables are? The answer is yes, one could make the unmeasured variables the same as some of the observed measures, and certain factor analysis methods have done that. That makes the issue of prediction for certain measures a trivial one, for we would be predicting variables using themselves as predictors. That is the situation that occurs in regression approaches to path analysis, where each measure is supposed to correspond directly to an underlying theoretical dimension. That is, in path analysis each underlying construct is treated as if it were the same as the observed measure/variable, for it is necessary to assume that variables are measured perfectly and without error. For example, in a path analysis interrelating ability and self-concept, a single measure of ability, whatever that measure happens to be, defines the ability construct, a single measure of self-concept defines the self-concept construct, and so on for all other measures.

As suggested in previous chapters, the primary shortcoming of path analysis is that each theoretical variable is operationalized by only a single measure. The result is that measurement error and specification error cannot be disentangled from variance tapping the theoretical variable of interest. By contrast, when multiple measures are available, different variance sources can be disentangled and reliabilities of measures can be estimated (e.g., Miller, 1995). There are problems separating variance components only when a factor is defined as identical to an observed measure. Then, some of the information that allows separating constructs from measures and partitioning of common, unique, and error variances is wasted.

Although the focus of this discussion is on how factor analysis techniques can be applied to improve structural models, it is important to remember that such uses have not been typical in that literature. Instead, factor analysis has been used most widely to represent a larger number of observed variables in terms of a smaller set of sources of common variance. In many instances, researchers started with a conceptual model they hoped to fit; in other instances, the research was much less driven by theoretical concerns. Regardless of whether the approach was exploratory or confirmatory, however, it was assumed that the resulting sources of common variance would have meaning that could be discerned from the pattern of relationships of the observed variables with the unobserved variables.

▌ Exploratory Factor Analysis

Because EFA approaches have little in common with the methods discussed in this text, they are not covered in much detail here. A nice introduction to EFA can be found in Ford, MacCallum, and Tait (1986), and readers interested in more details linking factor and structural equation models should see Loehlin (1992). Here, the focus is on EFA approaches, their prominent features, and how they compare to the types of models we have discussed throughout the text.

Perhaps the first defining feature of EFA is that most research using EFA has extracted factors that are **orthogonal,** that is, uncorrelated with or independent of one another.[9] The idea of uncorrelated predictor variables was discussed earlier as part of the discussions of collinearity. For the present discussion, note that if a structural equation path model were to extract uncorrelated factors, then it would be pretty boring given that there would be no paths between any of the theoretical variables. In other words, structural equation approaches stand in marked contrast to EFA insofar as the variables of interest (factors) in structural equation models usually will be hypothesized as correlating with one another.

Second, there are a number of different assumptions made that shape the type of EFA technique used. If one assumes that there is no unique variance, as is done in **principal components analysis,** then the "error" part of the factor model disappears. Once again, given the importance of dealing effectively with imprecision of measurement and the likelihood of imprecision actually occurring, components analysis has little to offer users of structural equation approaches. By contrast, consistent with path modeling approaches, a **principal factors** approach extracts common and unique variance components.

Third, and a point of particular importance to structural equation users, in EFA the model that is tested is underidentified, which means that there is no unique solution but rather an infinite number of possible solutions, each of which fits the data equally well. Part of the challenge of this type of factor analysis is to pick one from the array of possible "equally good fit" solutions that gives a solution that is interpretable.

Fourth, in most types of EFA, all measures are related to every factor. It is, of course, hoped that most of the relationships are trivial so that each measure is substantially linked only to one or, at most, a few of the factors. The approach that tries to attain such a solution has been called attaining **simple structure.** Because there is an infinite number of solutions that are mathematically equivalent, factor analy-

---

9. Although not really relevant to the present discussion, it is important to note that, when taking composites of items to form factors, the factors that emerge from an orthogonal factor analysis may be intercorrelated.

sis has methods, called **factor rotation**, for moving from one solution to another in an attempt to attain a simple structure. That is, **rotation** moves from an initial solution to another that fits equally well but has somewhat different properties in an attempt to find a solution in which each measure is trivially related to most of the underlying factors but substantially related to one factor. By contrast, a confirmatory use of factor analysis hypothesizes particular relationships between measures and factors and then typically will set all the other relationships between measures and factors to zero. Rotation is not possible when there is a unique solution, for any other solution would not have the same fit.

Given the difficulties inherent in selecting the "best" solution and in naming factors, it seems clear that confusion about factor analysis can occur when factor analytic approaches are used for data exploration. In their worst form, such approaches might be characterized as the "I'm not sure what is here and there are too many measures to make sense of, so let's do a factor analysis and reduce the measures to a more restricted set of variables and see what emerges" approach. Given that such approaches are characterized so negatively, readers may be wondering why factor analysis has been so widely used. In part, the answer is that a number of reasons, including methodological/analytic limitations, have restricted the use of factor analysis approaches for model testing (and they still impose some constraints on the number of measures and variables that can be considered at one time), with the result that factor analysis was for a time the most accepted way of matching observed measures to underlying dimensions. It was used even when a strong a priori theoretical model had been used to generate the data. It is interesting that recent work (Gerbing & Hamilton, 1996) suggests that, when an a priori structure is hypothesized, these types of factor analysis techniques provide a useful first step to complement more sophisticated types of CFA described later in this chapter.

Overall, then, variants of EFA have many features that structural equation approach users want to avoid in a methodology: orthogonal factors, an underidentified solution that is not uniquely solvable, and relationships between factors and measures that are incompletely specified. At the same time, however, Gerbing and Hamilton (1996) recently found that EFA techniques can be valuable when used in anticipation of use of the hypothesis testing confirmatory techniques that are described next. In conclusion, then, factor analysis techniques contributed much to the logical foundations of structural equation modeling (SEM). Nevertheless, it was not until CFA techniques were developed that much of the value of path modeling was produced.

Confirmatory Factor Analysis

With the relatively recent development of powerful computers and software, there has been a shift to alternative factor analysis approaches that attempt to test the viability of a priori structures. These latter types of factor analysis are called **confirmatory factor analysis.** CFA approaches examine whether or not existing data are consistent with a highly constrained a priori structure that meets conditions of model identification. This fitting process sometimes is referred to somewhat inaccurately as "confirming" a model or hypothesized structure. In fact, as mentioned earlier, a model never can be confirmed. It can be disconfirmed (it does not fit the observed data), or it can fail to be disconfirmed (it fits). The most important points for the current discussion, however, are that CFA approaches begin with a theoretical model that has to be identified (and therefore be uniquely solvable) and must attempt to see whether or not data are consistent with that theoretical model.

If CFA approaches sound a lot like path models, it is for good reason. General CFA models are a form of path models that hypothesize relationships between unmeasured constructs and observed measures. The difference between CFA models and latent variable path models is that in path models the latent variables (unmeasured constructs) are hypothesized to be causally interrelated, whereas in CFA models they are intercorrelated. Said differently, in CFA models all the latent variables are viewed as exogenous. As is true of exogenous variables in any model, CFA models do not attempt to disentangle the causes of hypothesized interrelationships among them. The strength of relationships among them, however, usually is of interest.

Even in CFA models where a priori underlying dimensions are operationalized through observed measures, there will be uncertainty about whether or not the measures are capable of assessing (or have assessed) the dimension(s) of interest (e.g., Cliff, 1983). In the factor analysis domain and, consequently, in analyses using latent variable structural equation approaches, one should be wary of factor labels and should provide as much construct validity information as is possible. For example, if I choose to put a label of "self-concept" on a factor/unmeasured variable, my assigning that label does not make the variable self-concept, and it certainly does not make the variable the same as other variables that also have been called self-concept. Furthermore, if I do not know the relationship of my measures of self-concept with other available measures of self-concept, then I am missing some valuable information about construct validity. (Note that, of course, construct validity information can be obtained from measures of other constructs as well via convergent and divergent/discriminant validity information.)

In summary, factor analysis provides a number of features that enrich structural equation approaches. First, it is a methodology that explicitly includes latent/unobserved variables plus observed measures and interrelates the two. Second, it draws attention to issues of operationalization of underlying variables and inherent shortcomings of path analysis models. Third, it illustrates how regression models can be extended to unmeasured variables. Fourth, CFA techniques provide a path modeling methodology for linking observed measures to underlying theoretical variables.

Use of Confirmatory Factor Analysis Techniques

CFA approaches were widely considered but little used until the 1970s. Precursor programs to the current LISREL program—ACOVS (Analysis of COVariance Structures), LISREL 1, and SIFASP (SImultaneous Factor Analysis across Several Populations)—all were developed at and distributed by Educational Testing Service in the early 1970s. At that point, CFA became a viable, if infrequently used, approach, for those programs provided a method for fitting data to hypothesized models. The first versions of the programs, however, were limited in the size of problems (e.g., number of measures, number of factors) they could address and were cumbersome and complicated to use, with the result that they were not widely used. By contrast, more recent versions of SEM programs are much more flexible, are easier to use, and handle much larger problems, making them much more accessible and practical to use.

CFA is straightforward to set up once the interrelationships are specified and the representative path model is constructed. Specifying the interrelationships should be easy, for the specifications come

directly from the theory underlying the model, which guides operationalization of the conceptual variables. Diagramming also should
be easy, for in this step the model just has to be set up as a path model
with the factors as independent variables and the observed measures
as dependent variables. Each dependent variable needs a residual path
(its uniqueness) as well as paths from other variables (factors). Current versions of SEM programs AMOS and EQS can produce model
estimates once users use the programs' drawing tools to draw the path
diagrams and link the observed measures to the diagrams. Even for
programs without drawing tools, the process of setting up a model
for analysis is not too difficult.

As an illustration of a CFA model, look at Figure 7.1. As can be
seen, the figure has three latent variables, or factors, each with three
indicators, or measures. The three latent variables are viewed as
intercorrelated. The paths from the factors to the measures are partial
regression coefficients; in this model, because each measure is caused
by only a single predictor, the paths reduce to simple regression
(correlations in the standardized case). The matrix of coefficients, as
noted earlier, is the factor pattern matrix. The e's are the residuals
(uniquenesses) for the endogenous variables.

So, how does one get from the diagram to factor analysis matrices
and to solving for the parameters? Begin with the basic equation listed
earlier,

$$Y = Pf + U. \tag{7.1}$$

The equations can be set up for each dependent variable in terms of
the three independent variables. In equation by equation form, looking like regression equations for each dependent variable, the elements of the matrices are as follows:

$$Y_1 = p_1{}^*f_1 + 0{}^*f_2 + 0{}^*f_3 + e_1$$
$$Y_2 = p_2{}^*f_1 + 0{}^*f_2 + 0{}^*f_3 + e_2$$
$$Y_3 = p_3{}^*f_1 + 0{}^*f_2 + 0{}^*f_3 + e_3$$
$$Y_4 = 0{}^*f_1 + p_4{}^*f_2 + 0{}^*f_3 + e_4$$
$$Y_5 = 0{}^*f_1 + p_5{}^*f_2 + 0{}^*f_3 + e_5$$
$$Y_6 = 0{}^*f_1 + p_6{}^*f_2 + 0{}^*f_3 + e_6$$
$$Y_7 = 0{}^*f_1 + 0{}^*f_2 + p_7{}^*f_3 + e_7$$
$$Y_8 = 0{}^*f_1 + 0{}^*f_2 + p_8{}^*f_3 + e_8$$
$$Y_9 = 0{}^*f_1 + 0{}^*f_2 + p_9{}^*f_3 + e_9$$

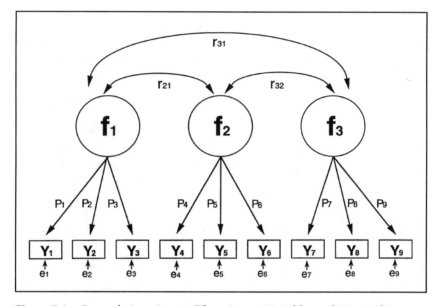

Figure 7.1. Interrelations Among Three Latent Variables and Nine Indicators

Put back in matrix form, $Y = Pf + e$, the Y's become a 1×9 vector, as follows:

$$Y = \begin{vmatrix} Y_1 \\ Y_2 \\ Y_3 \\ Y_4 \\ Y_5 \\ Y_6 \\ Y_7 \\ Y_8 \\ Y_9 \end{vmatrix}$$

The factors become a 1×3 vector:

$$f = \begin{vmatrix} f_1 \\ f_2 \\ f_3 \end{vmatrix}$$

The errors are a 1×9 vector:

$$U = \begin{vmatrix} e_1 \\ e_2 \\ e_3 \\ e_4 \\ e_5 \\ e_6 \\ e_7 \\ e_8 \\ e_9 \end{vmatrix}$$

The estimated coefficients are a 3×9 factor pattern matrix:

$$P = \begin{vmatrix} p_1 & 0 & 0 \\ p_2 & 0 & 0 \\ p_3 & 0 & 0 \\ 0 & p_4 & 0 \\ 0 & p_5 & 0 \\ 0 & p_6 & 0 \\ 0 & 0 & p_7 \\ 0 & 0 & p_8 \\ 0 & 0 & p_9 \end{vmatrix}$$

Note that most of the coefficients in the factor pattern matrix are fixed to 0 and that, as in the diagram, each measure is directly related to only a single factor. Because the measures are clustered, with indicators of each factor together, the factors can be readily discerned from the matrix.

Unfortunately, in this form, there is not enough information (nine equations but more than nine unknowns) to uniquely solve all the pattern matrix (P) coefficients and factor correlations. Furthermore, the factor correlations do not appear anywhere in the equations, so it would seem to be difficult to solve for them. The equation can be turned into a solvable form by multiplying each side by its transpose (because the two sides are equal, their transposes also are equal); that changes the left side to the variance/covariance or intercorrelation matrix of the observed measures, which then gives enough information to solve for the model. Thus,

$$YY' = (Pf + U)(Pf + U)'. \tag{7.2}$$

Expanded, the equation becomes

$$YY' = (Pf)(Pf)' + (Pf)U' + U(Pf)' + UU'. \qquad (7.3)$$

Because the errors are by definition independent of the factors, the two middle terms on the right side of the equation—$(Pf)U'$ and $U(Pf')$—both drop out, for they are zero, leaving

$$YY' = (Pf)(Pf)' + UU'. \qquad (7.4)$$

Using rules of matrix algebra, the equation becomes

$$YY' = Pff'P' + UU', \qquad (7.5)$$

where UU' represents the variance covariance matrix of the residuals and ff' represents the variance covariance matrix of the factors. That matrix is pre- and postmultiplied by the factor pattern matrix (P and P'). Thus, we have reached a "traditional" form for factor analysis in which the variance covariance matrix of the observed measures is expressed in terms of a factor pattern matrix, a factor variance covariance matrix, and a residual variance covariance matrix.

Using sigma (Σ) to represent the variance covariance matrix of observed measures, phi (Φ) to represent the factor variance covariance matrix, and psi (Ψ) to represent the residual matrix, the equation is

$$\Sigma_{YY} = P\Phi P' + \Psi. \qquad (7.6)$$

To repeat, sigma is the variance covariance (or correlation) matrix of the Y vector that appears in the preceding. Psi is the variance/covariance matrix of the residuals, that is, the U vector. Phi is the covariance matrix of the f vector. Because it is symmetric, only the lower triangular part is presented to illustrate it:

$$\Phi = \begin{vmatrix} \Phi_{11} & & \\ \Phi_{21} & \Phi_{22} & \\ \Phi_{31} & \Phi_{32} & \Phi_{33} \end{vmatrix}.$$

Because the factors are unmeasured, values for the variances can be specified in a number of ways. The variances do, however, have to be fixed in some way, for not specifying them leaves an indeterminacy problem between the factor loading and the factor variance; it is analogous to a two-indicator factor model described later in this chapter. The simplest way is to set the variances to unities, which would make phi a correlation matrix and the off-diagonal elements correlations. Another way, using what are called reference indicators, will be described later.

If we assume that the diagonal elements of phi all are fixed to 1.0, then all the elements of the diagram have been specified sufficiently to allow estimation of the model provided that it is identified. For that, we can revisit the identification issues from path models, here recast in terms of the factor model. With multiple measures of each factor and no residual covariances, identification is straightforward. The covariance matrix of the observed measures, the Y's, has available $\{[(v(v + 1)] / 2\}$ degrees of freedom; this formula is the total number of nonredundant elements in the matrix, including the variances and the covariances. In the present example, the available degrees of freedom is $9 \times 10 / 2 = 45$. A total of 3 degrees of freedom are lost to estimate the phis, 9 for the elements of P, and 9 for the elements of psi, leaving 24 degrees of freedom in the model. Thus, this model is overidentified and can be estimated.

Finally, there are implications of the fact that at least some of the factors estimated in CFA are likely to be hypothesized as correlating with one another. First, as can be illustrated by the model in Figure 7.1, the intercorrelations between factors can account for relationships between measures that cross factors in the model. Even though most of the loadings in the pattern matrix corresponding to Figure 7.1 are zero, relationships that cross factors would not be zero unless the factors are uncorrelated. Because in Figure 7.1 the factors are correlated, all the measures will correlate with one another. The magnitude of the cross-construct correlations depends on how strongly the factors are interrelated. Standard rules for tracing paths can be used to estimate the correlations. For example, the model predicts the relation between Y_1 and Y_7 to be ($p_1 \times r_{31} \times p_7$). Note that for each cross-factor relationship, there is only one path connecting each pair of measures, and it goes from the first measure via its loading to the first factor (e.g., p_1), from that factor to the second factor via the correlation between them (e.g., r_{31}), and on to the second measure via its loading on that second factor (e.g., p_7). (Remember that the tracing rules do not allow paths that go through two curved arrows.)

Second, because the factor correlations typically will be substantially less than unity insofar as factors will be distinct rather than highly similar, the relationships of measures across factors will in general be less than the relationships of measures within factors. This issue will be revisited when MTMM matrices are presented.

Finally, for readers familiar with EFA, the CFA model presents the factor structure versus factor pattern matrix issue in a way that, to me, has seemed particularly clear. For this assumption, I will assume that a correlation matrix is being analyzed. The factor pattern matrix contains standardized (partial regression) coefficients to reproduce the measures from the factors. When factors are orthogonal, elements of the factor pattern matrix become correlations (essentially simple standardized regression coefficients) between factors and measures, which makes them relatively easy to interpret.

Whenever factors are allowed to correlate, the coefficients in the pattern matrix take into account the relationships among the factors, making their interpretation more difficult, for in EFA every factor "causes" each measure. To aid interpretation, researchers suggest also interpreting the **factor structure matrix,** which is the product $P(ff')$ (or $P\Phi$), namely, the factor pattern matrix (P) multiplied times the factor correlation (covariance) matrix. Note that when factors are uncorrelated, ff' is an identity matrix (I), and $P(ff') = PI = P$. That is, the structure and pattern matrices are identical, and the structure versus pattern distinction is meaningless.

When factors are correlated, the pattern matrix coefficients essentially become *partial* regression coefficients, and the structure matrix contains information combined with the strength of the correlations among factors as well as strength of associations between measures and factors. The different complexity in interpreting information from oblique solutions is one reason why orthogonal factoring is used so often in EFA. A second is that unlike CFA, in which there is a unique estimate for each relationship among the factors, the solution can be rotated to change the magnitude of the correlations between factors (as noted earlier, that capability results from under-identification) as well as between factor loadings. Selecting a particular magnitude of relationship between factors to interpret is difficult and can seem arbitrary.

With respect to structural models, the structure versus pattern issue is largely irrelevant. Both the weights and the factor relationships are of interest. Therefore, there is little interest in the factor structure matrix except as part of a process for reconstructing the relationships among observed measures (i.e., model fitting).

In summary, CFA develops from theory that specifies exactly the nature of the relationships between measures and factors, and it can be done only if the model is identified, yielding a unique solution. In other words, CFA is a form of latent variable SEM. In CFA, the constructs are not causally interrelated but are allowed to covary/correlate. The theory dictates a model that can be presented as a path model. That model is tested for plausibility by the data collected, and it uses the equation

$$\Sigma_{YY} = P\Phi P' + \Psi, \tag{7.6}$$

which will provide the fundamental elements of latent variable SEM approaches that "causally" interrelate latent variables.

■ Constraining Relations of Observed Measures With Factors

Before turning to algebraic ways of assessing plausibility of factors and the size of relations between measures and factors, a second topic from test theory and factor analysis is relevant. That topic deals with the expected nature of the relations of different measures of a factor with that factor. In some instances, for example, researchers may believe that different observed measures will relate to a factor in exactly the same way. If so, they can examine plausibility of stronger assumptions. That is, the basic assumption is that indicators will be substantially related to the factors they purportedly measure. A stronger assumption, for example, would be that not only are they related, but the strengths of their relations to those factors are equal (e.g., Jöreskog, 1971).

First, consider the highly restricted condition in which, for a factor or latent variable, the relations of each of the different measures with the factor are expected to be exactly the same *and* the magnitude of the residuals is expected to be exactly the same. In this case, the researcher needs to be able to assume that the true score component of each measure is the same and that the remaining parts of each measure are the same. If these assumptions can be the measures are said to be **parallel tests** of the variable. 7.2, the measures of the factor would be parallel if $a = b =$ if $e_1 = e_2 = e_3 = e_4$. Note that instead of estimating four factor loadings, there now is only one to estimate. That ch

3 new degrees of freedom in the model that is estimated. For a variance/covariance matrix, the constraints on the residuals give 3 more degrees of freedom.[10] Thus, the parallel test model has more degrees of freedom than does a basic (unconstrained) model, for only one loading and one residual are estimated.

Second, if only the relations of measures with the variable are the same ($a = b = c = d$), then the measures are called **tau equivalent**. For tau equivalent models, the true score components of the models again are assumed to be the same, but error components are allowed to differ. Note that if measures are standardized, then it makes no sense to constrain the loadings without also constraining the residuals, for each totals to the same value (a variance of 1.0). Tau equivalent models also have more degrees of freedom than does the basic model.

Finally, if no constraints are imposed, then the tests are called **congeneric**. This is the basic and most common model. In many instances, not enough is known about the indicators to impose assumptions about equal loadings on them. In many others, researchers know that the assumption of equality of relationships does not make sense for their data.

The three models can be compared for a single set of data. That could be done by moving from least restrictive (congeneric) to most restrictive (parallel), assessing whether or not adding restrictions of equality on the loadings and residuals is realistic. If the fit of the model to the data becomes worse as the model is made more restrictive, then the constraints are not plausible for the data. As will be explained later, "worse" can be defined by a number of fit indexes that can be calculated in structural equation models.

Confirmatory Factor Analysis and Method Factors

The Basic Confirmatory Factor Analysis Path Model for Multitrait-Multimethod Matrices

If we assume that traits and methods combine additively, then we can integrate MTMM matrices with path models and diagram the model

---

10. For standardized data, because the total variance for each variable is fixed to 1.0 and the residuals are defined by the common loadings (they are sqrt[$1 - R^2$]), additional degrees of freedom are not gained by constraining the residuals.

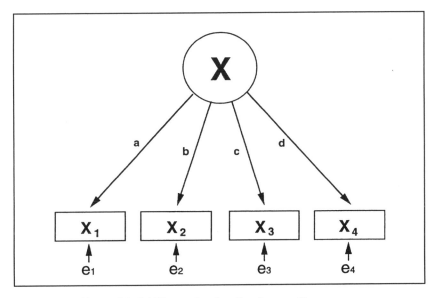

Figure 7.2.   Factor Model Illustration for Consistency Tests

as a confirmatory factor model, illustrated in Figure 7.3. Although an additive model is a reasonable one to hypothesize, MTMM matrices have not proven to be as straightforward as they at first seem to be. First, there are arguments for traits and methods combining in multiplicative fashion (e.g., Campbell & O'Connell, 1967). Second, there are nonobvious issues of identification that need to be addressed when using a full trait × method model (e.g., Kenny & Kashy, 1992). Nevertheless, for now we assume that they combine in additive fashion and that the model is identified, for the principle of separating trait variance from method variance illustrated here is a general one and works successfully in situations other than the full trait × method model. Illustrations of CFAs of MTMM matrices have been provided by Cole (1987), Dunn, Everitt, and Pickles (1993), and Marsh and Byrne (1993). Dunn et al. (1993) looked at basic variations of MTMM models, adding or excluding relations among methods, among traits, and between traits and methods, illustrating what happens under different assumptions.

Figure 7.3 contains three trait factors (above the measures) and three method factors (below the measures). It is set up to be consistent with Table 5.1. So, for example, the first, fourth, and seventh meas-

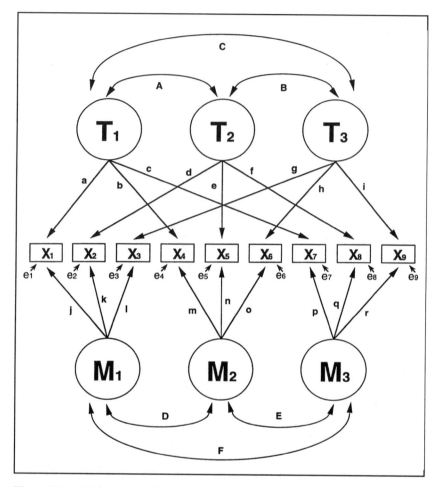

Figure 7.3. Multitrait-Multimethod Matrix Modeling Using Confirmatory Factor Analysis

ures are the ones measuring the first trait. Each measure assesses (loads on) a trait and a method. The diagram assumes that traits are independent of methods, thus including no paths from trait factors to method factors. Methods are allowed to correlate, as, of course, are traits, for the model would be uninteresting if the traits assessed were independent of one another.

By using the tracing rule for path models, the different types of relationships can be seen as reflecting different combinations of paths. Remember, as the relationships are interpreted, that in the standardized metric in which we are working all the paths should be less than 1. To illustrate through examples how the path model decomposes relationships within the matrix:

Monotrait-Heteromethod: $r_{41} = ab + jDm$.

Note that assuming Campbell and Fiske's (1959) Condition 1 as described in Chapter 5, Paths a and b, trait loadings, should be relatively large, for the measures should be substantially related to the traits that they are supposed to assess. The second term on the right side of the equation depends on both the strength of the method factors and their relationship. Because it combines three elements less than 1, it is likely to be smaller than the ab term. If the methods are independent of one another, then the right term would disappear, leaving only the trait variance.

Heterotrait-Monomethod: $r_{21} = aAd + jk$.

As was true in the preceding illustration, the sizes of Paths j and k depend on the strength of the method variance. The first term on the right side of the equation contains two elements, trait loadings, that ought to be substantial assuming Campbell and Fiske's Condition 1. Thus, the size of the first term depends heavily on the strength of the relationship between the traits, which usually should be neither too strong nor zero but could well be substantial.

According to Condition 3 of Campbell and Fiske (1959), r_{41} should be greater than r_{21}. From the CFA perspective, however, such a condition is unnecessary. It would not necessarily be bad in terms of validity for Traits 1 and 2 to be moderately interrelated and for the method variance of Method 1 to be substantial (which could result in r_{21} being large) or for the methods to be independent (which would reduce the size of r_{41}).

Heterotrait-Heteromethod: $r_{51} = aAe + jDn$.

In this case, both terms on the right side of the equation combine three elements less than 1, so these terms should tend to be less than either of the two other types just described.

Monotrait-Monomethod: $r_{11} = a^2$.

In the model of Campbell and Fiske, these terms are reliabilities (they are working from a correlation matrix). In the path model approach, the solution process extracts trait and method variance and leaves a residual, which in Figure 7.3 is the e terms. Reliability can be determined from the residuals in path modeling using $1 - e^2$.

▌ *Confirmatory Factor Analysis Approaches to Multitrait-
Multimethod Matrices and Model Identification*

Kenny and Kashy (1992) provided a detailed discussion of identification of MTMM matrices. Initially, for the 3 (traits) x 3 (methods) MTMM model, Kenny and Kashy noted that a model attempting to correlate trait factors with method factors will not be identified. Furthermore, if researchers attempt to estimate a solution with traits independent from methods but in which all the loadings on a single factor are forced to be equal, then underidentification will result. Finally, even for a model like the one presented in Figure 7.3 in which, due to independence of trait and method factors, empirical identification problems seem less likely, Kenny and Kashy suggested that most data sets have had problems in finding viable solutions. In the structural equation literature, a viable solution is one in which all coefficients are acceptable. Unacceptable values include negative variances, for either residuals or factors, and covariances that exceed the product of the standard deviations of the variables that covary (i.e., equivalent to a correlation with an absolute value greater than 1.0). For MTMM matrices, assuming that trait measures correlate positively with one another, loadings within trait factors with differing signs also indicate that there likely were problems in estimation.

As the clearest illustration of the likelihood of problems, Wothke (1987) examined 23 different MTMM data sets, attempting to fit them to CFA models with traits independent of methods. Although the problems varied from data set to data set, he reported failure to obtain an acceptable solution in all 23 cases. Kenny and Kashy (1992) suggested that identification in such MTMM models is most likely to occur if the loadings of measures within factors diverge. Otherwise, the solution approximates the equal loading one that they showed not to be identified, with the consequence that problems of empirical identification (the data set producing identification problems in a model that could be identified) emerge. But even in the final instance, with divergent loadings, Kenny and Kashy suggested that there still might be other problems in reaching a solution.

Given problems that emerged with 3 × 3 MTMM matrices, one might decide to abandon MTMM models altogether. Such a solution seems misguided, for the problem described appears only in the fully crossed model. So, for example, if one method were to exert little common influence on measures (i.e., be weak) and could be dropped, then the model could be identified. Furthermore, given the intuitive appeal of the MTMM CFA model, abandoning MTMM models seems severe and simplistic, for we know that there are sources of common method variance that will bias our solutions if they are ignored. Unfortunately, however, there are not ideal structural equation alternatives (see also Marsh & Grayson, 1995). First, researchers may as well examine plausibility of their data's fit to an additive model, but they might well expect to encounter problems in estimation. If such problems occur, then they can try one of several alternatives.

Kenny and Kashy (1992) suggested, as a first alternative, specifying methods as residual covariances in the structural model rather than specifying them as methods factors. Such an approach will produce a solution but has two weaknesses. First, as described earlier in this chapter, a residual covariance approach can fit data that display structures other than common method factors. Second, the approach requires that methods be independent of one another; if methods correlate, then the solution will be biased, likely overestimating convergent validity and underestimating discriminant validity.

A second alternative suggested by Kenny and Kashy (1992) is to drop one of the factors, choosing from among the methods factors because it makes little sense to drop a trait factor. In fact, I have encountered such an instance (Maruyama, 1982), for one of the methods employed was a free response method that in fact produced no method variance. Barring a source of an easy decision such as that one, however, Kenny and Kashy described an approach that drops a factor without actually dropping a factor. That approach, similar to effect coding in analysis of variance, assigns weights of +1 and −1 to various methods factors so that the methods factors actually end up contrasting various methods. For such an approach, a covariance matrix rather than a correlation matrix should be analyzed. Kenny and Kashy suggested that, because of the restrictive assumptions made in contrasting methods, this approach tends inaccurately to lower discriminant validity and increase convergent validity as well as to lower estimates of method variance. Finally, if no variant of an additive model fits, then nonadditive effect models could be examined for plausibility.

■ Summary of Confirmatory Factor Analysis and Multitrait-Multimethod Models

In summary, this section introduced formal ways to think about and handle effects of common method variance within structural equation models. Even though problems may appear if the data include a fully crossed set of methods and traits, it is important to consider specifying methods effects in models as a means of teasing apart trait true score variance from other sources of variance that obscure the nature of trait relationships. That is, additive effects models such as the MTMM model described in this chapter can readily handle prominent method variance provided that methods are not fully crossed with traits.

■ Initial Testing of Plausibility of Models: Consistency Tests

One of the primary advantages of introducing multiple measures of latent variables is that information from them can be used to examine whether or not those measures define an underlying variable in a consistent way. This section demonstrates one way in which multiple indicators can be used to "test" for consistency. The perspective presented was developed primarily by Costner and his colleagues (e.g., Costner, 1969; Costner & Schoenberg, 1973). There are formal tests that can be used to test consistency using canonical correlation or structural equation models. For this discussion, however, knowing how to use those tests is less important than gaining a good understanding of what multiple indicators provide in the way of information and how those indicators can be used to examine viability of constructs. The approaches described illustrate, in a more simple way, the processes that are used in latent variable structural equation models. As noted earlier in this chapter, readers who want information beyond what is presented should consider Kenny (1979). This section is presented assuming a correlation metric, and this is the way in which the approach was developed.

Number of Indicators and Consistency Tests

Figure 7.2 can be used to illustrate how consistency tests can be performed. Because only *X*'s appear in the figure, any correlations presented will be expressed using only the numbers, for example, r_{12} rather than rX_1X_2. Consider the model first imagining that only X_1 is available to measure X. In that case, X needs to be defined exactly by X_1, so path *a* is fixed to unity and e_1 is fixed to zero.[11] Assuming measures and constructs are the same is what is done by path analysis. In doing path analysis, therefore, researchers have to hope that X_1 is at least a close approximation of X.

Second, imagine that only X_1 and X_2 are available. In that instance, there is one correlation between the two measures (r_{12}) and two paths to estimate (*a* and *b*). What results when the tracing rules from path analysis are applied to the model is one equation in two unknowns, $r_{12} = ab$, which is an underidentified model. It can be estimated by assuming that the paths are equal (*a* = *b*); by selecting two values that, when multiplied together, yield the correlation; or by fixing one of the two paths to unity (1.0). If the first case, then each of the two paths is the square root of the correlation and, using the terminology introduced earlier, the indicators are assumed to be **parallel.** If the last case, then the path that is not fixed becomes the correlation. The middle case works but is very difficult to justify, for selection of the two values is arbitrary, as is their assignment to the two measures. In summary, having two indicators provides some flexibility and is markedly better than having only a single indicator, but it still is less than ideal.

Continuing the progression of adding new indicators, imagine that the first three indicators of X are available. In this case, there are three correlations between indicators, yielding three equations and three unknowns. The model then is just identified. From the tracing rules, the equations are

$$r_{12} = ab \text{ (same as the two-indicator model)},$$
$$r_{13} = ac, \text{ and}$$
$$r_{23} = bc.$$

Thus, the model can estimate *a*, *b*, and *c*; those estimates can be seen most easily in terms of their squares:

---

11. There are alternatives such as adjusting for unreliability, but, as noted earlier in this book, such corrections are risky, for they may be inaccurate.

$$a^2 = (r_{12} \times r_{13}) / r_{23} = abac / bc = aa,$$
$$b^2 = (r_{12} \times r_{23}) / r_{13} = abbc / ac = bb, \text{ and}$$
$$c^2 = (r_{13} \times r_{23}) / r_{12} = acbc / ab = cc.$$

The estimates are not independent of one another, for they all involve the same three correlations. Furthermore, as is true of all just-identified models, there is only a single way in which to estimate each path, and no test of fit is possible. Thus, having available three indicators is valuable, for it yields estimates of each of the three paths. On the other hand, within a single factor model there is no way in which to judge fit of those estimates, for the model is just identified and will fit perfectly.

Adding a fourth indicator allows tests of the consistency of estimates, for there now are more degrees of freedom than paths (six correlations and four paths). Any number of indicators greater than four, of course, allows similar tests and more of them. The equations are as follows (the first three are the same as from the three-indicator model):

$$r_{12} = ab,$$
$$r_{13} = ac,$$
$$r_{23} = bc,$$
$$r_{14} = ad,$$
$$r_{24} = bd, \text{ and}$$
$$r_{34} = cd.$$

Estimating the paths as before yields squares of the paths:

$$a^2 = (r_{12} \times r_{13}) / r_{23} = (r_{12} \times r_{14}) / r_{24} = (r_{13} \times r_{14}) / r_{34},$$
$$b^2 = (r_{12} \times r_{23}) / r_{13} = (r_{12} \times r_{24}) / r_{14} = (r_{23} \times r_{24}) / r_{34},$$
$$c^2 = (r_{13} \times r_{23}) / r_{12} = (r_{13} \times r_{34}) / r_{14} = (r_{23} \times r_{34}) / r_{24}, \text{ and}$$
$$d^2 = (r_{14} \times r_{24}) / r_{12} = (r_{14} \times r_{34}) / r_{13} = (r_{24} \times r_{34}) / r_{23}.$$

There are three ways of estimating each of the paths. (Do not forget to take square roots to get the paths.) If the model fits the data, then the various estimates of each coefficient should be consistent with one another (i.e., approximately the same). If, however, the different ways of estimating a coefficient yield markedly different estimates, then there are problems in the model.

Although consistency could be assessed by calculating each estimate of a, b, c, and d in all possible ways, that approach is not optimal because the different estimates are not independent of one another; there are only 2 degrees of freedom in the model. A more efficient way in which to examine consistency is to use the three different pairs of correlations that should be equal. Starting from any of the equations, deleting the redundant term, and moving all terms from the denominator will result in two of the three pairs of correlations. The three pairs are

$$r_{12}r_{34} = r_{13}r_{24} = r_{14}r_{23}.$$

For example, consider

$$r_{12}{}^*r_{13} / r_{23} = r_{12}{}^*r_{14} / r_{24}.$$

The r_{12} can be deleted (by dividing both sides by r_{12}) from both sides of the equation, leaving

$$r_{13} / r_{23} = r_{14} / r_{24}.$$

Multiplying by $(r_{23} \times r_{24})$ yields

$$r_{13}r_{24} = r_{14}r_{23}.$$

Note that all four measures appear in the subscripts on each side of the equation.

The equality $r_{12}r_{34} = r_{13}r_{24} = r_{14}r_{23}$ yields three of what Kenny (1979) called "vanishing tetrads," for the differences between the pairs of correlations should be 0 if the model is in fact true and a single factor fits the data. Because the four indicators all define a single factor, this consistency test can be thought of as *consistency within* a construct. The vanishing tetrads are

$$r_{12}r_{34} - r_{13}r_{24} = 0$$
$$r_{12}r_{34} - r_{14}r_{23} = 0, \text{ and}$$
$$r_{13}r_{24} - r_{14}r_{23} = 0.$$

The tetrads are not independent, for the model has only $6 - 4 = 2$ degrees of freedom. Nonetheless, they provide valuable information about plausibility of a single-factor model. If the tetrads approximate zero, then the single-factor model seems plausible.

Before reading further, readers should attempt Exercise 7.2, in which path estimates and vanishing tetrads are calculated.

▎ Costner's Original Consistency Model

The "classic" model developed by Costner and his colleagues (Costner, 1969; Costner & Schoenberg, 1973) appears in Figure 7.4. Note that if X and Y are the same variable ($e = 1$), then Figures 7.2 and 7.4 would be identical and there would be nothing new to discuss. Assuming that they are not identical, this model tests *consistency between* constructs.

As was done for the previous model, the logic of path analysis can be used to trace the paths and represent the relationships between the observed measures. The model has six correlations and five paths to estimate, thus leaving only 1 degree of freedom. The equations are

$$rX_1X_2 = ab,$$
$$rX_1Y_1 = aec,$$
$$rX_1Y_2 = aed,$$
$$rX_2Y_1 = bec,$$
$$rX_2Y_2 = bed, \text{ and}$$
$$rX_1Y_2 = cd.$$

Although it may not be immediately obvious, these equations can be combined to yield the following equality:

$$rX_1Y_1 \times rX_2Y_2 = rX_1Y_2 \times rX_2Y_1 \qquad \text{or}$$
$$aec \times bed = aed \times bec = abcde^2.$$

Because both sides should be the same, their difference should be zero. If this difference approximates zero, then the model fits (i.e., there seems to be no nonrandom measurement error in the model).

Finally, Kenny (1979) introduced yet a third model variation that can be used for consistency tests. This variant begins with a three-indicator, just-identified model and adds a fourth indicator that comes from a different conceptual variable, as illustrated in Figure 7.5.

Figure 7.5 also is a model with 6 available degrees of freedom and five paths and, thus, seemingly would have 1 degree of freedom.

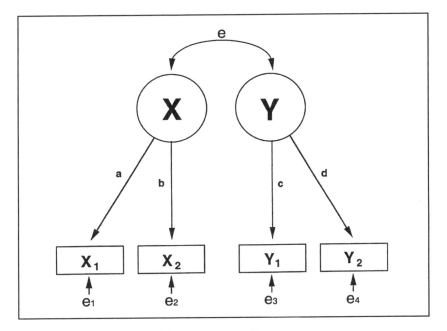

Figure 7.4. Costner Model for Consistency Tests

In fact, there are 2 degrees of freedom coupled with underidentification, for the d and e paths cannot be uniquely solved; only the de product can be determined.

The X_1, X_2, and X_3 relationships are exactly the same as in the three-indicator, single-factor model, and their relationships with Y_1 are

$$rX_1Y_1 = aed,$$
$$rX_2Y_1 = bed, \text{ and}$$
$$rX_3Y_1 = ced.$$

The equality for this model is

$$rX_1X_3 \times rX_2Y_1 = rX_1X_2 \times rX_3Y_1 = rX_2X_3 \times rX_1Y_1 \qquad \text{or}$$
$$ac \times bed = ab \times ced = be \times aed = abcde,$$

which could yield two vanishing tetrads. This model allows testing consistency of indicators on constructs with only three available indicators. Kenny (1979) called this consistency of the **epistemic**

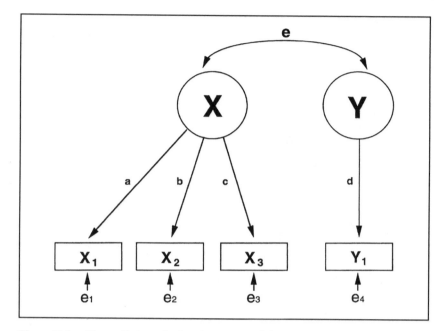

Figure 7.5. Kenny Epistemic Consistency Model

correlation, which is the relationship of an indictor with the underlying construct.

In summary, the consistency tests illustrate the information that is gained by the availability of multiple indicators. They also allow investigators to examine plausibility of their models at a model development stage. They can be used during development of constructs to establish plausibility of single "factoredness" or to identify indicators that could be problematic in structural equation models. If, for example, "extra" indicators are available, then consistency information could be used to decide whether or not to drop indicators before building models or to add to a model additional factors representing influences such as method variance.

Most important for many investigators, the "consistency" approaches can remove much of the mysticism that comes from structural equation models generally and from large models particularly by giving investigators a better feel for their data. They can be used to examine sources of problems when models are not fitting well. They also serve a valuable prospective function, for investigators can use these methods with pilot data to get a sense of the factor structure.

(In such instances, inspection of outliers is particularly important, for single outliers can markedly change correlations in small samples.) Finally, full-information solutions like those used with latent variable structural equation models estimate paths using information from all the different ways of estimating them, in effect trying to reconcile the different ways of estimation. Thus, to the degree that different estimates are not consistent, fit suffers and estimates can become less stable.

Readers should now try Exercise 7.3, which takes the information from the consistency tests and uses it to demonstrate how overall model fit is calculated. This illustration is very important, for it demonstrates how SEM programs calculate the goodness-of-fit statistics and indexes that they do.

At this point, all the background information to prepare readers to become SEM researchers has been provided. Readers should be familiar with the logic underlying basic path models, how those models can be decomposed into direct and indirect causal effects plus noncausal effects, options (nonrecursive models or longitudinal panel models) to consider when two or more variables seem to cause each other, the importance of having available multiple measures of constructs of interest, and how to model residual covariances stemming from additional sources of common variance. Finally, before turning to full latent variable structural equation models, it is important to again issue the reminder that SEM approaches begin with and are driven by theory. They are intended to be confirmatory (i.e., to test existing models of reality), not to tinker with to generate models of reality.

E X E R C I S E   7 . 1

Setting Up Matrices for Confirmatory Factor Analysis

Matrices for the MTMM CFA model are set up in exactly the same way as was done in an earlier section of this chapter. Set up the matrices for Figure 7.3. Call the factor pattern matrix lambda, and set it up. (Hint: There are trait-plus-method number of factors.) Call the factor correlation matrix phi, and set it up. Call the residual matrix theta, and set it up.

E X E R C I S E   7 . 2

Consistency Tests

Using the approach outlined in this chapter, estimate the loadings of the *first* and *last* measures of each construct in *all* possible ways (four variables should yield three ways, and five variables should yield six ways). If readers want to look at a relevant diagram, they should look at Figure 7.2. For the first example, just add an additional indicator X_5 with a path e; for the second illustration, imagine that the X's are Y's.

Get the pooled estimate of those loadings by summing numerators and denominators from the various estimates separately. Finally, calculate the "vanishing tetrads" generated from Measures X_1-X_4 for each construct, and, by inspection, assess plausibility of a single-factor model.

Construct 1: Academic Achievement Values

X_1 = studying consistently to become well educated
X_2 = working hard to achieve academic honors
X_3 = striving to get top grade point average
X_4 = studying hard to get good grades
X_5 = hours spent on homework

	X_1	X_2	X_3	X_4	X_5
X_1	1.00				
X_2	.47	1.00			
X_3	.41	.55	1.00		
X_4	.46	.56	.59	1.00	
X_5	.06	.10	.08	.10	1.00

Construct 2: Family Social Class

Y_1 = home richness index
Y_2 = family finances
Y_3 = father's education
Y_4 = mother's education

	Y_1	Y_2	Y_3	Y_4
Y_1	1.00			
Y_2	.42	1.00		
Y_3	.32	.31	1.00	
Y_4	.27	.35	.55	1.00

EXERCISE 7.3

Calculating Residual Matrices Used in Fit Tests

Use the following estimates of the paths from the measures to the underlying factor/construct for the first part of Exercise 7.2 (i.e., the Academic Achievement Values construct):

$$X_1, \text{path} = .585$$
$$X_2, \text{path} = .762$$
$$X_3, \text{path} = .723$$
$$X_4, \text{path} = .782$$
$$X_5, \text{path} = .118.$$

Use the above paths to estimate what each of the correlations between each pair of measures is *according to the model*. That is done by using the tracing rules, for example, $r_{12} = .585 \times .762$. In Figure 7.2, $r_{12} = a \times b$. Similarly, $r_{13} = a \times c$, and so forth. Put each correlation into matrix form paralleling the matrix in the first part of Exercise 7.2. When all 10 correlations have been computed, the result is a predicted variance/covariance matrix (call it Σ) for the model. Compare the matrix predicted by the model and the one observed (call it S). The difference between the predicted and observed covariance matrices ($\Sigma - S$) is the residual. That residual is what is tested for significance in structural equation programs. Because the test is a test of the residual, significance is not wanted, for that means that the residual is different from 0, which means that the model does not fit; it leaves unexplained appreciable variability. Thus, it is a significance test that seems "backward."

Does your inspection of the differences lead you to the same conclusion that the vanishing tetrads did?

In maximum likelihood programs such as LISREL, the fitting function is of the form

$$F = \ln|\Sigma| - \ln|\Sigma| + \text{tr}(S\Sigma^{-1}) - n,$$

where Σ is the predicted variance/covariance matrix, S is the observed variance/covariance matrix, and n (or $p + q$ if exogenous and endogenous variables are separated) is the size of the input matrix. In English, the equation says that the function is the log of the determinant of Matrix Σ minus the log of the determinant of Matrix S plus the trace of the Matrix S times Matrix Σ^{-1} minus n (where n is the size of the observed matrix). Regardless of whether or not readers follow all the matrix operations, the logic of minimization is that as S and Σ converge, their determinants also converge, and the difference between the first two terms goes to 0. Also as they converge, Σ^{-1} approaches S^{-1}, which makes $S\Sigma^{-1}$ approach an identity matrix. Because the trace is the sum of the diagonal elements, it approaches n, and their difference also goes to 0.

SOLUTIONS TO EXERCISES

Exercise 7.1

	T_1	T_2	T_3	M_1	M_2	M_3
Lambda						
X_1	a	0	0	j	0	0
X_2	0	d	0	k	0	0
X_3	0	0	g	l	0	0
X_4	b	0	0	0	m	0
X_5	0	e	0	0	n	0
X_6	0	0	h	0	o	0

	T_1	T_2	T_3	M_1	M_2	M_3
X_7	c	0	0	0	0	p
X_8	0	f	0	0	0	q
X_9	0	0	i	0	0	r

Phi

	T_1	T_2	T_3	M_1	M_2	M_3
T_1	1.0					
T_2	A	1.0				
T_3	C	B	1.0			
M_1	0	0	0	1.0		
M_2	0	0	0	D	1.0	
M_3	0	0	0	F	E	1.0

Theta (diagonal)

[e_1 e_2 e_3 e_4 e_5 e_6 e_7 e_8 e_9]

Exercise 7.2

A solution for Construct 1 appears in Exercise 7.3. Of most importance is that the model fits well in Construct 1 despite having one item that correlates poorly with all other indicators. Its low loading likely suggests it should be dropped from the model, yet it does not lead to a poor fit—an important point to remember when thinking about overall model fit. Construct 2 yields discrepant estimates for paths as well as nonvanishing tetrads. It is not single-factored.

Exercise 7.3

Consistent with the findings from Exercise 7.2, all the residuals are very small, supporting the single-factor interpretation.

Illustration 3:   Peer Popularity and Academic Achievement

Confirmatory Factor Analysis

This illustration continues analysis of a single data set with different methods. As was done with the prior two illustrations with this data set, the model set up for the SEM program LISREL appears as an appendix. LISREL output is added to the appendix. The matrices presented correspond directly to Equation 7.6 presented earlier:

$$\Sigma_{YY} = P\Phi P' + \Psi,$$

where Σ_{YY} is the variance/covariance matrix of observed measures, P (and P') is the factor pattern matrix, Φ is the factor correlation matrix, and Ψ is the residual variance/covariance matrix.

On the basis of other analyses, the theoretical variable of Family Social Class was dropped from the model because it was not related to any other variable, either in the observed variable models or in the latent variable models. The remaining eight latent variables (which cross three time periods) appear in Figure 7.6. Readers should note that they are the same variables as appear in Figure 9.3 but that those appear in a path model rather than in a confirmatory factor model. Their measures are as follows:

1.   Academic Ability, measured by the Peabody PVT (16) and the Raven Progressive Matrices (17);
2-4. Acceptance by Peers, measured by choices for seating, schoolwork, and playground choices (three waves: 13, 14, 15; 4, 5, 6; 7, 8, 9);
5-7. Academic Achievement, measured by performance on standardized verbal achievement tests and verbal grades (also three waves: 27, 28; 18, 19; 20, 21); and
8.   Teacher Ratings, measured by the semantic differential scale score (30) and a general expectation rating (32).

Although the greatest interest in these data stems from the structural model relationships between peer acceptance and achievement, they also are amenable to CFA. As will be explained in detail in Chapter 10, the fit of the CFA model would be identical to the fit of a just-identified structural model causally linking the variables.

The solution that results from the program and model is as follows:

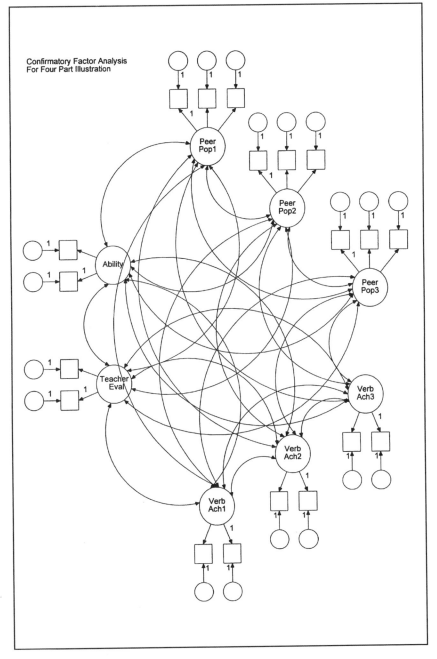

Figure 7.6. Confirmatory Factor Analysis for Four-Part Illustration

LISREL Estimates (maximum likelihood):
Relations of measures to constructs (lambda Y)

| | Latent Variable | | | | | | | |
	Ability	PeerAcc1	Achieve1	PeerAcc2	Achieve2	PeerAcc3	Achieve3	TEvaluat
VAR 16	1.00	—	—	—	—	—	—	—
VAR 17	.60	—	—	—	—	—	—	—
	(.25)							
	2.41							
VAR 13	—	1.00	—	—	—	—	—	—
VAR 14	—	.69	—	—	—	—	—	—
		(.14)						
		4.85						
VAR 15	—	.84	—	—	—	—	—	—
		(.16)						
		5.39						
VAR 27	—	—	1.00	—	—	—	—	—
VAR 28	—	—	.98	—	—	—	—	—
			(.24)					
			4.13					
VAR 4	—	—	—	1.00	—	—	—	—
VAR 5	—	—	—	1.00	—	—	—	—
				(.11)				
				9.05				
VAR 6	—	—	—	1.06	—	—	—	—
				(.11)				
				9.72				
VAR 18	—	—	—	—	1.00	—	—	—
VAR 19	—	—	—	—	1.11	—	—	—
					(.15)			
					7.22			
VAR 7	—	—	—	—	—	1.00	—	—
VAR 8	—	—	—	—	—	.95	—	—
						(.13)		
						7.12		
VAR 9	—	—	—	—	—	.88	—	—
						(.12)		
						7.25		
VAR 20	—	—	—	—	—	—	1.00	—

LISREL Estimates (continued)

| | *Latent Variable* | | | | | | | |
	Ability	*PeerAcc1*	*Achieve1*	*PeerAcc2*	*Achieve2*	*PeerAcc3*	*Achieve3*	*TEvaluat*
VAR 21	—	—	—	—	—	—	.61	—
							(.14)	
							4.21	
VAR 30	—	—	—	—	—	—	—	1.00
VAR 32	—	—	—	—	—	—	—	.61
								(.15)
								4.08

| | *Latent Variable* | | | | | | | |
	Ability	*PeerAcc1*	*Achieve1*	*PeerAcc2*	*Achieve2*	*PeerAcc3*	*Achieve3*	*TEvaluat*
Ability	.46							
	(.22)							
	2.05							
PeerAcc1	.15	.71						
	(.09)	(.17)						
	1.64	4.06						
Achieve1	.24	.16	.30					
	(.09)	(.08)	(.13)					
	2.71	1.97	2.32					
PeerAcc2	.04	.14	.08	.69				
	(.08)	(.09)	(.07)	(.14)				
	0.42	1.62	1.09	4.79				
Achieve2	.30	.14	.37	.09	.50			
	(.09)	(.08)	(.09)	(.07)	(.12)			
	3.39	1.83	4.01	1.33	4.17			
PeerAcc3	−.04	.05	.06	.14	−.03	.72		
	(.09)	(.09)	(.08)	(.09)	(.07)	(.16)		
	−0.47	0.56	0.81	1.68	−0.36	4.54		
Achieve3	.25	.27	.55	.20	.57	.00	.85	
	(.11)	(.11)	(.14)	(.10)	(.12)	(.10)	(.23)	
	2.27	2.52	3.97	2.04	4.71	0.02	3.67	
TEvaluat	.25	.27	.38	.10	.42	.02	.63	.64
	(.10)	(.10)	(.10)	(.09)	(.10)	(.09)	(.13)	(.19)
	2.56	2.76	3.83	1.19	4.37	0.24	4.96	3.48

NOTE: Standard errors are in parentheses. *t* values are in rows under standard errors.

The covariance metric makes it more difficult to interpret the size of the relationships. One could easily ask for the scaled solution, which provides estimates in which the latent variables are scaled to unit variance.

Although the chi-square is pretty good—chi-square with 115 degrees of freedom = 117.14 ($p = .43$)—other information from the solution suggests that the model could be improved. In other words, given the existing measurement structure, there is no solution that would provide a better fit. Because there are no degrees of freedom in the relationships among the theoretical variables, improving the model would require some type of reconceptualization of the measurement model. That could be done by adding residual covariances to the existing measurement model or by changing the basic measurement model.

A P P E N D I X 7 . 1

LISREL Setup and Output From Illustration

$$\text{Model: } \Sigma_{YY} = P\Phi P' + \Psi,$$

where

Σ_{YY} is the variance/covariance matrix of observed measures
P (and P') is the factor pattern matrix, designated by the letters LY in LISREL
Φ is the factor correlation matrix, designated by PS in LISREL
Ψ is the residual variance/covariance matrix, designated by TE in LISREL

The matrix for these analyses is on the opposite page.

The LISREL control cards (although the measures are selected from a larger matrix called MAfullmt.rx containing additional measures, which accounts for the 33 measures and the need for an SE line, plus the selection that follows it) are as follows:

Mexican American data, runs for choices of whites, CFA, with reference indicators

```
DA NI=33 NO=100 MA=CM
KM FU FO FI=a:MAfullmt.rx
(8F10.7)
SD FO
```

Covariance Matrix to Be Analyzed

	VAR 16	VAR 17	VAR 13	VAR 14	VAR 15	VAR 27	VAR 28	VAR 4	VAR 5	VAR 6	VAR 18	VAR 19	VAR 7	VAR 8	VAR 9	VAR 20	VAR 21	VAR 30	VAR 32
VAR 16	1.00																		
VAR 17	.28	1.00																	
VAR 13	.16	.10	1.00																
VAR 14	.03	.04	.52	1.00															
VAR 15	.15	.05	.59	.36	1.00														
VAR 27	.31	.24	.08	.10	.16	1.00													
VAR 28	.15	.06	.15	.04	.36	.30	1.00												
VAR 4	.01	.05	.12	.04	.10	.10	.07	1.00											
VAR 5	.02	.03	.16	.05	.08	.11	.00	.68	1.00										
VAR 6	.04	.01	.16	.09	.12	.12	.11	.73	.72	1.00									
VAR 18	.28	.13	.12	-.01	.17	.33	.36	-.05	.08	.03	.81								
VAR 19	.31	.25	.17	.01	.21	.42	.46	.12	.13	.16	.55	.82							
VAR 7	-.03	-.01	.00	.11	.16	.00	.18	.19	.12	.08	-.05	-.04	1.05						
VAR 8	-.02	.09	.02	.14	.12	.08	.05	.20	.12	.20	.03	.04	.69	1.10					
VAR 9	-.12	-.02	-.05	.04	.04	.04	.02	.20	.11	.22	-.10	-.04	.62	.60	.96				
VAR 20	.22	.20	.23	.17	.37	.43	.54	.19	.21	.23	.52	.61	-.01	.04	-.02	1.24			
VAR 21	.16	.06	.14	.02	.23	.36	.32	.19	.10	.07	.43	.42	.10	.00	-.06	.51	1.44		
VAR 30	.24	.12	.17	.13	.29	.30	.41	.11	.10	.10	.42	.50	.01	-.03	.04	.68	.29	1.00	
VAR 32	.22	.11	.31	.36	.28	.35	.28	.09	.03	.14	.21	.17	.04	.05	.11	.33	.11	.39	1.00

```
(11F7.5)
1.0 1.0 1.0 1.0 1.0 1.0 1.025 1.049 .981 1.0 1.0
1.0 1.0 1.0 1.0 1.0 1.0 .901 .907 1.114 1.200 .911
.936 .766 .875 .926 1.0 1.0 1.0 1.0 .705 1.0 1.0
SE
16 17 13 14 15 27 28 4 5 6 18 19 7 8 9 20 21 30 32 /
MO NY=19 NE=8 LY=FU,FI BE=FU,FI PS=SY,Fr TE=SY,FI
FR LY 2 1 LY 4 2 LY 5 2 LY 7 3 LY 9 4 LY 10 4 C
ly 19 8 ly 12 5 ly 14 6 ly 15 6 ly 17 7
FR TE 1 1 TE 2 2 TE 3 3 TE 4 4 TE 5 5 TE 6 6 TE 17 17
   TE 18 18 C
TE 7 7 TE 8 8 TE 9 9 TE 10 10 TE 11 11 TE 12 12 TE 13
   13 TE 14 14 TE 15 15 C
TE 16 16 TE 17 17 TE 11 6 TE 12 7 TE 13 8 TE 14 9 TE
   16 6 C
TE 17 7 TE 15 10 TE 16 11 TE 17 12 te 18 18 te 19 19
ST 1.0 LY 1 1 LY 3 2 LY 6 3 LY 8 4 LY 11 5 LY 13 6 LY
   16 7 C
LY 9 4 LY 8 4 LY 18 8
ST .7 LY 4 2 LY 7 3 LY 5 2
ST .3 LY 2 1
ST 1.0 PS 1 1 PS 2 2 PS 3 3 PS 4 4 ps 5 5 ps 6 6 ps
   7 7 ps 8 8
ST .7 TE 1 1 TE 2 2 TE 3 3 TE 4 4 TE 5 5 TE 6 6 TE 7
   7 TE 8 8 TE 9 9 C
TE 10 10 TE 11 11 TE 12 12 TE 13 13 TE 14 14 TE 15 15
   TE 16 16 TE 17 17
ST .6 TE 18 18 TE 19 19
path diagram
OU PT SE TV AD=OFF LY=SMACFA1m BE=SMACFA1m PS=SMACFA1m
   TE=SMACFA1m
```

The fit indexes for the CFA analysis (to review after reading Chapter 1?) were as follows:

```
F FIT STATISTICS
WITH 115 DEGREES OF FREEDOM = 117.14 (P =

N-CENTRALITY PARAMETER (NCP) = 2.14
NFIDENCE INTERVAL FOR NCP = (0.0 ; 31.84)
```

171

MINIMUM FIT FUNCTION VALUE = 1.18
POPULATION DISCREPANCY FUNCTION VALUE (F0) = 0.022
90 PERCENT CONFIDENCE INTERVAL FOR F0 = (0.0 ; 0.32)
ROOT MEAN SQUARE ERROR OF APPROXIMATION (RMSEA) =
  0.014
90 PERCENT CONFIDENCE INTERVAL FOR RMSEA = (0.0 ;
  0.053)
P-VALUE FOR TEST OF CLOSE FIT (RMSEA < 0.05) = 0.93
EXPECTED CROSS-VALIDATION INDEX (ECVI) = 2.70
90 PERCENT CONFIDENCE INTERVAL FOR ECVI = (2.68 ;
  3.00)
ECVI FOR SATURATED MODEL = 3.84
ECVI FOR INDEPENDENCE MODEL = 8.26
CHI-SQUARE FOR INDEPENDENCE MODEL WITH 171 DEGREES OF
  FREEDOM = 779.49
INDEPENDENCE AKAIKE INFORMATION CRITERIA (AIC) =
  817.49
MODEL AIC = 267.14
SATURATED AIC = 380.00
INDEPENDENCE CAIC = 885.99
MODEL CAIC = 537.53
SATURATED CAIC = 1064.98
ROOT MEAN SQUARE RESIDUAL (RMR) = 0.056
STANDARDIZED RMR = 0.056
GOODNESS OF FIT INDEX (GFI) = 0.90
ADJUSTED GOODNESS OF FIT INDEX (AGFI) = 0.83
PARSIMONY GOODNESS OF FIT INDEX (PGFI) = 0.54
NORMED FIT INDEX (NFI) = 0.85
NON-NORMED FIT INDEX (NNFI) = 0.99
PARSIMONY NORMED FIT INDEX (PNFI) = 0.57
COMPARATIVE FIT INDEX (CFI) = 1.00
INCREMENTAL FIT INDEX (IFI) = 1.00
RELATIVE FIT INDEX (RFI) = 0.78
CRITICAL N (CN) = 130.47

PART 4

LATENT VARIABLE
STRUCTURAL
EQUATION
MODELS

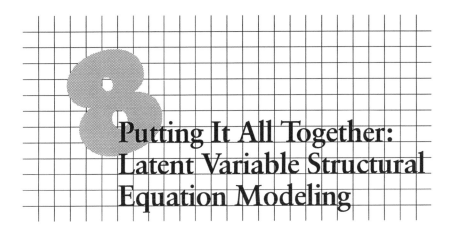

Putting It All Together: Latent Variable Structural Equation Modeling

Moving to latent variable structural equation modeling (SEM) is now but a small step from methods and ideas that have been covered thus far. That step integrates the logic of factor analysis from Chapter 7 with the logic of path modeling. In latent variable modeling, the variables that appear in the path models actually are factors extracted through confirmatory factor analysis (CFA). The factors/variables are defined by a set of observed measures. Each measure is specified a priori as being related to one or more of the factors. The relationships between factors and measures are specified by equations exactly like the factor analysis model, $Y = Pf + e$. The factors then are interrelated using an equation that parallels the traditional regression equation, $Y = AX + BY + E$ (Y here is *not* the same Y as in the factor analysis equation). What prevents the solution from being a simple regression model is that the X's and Y's in the regression equation are not measured directly but rather are latent variables tapped only through the observed measures that are intended to operationalize them.

There are a couple of additional complications associated with the transition to latent variable SEM. First, there are two sets of factors extracted, one for endogenous variables (in typical factor analysis terminology, $Y = Pf + e$) and the other for exogenous variables ($X = P'f' + e'$, with primes intended only to distinguish the coefficients in the X model from those in the Y model). Those factors (f' and f) then become the respective X and Y variables that are interrelated using the regression model ($f = Af' + Bf + E$). Second, the different computer programs for analyzing latent variable SEMs have used various sets of symbols and formats to present the equations. This book uses the notation of the LISREL program (e.g., Jöreskog & Sörbom, 1988, 1993), the first and most widely used of the SEM programs. LISREL presents the matrices using Greek letters to signify vectors and matrices. The issues are presented in a way that users of earlier versions, as well as the most recent versions, of the LISREL computer program should be able to understand and apply them.

This chapter presents the basics of latent variable SEM. Estimation in SEM is done using **full information** approaches (i.e., estimation of each parameter uses all available information from the covariance matrix in determining the estimate), which means that the factor and regression components of the models are estimated simultaneously. Nevertheless, as is commonly done by SEM programs, the presentation is divided up into two components. The component relating observed measures to latent variables is presented first, followed by the component interrelating latent variables. The importance of **reference indicators,** or measures used to provide a scale or metric for unmeasured variables, also is presented. Then the full model is illustrated through an example. The illustration covers issues of model specification and identification and sets up the matrices that are needed for latent variable SEM. Finally, basic issues of model fitting are discussed.

The Basic Latent Variable Structural Equation Model

The Measurement Model

The measurement model is the model discussed in Chapter 7 relating measures to theoretical variables or factors. It contains information about how theoretical variables are operationalized in each study. Although in path analysis information about operationalization can be hidden by labels (e.g., by calling a measure of school grades "achievement" and using that label in any figures and discussion), in latent variable models such information is more readily apparent.

Each indicator needs to be described, and its relationship to the conceptual variable(s) it is supposed to assess needs to be specified. With respect to written research reports, the description of constructs/latent variables and the measures that operationalize them should appear in the introduction and methods sections. Consistent with notions that researchers need to specify the nature of relationships of measures with variables, inaccuracies or imprecision in defining latent variables usually is called **specification error**. A second type of specification error comes from inaccurately defining the relationships among latent variables. Thus, when researchers mention misspecified models, they are suggesting that there is inaccuracy in specifying relations of measures either to variables or among variables.

In the LISREL measurement model, two CFA models are built, one for exogenous variables and the other for endogenous variables. Actually, separating variables is not necessary; one can treat exogenous variables as if they were endogenous and thereby include the full factor model in a single set of equations. The approach is mathematically equivalent to the two sets of factors approach that is the basic one for computer programs such as LISREL. Because introducing the two approaches together can be confusing to readers, however, presentation of what will be called "an all Y model" is delayed until later and is covered only briefly because most other SEM programs are equation based rather than matrix based, making the distinction unnecessary. That is, because other SEM programs such as AMOS (Arbuckle, 1994, 1997), EQS (e.g., Bentler, 1989), and the SIMPLIS language of LISREL (Jöreskog & Sörbom, 1993) are set up by defining individual equations rather than specifying elements of matrices, this distinction between measurement models is irrelevant. Despite their appearance, however, the programs actually use matrices equivalent to those presented in LISREL to solve for estimated parameters.

In all SEM programs, including LISREL and EQS, the measurement model is a series of regression equations linking measures to factors—the traditional factor analysis approach. Relationships can be specified either in a series of equations, one for each observed measure because in factor analysis observed measures are the dependent variables, or in matrix form consistent with the basic factor analysis formula. Whereas AMOS, EQS, and the SIMPLIS version of LISREL, for example, have researchers define their models equation by equation, the basic LISREL program has researchers specify row and column coordinates of parameters to be estimated within matrices.

Using LISREL terminology, in matrix form the factor analysis equations of the form $Y = Pf + e$ are

$$Y = \Lambda_y\eta + \varepsilon \text{ for the endogenous variables and} \qquad (8.1)$$
$$X = \Lambda_x\xi + \delta \text{ for the exogenous variables.} \qquad (8.2)$$

To explain the Greek letters while stating Equations 8.1 and 8.2 in narrative form, the equations are as follows: Equation 8.1—Y equals lambda Y times eta plus epsilon; Equation 8.2—X equals lambda X times xi plus delta. The two lambda matrices are the factor pattern matrices (the P's), eta is the vector of endogenous variables (factors), xi is the vector of exogenous variables (factors), and epsilon and delta are the residuals (e's) for the observed measures.

The single model used for SEM can handle path models with and without measurement error as well as models with nonrandom measurement error. If a model contains measurement error, then the residuals (epsilon and delta) are made up of both error and unique true score variances. If there is nonrandom error, then the variance/covariance matrices of those residuals can allow residuals within matrices to covary with one another.[12] They will not be just a vector of residual variances representing the diagonal elements of the matrices but rather will have off-diagonal elements that are nonzero.

To be able to work with the residual variance/covariance matrices, the equations for X and Y need to be expressed in terms of variance/covariance matrices of observed measures. They can be expressed that way by postmultiplying each side of the factor analysis equation by its transpose and taking expected values. The algebra for this operation is exactly the same as has been illustrated in Chapter 7 and, therefore, will not be repeated here. Thus, for $Y = \Lambda_Y \eta + \varepsilon$, the resulting equation is

$$\Sigma_{YY} = \Lambda_Y \eta\eta'\Lambda_Y' + \Theta\varepsilon; \qquad (8.3)$$

---

12. One reason for combining the exogenous and endogenous variables into a single-factor model is so that residuals can covary across matrices. This reason is obviated in LISREL 8, which allows residuals to covary *between* the two matrices of residuals and in equation form programs such as AMOS and EQS, in which the residual covariances can be named in a straightforward fashion.

for $X = \Lambda_X \xi + \delta$, the resulting equation is

$$\Sigma_{XX} = \Lambda_X \xi\xi'\Lambda_X' + \Theta\delta. \tag{8.4}$$

Finally, to define the new terms: the expected value of $\varepsilon\varepsilon'$ is a variance/covariance matrix called $\Theta\varepsilon$, and the expected value of $\delta\delta'$ is $\Theta\delta$. In addition, the expected value of $\xi\xi'$ is defined as a factor variance/covariance matrix Φ; thus, the latter equation can be expressed as $\Sigma_{XX} = \Lambda_X \Phi \Lambda_X' \Theta\delta$. Finally, as is illustrated later in this chapter when the structural model is presented and explained, the expected value of $\eta\eta'$ cannot be expressed so simply, for it is a function of a number of other matrices.

Before presenting the structural model that interrelates theoretical variables, the issue of reference indicators is revisited and more fully explained and illustrated. Reference indicators provide a critical link between the measurement model's observed variables and the structural model's unmeasured theoretical variables. Without reference indicators, it is not possible to attain identification of latent variable models, for reference indicators provide a scale or metric for latent variables. Many users of SEM techniques seem to have trouble understanding why reference indicators are needed, how reference indicators operate, and what it means to say that selection of a reference indicator is arbitrary—the issues covered in the next section.

Reference Indicators

As noted in the preceding section, scaling of latent endogenous variables can cause problems, for there is no covariance matrix of latent endogenous variables (of etas) in which to specify the variances as set to particular values. Therefore, one needs to scale latent endogenous variables by fixing the relationship between an indicator and each latent variable. Table 8.1 provides an artificial illustration of how proportionality is maintained across selection of different indicators.

For Table 8.1, imagine that we have a single factor with three indicators. (Readers who like to visualize the model can refer to Figure 7.2, assuming that only three indicators—X_1, X_2, and X_3—are available.) The illustration is a CFA model, for there is no structural model with only a single latent variable. In CFA problems, latent variables can be scaled by fixing their variances to some constant. In

TABLE 8.1 Illustration of Reference Indicators

(a) Correlation Matrix

	X_1	X_2	X_3
X_1	1.00		
X_2	.42	1.00	
X_3	.48	.56	1.00

(b) Equivalent Versions of the Model

Reference Indicator	None	X_1	X_2	X_3	Residual Variance
Loading					
X_1	.60	1.00	.60 / .70	.60 / .80	.64
X_2	.70	.70 / .60	1.00	.70 / .80	.51
X_3	.80	.80 / .60	.80 / .70	1.0	.36
Variance latent variable	1.00	$.60^2$	$.70^2$	$.80^2$	

the first column of the example, the variance of the latent variable is fixed to 1.0. By contrast, in structural models that hypothesize causal paths between latent variables, fixing the variance of endogenous variables is not an option. In those models, the variance of endogenous latent variables is a function of explained and unexplained variance and needs to be scaled by using a reference indicator. In other words, the solution in the first column is not possible for endogenous variables in structural models, for they cannot be fixed to a defined value. The solution would require selecting and scaling one of the indicators, yielding one of the solutions found in the second, third, and fourth columns.

What I have done in the illustration is to begin with values for the relations of X_1, X_2, and X_3 with X (Paths a, b, and c in Figure 7.2) of .60, .70, and .80, respectively. Then, using the tracing rule, the correlation between each pair of measures is the product of the paths between them. That is, $r_{12}(ab) = .60 \times .70 = .42$, $r_{13}(ac) = .60 \times .80 = .48$, and $r_{23}(bc) = .70 \times .80 = .56$. The same values can be drawn from the path model consistency tests described at the end of Chapter 7. Although that model typically is used to solve for the paths (a, b, and c), it can be done "backward." As was shown in Chapter 7, a, b, and c are related to the correlations: $a^2 = (r_{12} \times r_{13} / r_{23})$, $b^2 = (r_{12} \times r_{23} / r_{13})$, and $c^2 = (r_{13} \times r_{23} / r_{12})$. The system of three equations in three unknowns (correlations) is solvable. For example, because a^2 is just .6 squared (i.e., .36), $.36 = (r_{12} \times r_{13} / r_{23})$. Then, multiplying a^2 times b^2, which is .49 (i.e., $.49 = (r_{12} \times r_{23} / r_{13})$), gives $.36 \times .49 = r_{12}^2$, or $r_{12} = $ sqrt(.1764) $= .42$. By a similar process, $r_{13} = .48$ and $r_{23} = .56$, all answers the same as by the tracing rule. These values for r_{12}, r_{13}, and r_{23} appear as the correlation matrix in Table 8.1, which yields factor loadings of .60, .70, and .80.

The matrix in Table 8.1 can be used in various structural equation programs to produce the columns of estimates that appear in the lower part of Table 8.1. The first column of numbers is what would be estimated if the variance of the latent variable were fixed to 1.00, the second if X_1 were made the reference indicator (for the second, third, and fourth columns, I have left the values as ratios rather than inserting their numerical values), the third if X_2 were made the reference indicator, and the fourth if X_3 were made the reference indicator. The final column contains the residual variances, which are unchanged across the four variations. The residuals are equal to the total variances (each of which is 1 given that the variables are standardized) minus the loading squared from the first column, in which the latent variable is scaled to unit variance. For example, the residual for X_1 is $1 - .60^2$, or $1 - .36 = .64$.

There are three important points to be made. The first is that designating an indicator the reference indicator does not make the indicator and the latent variable the same unless the reference indicator's residual variance is fixed to 0. That is *not* done in this example and should not be done when multiple indicators are available. With multiple indicators, there is no need to fix residual variances to zero; fixing the residual to zero makes the latent variable and observed variable the same, which ignores important information about reliability of the reference indicator. Second, the proportionality of the indicators is unchanged by selection of a reference indicator. As can be seen from Table 8.1, their relative sizes are maintained regardless of which becomes the reference indicator. Third, the residual variance is unchanged by selection of a reference indicator. Only the variance of the latent variable changes. That change, of course, would alter the nonstandardized paths to and from Variable X; however, if one standardizes the latent variables by converting their variances to unity, then all variations would produce the same solution. Most SEM programs provide scaled solutions in which latent variables are re-scaled to unit variance. Such a rescaling imposed on solutions from any of the second, third, or fourth columns would yield as loadings of the indicators the same values as are found in the solution of the first column.

For readers who have access to an SEM program, I would suggest as an exercise inputting the simple 3×3 correlation matrix and estimating the solution by fixing the variance to 1.0 and by fixing different indicators as reference indicators. Incidentally, even if the model were overidentified, the fit indexes and statistics of the different models would be identical, as is the case for just-identified models such as the one illustrated in Table 8.1.[13]

It is hoped that the illustration helps demystify selection of reference indicators. Because selection is arbitrary, the issue of reference indicators should be a simple one to remember, for it is the same regardless of the type of structural model. *For each endogenous variable, specify one indicator as a reference indicator and fix its relationship with the latent variable to some value, typically 1.* Selecting the most reliable indicator as the reference indicator increases the variance of the latent variable and lowers the loadings of indicators on it but has no effect on the relative loadings or on overall model fit. With respect to structural paths, selecting different reference indicators changes the unstandardized paths to and from the latent variable but does not affect either significance of paths or the size of paths if the latent variable is rescaled to unit variance.

At this point, the complete measurement model has been described. In other words, in setting up this part of the SEM model, the factors/latent variables have been operationalized (i.e., linked to observed measures), so attention can be turned to the interrelationships among the latent variables in the structural model.

▌ The Structural Model

The structural model is the regression part of latent variable SEM. The primary differences between latent variable structural models and basic path analytic models are that (a) the variables in latent

---

13. Using LISREL 7, I had some trouble getting the solution for the first column, in which I fixed the variance of the latent variable to unity. Readers also might encounter problems if they try that version of the program.

variable models typically are not measured (the exception is where there is only a single indicator of a conceptual variable) and that (b) when calculating values for parameter estimates, no distinction needs to be made between recursive and nonrecursive models or models with residual covariation among latent variables. All models can be handled by the general regression equation.

The variables in the regression equation are the etas and xis from the measurement model. Those variables are related through the general regression equation presented earlier in this chapter ($Y = AX + BY + E$), but once again the Greek terminology may make them seem different. The equation in LISREL for the structural model, which perfectly parallels the regression equation and differs only by using different symbols, is

$$\eta = \beta\,\eta + \Gamma\,\xi + \zeta. \qquad (8.5)$$

Compare that with

$$Y = B\,Y + A\,X + E.$$

In LISREL terminology, beta (β) is the matrix of regression weights interrelating endogenous (η) variables, gamma (Γ) is the matrix of regression weights relating exogenous (ξ) to endogenous (η) variables, and zeta (ζ) is the vector of residuals for the endogenous latent variables. If the beta matrix is or, by interchanging rows, can be made lower triangular (i.e., all elements above the main diagonal are 0), then the model is recursive and has unidirectional flow; if it cannot be made lower triangular, then the model is nonrecursive. Unlike regression approaches, regardless of recursivity, the model is estimated in the same way. As was true of regression approaches, however, for nonrecursive models there are additional concerns related to identification.

An alternative form of the structural model equation moves all the etas to the left side of the equation, yielding

$$(I - B)\eta = \Gamma\,\xi + \zeta. \qquad (8.6)$$

For any readers familiar with the early versions of the LISREL program, this is the form of the equation that was used except that the matrix preceding eta was called B rather than $I - B$. By calling the matrix B rather than $I - B$, all the coefficients in the beta matrix had to have their signs reversed before interpreting them, for the values in the matrix would be correct but have signs opposite to their true signs ($-\beta$). By contrast, the form presented first (i.e., with the coefficients interrelating the endogenous variables on the right side of the equation) yields estimates with the correct signs. Later versions of LISREL switched because having to remember to reverse signs was an unneeded complication for researchers not completely comfortable with SEM approaches. (For the rest of us, reminiscing about how beta was different will define us as "old-timers.")

The $I - B$ form of the structural model is useful for expressing the structural model in terms of covariances. If the equation is changed to express covariances in a fashion paralleling the measurement model and the factor model in Chapter 7, then the equation becomes

$$\eta\eta' = (I - B)^{-1}\Gamma\xi\xi'\Gamma'(I - B)^{-1'} + (I - B)^{-1}\zeta\zeta'(I - B)^{-1'}. \quad (8.7)$$

Taking expected values, replacing $\xi\xi'$ with Φ and $\zeta\zeta'$ with Ψ, the equation becomes

$$\Sigma_{\eta\eta'} = (I - B)^{-1}\Gamma\Phi\Gamma'(I - B)^{-1'} + (I - B)^{-1}\Psi(I - B)^{-1'}. \quad (8.8)$$

As noted earlier, the covariance matrix of the etas could not be directly specified. It is a function of the explained variance (the first term on the right side of the equation, $(I - B)^{-1}\Gamma\Phi\Gamma'(I - B)^{-1'}$) and the unexplained variance (the second term on the right side, $(I - B)^{-1}\Psi(I - B)^{-1'}$) in the structural model.

One consequence of not being able to directly specify elements of the eta covariance matrix is that it is somewhat tricky to provide those variables with a scale or metric. Because they are unmeasured, they have no inherent scale. Yet, if they are not assigned a metric, then the model will be underidentified. To assign a metric, one of the indicators of each endogenous latent variable needs to have its reliable component tied in some fashion (usually set equal) to the variance of the latent variable. Its reliable component can, for example, be set equal to the variance of the latent variable by fixing the loading in the lambda matrix to 1.0. The indicator whose loading is fixed is called a **reference indicator**, for it provides a point of reference for the latent variable. *All latent endogenous variables need to have a reference indicator selected and that measure's loading fixed for the* *solution to be identified.*[14] By contrast, variances of exogenous latent variables can be scaled by fixing diagonal elements in the phi matrix as well as by specifying reference indicators.

In summary, latent variable SEM methods represent a logical coupling of regression and factor analytic approaches. They provide researchers with the capacity to overcome many of the problems and shortcomings of path model approaches, such as measurement and specification error, and provide a model general enough to deal with both nonrecursive and recursive models. Once one gets past the Greek terminology for matrices used by the LISREL program, the basic model can be seen as a straightforward combination of regression and factor analysis. If the techniques had been available earlier, then latent variable SEM could have saved path analysis approaches from much criticism about deficiencies in their methods. Unfortunately, its development had to wait for availability of both computer technology and programs that could use that technology. It was Jöreskog (1969, 1973), Bock and his students (e.g., Keesling, 1972), and Wiley (1973) who opened the door to latent variable SEM methods.

An Illustration of Structural Equation Models

Model Specification

Imagine, for example, that we decide that we want to examine the relationships of two exogenous variables (family social class and student ability) with two endogenous variables (student peer status and student achievement). Imagine further that we decide to collect information on parents' educational attainment, parents' job status, and family income as measures of social class; two ability or intelligence tests, the Peabody Picture Vocabulary Test (PPVT) and the Raven Progressive Matrices, as measures of ability; sociometric peer ratings on school work, play, and friendships as measures of peer status; and mathematical, verbal, and analytic reasoning dimensions of a standardized achievement test.

---

14. The most recent version of LISREL, LISREL 8, will select a reference indicator for researchers as part of its estimation process.

Our measurement model appears as Figure 8.1. In Figure 8.1, there has been no distinction made between exogenous and endogenous variables, for at this point there are no arrows connecting the latent/conceptual variables. If the latent variables were to be connected by curved, double-headed arrows, then we would have a CFA model with four factors. As can be seen in Figure 8.2, however, the hypothesized model is in fact a causal one, with paths from exogenous to endogenous variables.

Once the hypothesized causal relationships are specified, the separation of exogenous and endogenous variables becomes obvious. One additional point of importance is that even though achievement and peer status are likely to be interrelated, it is not immediately obvious how to specify the nature of their interrelationship in the model. First, there is no compelling justification for specifying either of them as causally preponderant over the other. Second, because the model specifies that they share common causes, they will be related in the model without any path that goes directly between them. (The magnitude of their relationship in the absence of a direct path between them can be calculated by using tracing rules described earlier in this book.) If those common causes are hypothesized to be strong enough, then no other path may be needed between them even if their relationship is substantial. On the other hand, if their hypothesized relationship exceeds the covariation they would be expected to share due to their common causes, then the additional relationship needs to be acknowledged in the model. A way to model such covariation without assigning causal preponderance is to connect their residuals. In terms of overall model fit, including the residual covariance is equivalent to putting a path either from peer status to achievement or vice versa.

Identification

As has been true for all types of structural models, for a model to be estimable, it needs to be identified. In latent variable structural models, degrees of freedom can be determined readily beginning with the formula for covariance matrices, $v(v + 1) / 2$ (where v is the number of measures), to determine possible degrees of freedom. SEM approaches assume that covariance matrices are being analyzed, so the variances are included in the formula for degrees of freedom. Thus, the appropriate formula is $v(v + 1) / 2$ rather than the

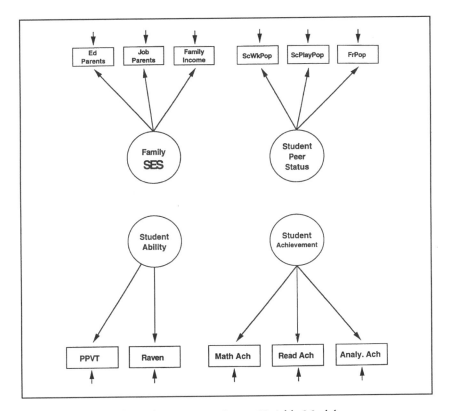

Figure 8.1. Hypothetical Four-Factor Latent Variable Model

$v(v-1)/2$ that is used for determining the number of correlations in a matrix.

Once total possible degrees of freedom are determined, then, by subtracting all coefficients to be estimated, one can determine the degrees of freedom for any particular model. In the present illustration, v is 11; thus, possible degrees of freedom are $11(12)/2 = 66$. From 66 we subtract 11 paths from latent variables to observed measures, 11 residuals on observed measures, and 6 paths (4 unidirectional and 2 representing covariances) and 2 residuals in the structural model, apparently leaving 36 degrees of freedom. Scaling the latent variables requires fixing reference indicators for each of the two endogenous variables, recapturing 2 degrees of freedom. Scaling of latent variables for the two exogenous variables is done by fixing two variances in the phi matrix; because these were not included as free parameters in the preceding calculations, no adjustment of

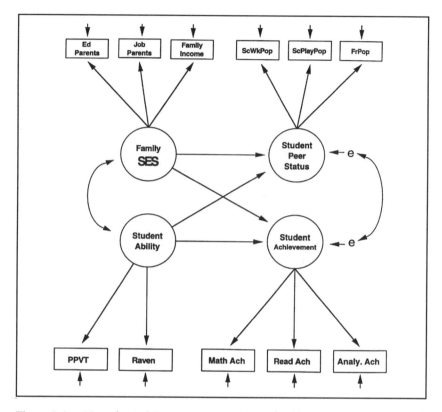

Figure 8.2. Hypothetical Four-Factor Latent Variable Model

degrees of freedom is needed. If they had been scaled through use of reference indicators, then 2 degrees of freedom would be gained for the two reference indicators, but the variances in the phi matrix would have to be freely estimated, and the two additional free parameters would take away the 2 degrees of freedom that were gained. Either way results in a model having $36 + 2 = 38$ degrees of freedom.

For complicated models, identification of all parameters may not be readily apparent. For example, not all parameters in models with positive degrees of freedom are necessarily identified (remember the example from the consistency tests called consistency of the epistemic correlation). In such instances, determining identification of a model is necessary (e.g., Bollen, 1989; Rigdon, 1995).

SEM programs supposedly provide information about identification. If a model is not identified, then the programs should not be able to determine a unique solution. As noted in Chapter 6, the acid test should be whether or not the program is able to calculate standard errors for the parameter estimates, for in order to produce standard errors, the information matrix (a matrix based on the matrix of estimates) needs to be inverted. If parameters are not identified, then one or more of them are linearly dependent on other parameter estimates, and the information matrix should be not invertible but, rather, singular. In other words, the computer programs should help determine model identification. Attaining a solution with standard errors should be evidence of identification of the model. Two cautions, however, are in order. First, if a model is not identified, then the programs should alert you to the presence of problems but may not properly point to the cause of the identification problems. Second, and more important, there has been considerable discussion among SEM researchers about whether or not the programs can be trusted to test for model identification. There seems to be widespread agreement that occasionally the programs produce solutions including standard errors for models that are not identified. A conservative approach, therefore, would be to determine model identification before using an SEM program.

One way in which to think about identification for researchers who would like to ensure identification before analyzing their data is to separate the measurement and structural models. If each one is identified independently, then the model is identified. Although there still seems to be some disagreement about how to establish necessary and sufficient conditions for identification of latent variable SEMs, a conservative view that I follow is that the measurement model never buys identification of the structural model. From that perspective, the structural model needs to be identified; assessing whether or not it is identified can be done using the conditions for identification introduced in Chapter 6. Provided there are available multiple indicators of the latent variables, identification of the measurement model should be no problem so long as the factors are scaled using the options of specifying reference indicators and/or fixing variances (for exogenous variables only).

In the present example, conditions of identification are readily met. The structural model is a recursive model, measures are linked only to single factors, and the residual covariance links two variables with no causal path between them; thus, all of the parameters are identified. The structural part of the model contains six paths: the covariance between the exogenous variables, the four paths from exogenous to endogenous variables, and the residual covariance between the two endogenous variables. If attention is focused only on the structural model, then the old rules for degrees of freedom that were learned in path analysis still hold. To be consistent with the covariance language of structural equation models, $v(v + 1) / 2$ can be used as the formula for available degrees of freedom, resulting in $4(5) / 2 = 10$ possible degrees of freedom, less six paths and four variances, leaving no degrees of freedom, a just-identified structural model. Note that if $v(v - 1) / 2$ from path analysis had been used, then the four variances would be ignored and the result, 0 ($6 - 6 = 0$) degrees of freedom, would be the same.

Because the structural model has no degrees of freedom, in this example all 38 degrees of freedom in the model test the fit of the measurement model. Any failure to fit results from imprecise specification of the measurement model, not from misspecifying the relationships among the latent variables. All just-identified structural models are equivalent and fully account for the relationships among the latent variables. This equivalence provides a "best fit" for the latent variables that is independent of the particular model that is specified, in effect simultaneously examining the best fit of an array of different models. Two points are worth noting. First, latent variable SEM approaches do *not* get around the "equivalent model" problem. The fit of the present model would be identical to the fit of a number of other structural models that are just identified. Second, the idea of knowing that all of the lack of fit is located in the measurement model is an appealing one. It means that no matter how the conceptual variables are interrelated, the only way in which to get a better fit would be to change the measurement model. Some of the indexes for examining model fit include just-identified structural models as one of a series of nested tests that help examine model adequacy and fit.

Equations and Matrices

Setting up the equations and corresponding matrices for the example follows exactly the methods used in the path analysis and CFA chapters. It provides a clear way in which to look at the degrees of freedom issue in detail. We begin with the measurement model, endogenous first. Equation by equation, which is the way in which models are set up in programs such as AMOS and EQS, the model is

$$ScWkPop = \lambda_1 \eta_1 + \varepsilon_1$$
$$ScPlPop = \lambda_2 \eta_1 + \varepsilon_2$$
$$FrPop = \lambda_3 \eta_1 + \varepsilon_3$$
$$MathAch = \lambda_4 \eta_2 + \varepsilon_4$$
$$ReadAch = \lambda_5 \eta_2 + \varepsilon_5$$
$$AnalyAch = \lambda_6 \eta_2 + \varepsilon_6.$$

In matrix form as used by LISREL, it is

$$Y = \Lambda_Y \eta + \varepsilon \qquad \text{or}$$

$$
\begin{vmatrix} ScWkPop \\ ScPlPop \\ FrPop \\ MathAch \\ ReadAch \\ AnalyAch \end{vmatrix}
=
\begin{vmatrix} \lambda_1 & 0 \\ \lambda_2 & 0 \\ \lambda_3 & 0 \\ 0 & \lambda_4 \\ 0 & \lambda_5 \\ 0 & \lambda_6 \end{vmatrix}
\begin{vmatrix} \eta_1 \\ \eta_2 \end{vmatrix}
+
\begin{vmatrix} \varepsilon_1 \\ \varepsilon_2 \\ \varepsilon_3 \\ \varepsilon_4 \\ \varepsilon_5 \\ \varepsilon_6 \end{vmatrix}.
$$

For $\Theta\varepsilon$, there are no residual covariances, so the matrix is diagonal and contains the variances of the epsilons (e.g., ε_1^2). To meet conditions for identification, one indicator in each column of lambda Y has to be fixed to a nonzero value. The one selected is arbitrary. As explained earlier in this chapter, regardless of the one selected, the three indicators will maintain proportionality with one another; just the reference point changes. Thus, in this part of the model, there are 10 parameters ($6 - 2 = 4$ lambdas and 6 theta epsilons) to be estimated.

For the exogenous variables, the equations are

$$EdParents = \lambda_7 \xi_1 + \delta_1$$
$$JobParents = \lambda_8 \xi_1 + \delta_2$$
$$FamIncome = \lambda_9 \xi_1 + \delta_3$$
$$PPVT = \lambda_{10} \xi_2 + \delta_4$$
$$Raven = \lambda_{11} \xi_2 + \delta_5.$$

In matrix form,

$$X = \Lambda_x \xi + \delta$$

$$
\begin{vmatrix} \text{EdParents} \\ \text{JobParents} \\ \text{FamIncome} \\ \text{PPVT} \\ \text{Raven} \end{vmatrix}
=
\begin{vmatrix} \lambda_7 & 0 \\ \lambda_8 & 0 \\ \lambda_9 & 0 \\ 0 & \lambda_{10} \\ 0 & \lambda_{11} \end{vmatrix}
\begin{vmatrix} \xi_1 \\ \xi_2 \end{vmatrix}
+
\begin{vmatrix} \delta_1 \\ \delta_2 \\ \delta_3 \\ \delta_4 \\ \delta_5 \end{vmatrix}
$$

Once again, $\Theta\delta$ is just the residuals, in this case the variances of the deltas. To scale the exogenous latent variables, either a reference indicator needs to be designated or the variances need to be fixed to a value in the phi (variance/covariance) matrix. The choice is another arbitrary one. In this case, assume that we decide to fix the variances in the phi matrix, so another 10 parameters (5 lambdas and 5 thetas) need to be estimated.

For the structural model, the equations are

$$
\eta_1 = \gamma_1 \xi_1 + \gamma_2 \xi_2 + \zeta_1 \text{ and}
$$
$$
\eta_2 = \gamma_3 \xi_1 + \gamma_4 \xi_2 + \zeta_2.
$$

In matrix form,

$$\eta = \beta\eta + \Gamma\xi + \zeta$$

$$
\begin{vmatrix} \eta_1 \\ \eta_2 \end{vmatrix}
=
\begin{vmatrix} 0 & 0 \\ 0 & 0 \end{vmatrix}
\begin{vmatrix} \eta_1 \\ \eta_2 \end{vmatrix}
+
\begin{vmatrix} \gamma_1 & \gamma_2 \\ \gamma_3 & \gamma_4 \end{vmatrix}
\begin{vmatrix} \xi_1 \\ \xi_2 \end{vmatrix}
+
\begin{vmatrix} \zeta_1 \\ \zeta_2 \end{vmatrix}.
$$

Note that beta is null, for there are no hypothesized causal relationships between the two latent variables. There are four relationships to solve for in gamma. In addition, the covariance matrices for the phis and psis need to be solved for:

$$
\Phi = \begin{vmatrix} 1.0 & \phi_{12} \\ \phi_{21} & 1.0 \end{vmatrix}.
$$

As is true for all covariance matrices, phi is symmetric and ϕ_{12} is the same as ϕ_{21}, so there is only one coefficient to estimate. If reference indicators had been specified in lambda X, then the variances in phi (ϕ_{11} and ϕ_{22}) would have to be freely estimated and the degrees of freedom would not change (+2 in lambda X and −2 in phi). For psi, the residual covariance matrix of the factors or latent variables, the matrix is

$$\zeta = \begin{vmatrix} \zeta_1^2 & \zeta_{12} \\ \zeta_{21} & \zeta_2^2 \end{vmatrix} \text{ or, using Greek psi, } \Psi = \begin{vmatrix} \psi_1^2 & \psi_{12} \\ \psi_{21} & \psi_2^2 \end{vmatrix}.$$

Once again, psi is a symmetric covariance matrix, so there are only three coefficients to estimate.

Adding up the parameters to estimate, the total is $10 + 10 + 4 + 1 + 3 = 28$, $66 - 28 = 38$ degrees of freedom in the model, the same total that was presented earlier.

■ Basic Ideas Underlying Fit/Significance Testing

At this point, assuming that the data have been collected and the matrices that link observed to latent variables and latent variables with one another have been specified, all that is needed to conduct the analyses is to set up the commands for the computer program selected. Because readers likely will be using a variety of different programs, no program is described in detail here. (In addition to the references already cited, readers also might see Byrne [1989], for LISREL and Byrne [1994], for EQS.) At the end of this chapter, illustrations using the LISREL program are presented; hopefully, users of other programs will be able to adapt the illustrations to set up the programs they are using. (In the next chapter, an illustration is set up for AMOS and EQS as well as LISREL.) The focus here is on the solution process (i.e., how the programs fit the model to the data and what the test statistics that are generated mean) rather than on setting up the program. In wrapping up this chapter, general principles of fit and significance testing are presented. A detailed discussion of the range of different fit statistics and indexes will be left until Chapter 10.

■ *Individual Parameter Significance*

Before addressing overall fit of the model, it is important to note that in latent variable SEM techniques, each individual parameter that is freely estimated will have a standard error attached to it. That standard error allows for assessing significance of each parameter estimated. Significance of parameters is most commonly done by judging discrepancy from zero in a traditional test of critical ratios of t's or Z's, which tests whether or not zero is contained within the confidence interval. For the larger samples that are expected for SEM, t's approach Z's. Therefore, as a general rule, if an estimate is greater than twice its standard error ($Z > 2.0$), it is deemed significant. The confidence interval also allows testing in different ways. For example, one could test whether or not a correlation between two variables is low enough that they could not be considered to be identical if tested by a confidence interval that does not include 1.0. Standard errors are available for all free parameters including residuals, variances, covariances, and paths.

Testing significance of individual paths is very different from testing overall fit of the model. Good fitting models can have insignificant parameters in places where significance and meaning were expected, whereas poorly fitting models still could find strong and important relationships between variables. Researchers need to balance their focus between significance of particular paths and that of overall model fit. In some instances particular parameters may be more important, whereas in others it may be overall model fit that is the primary issue.

▌ Model Fitting

As was illustrated in Exercise 7.3, statistical tests *of the model* for all tests are tests of differences between the variance/covariance matrix predicted by the model and the sample variance/covariance matrix from the observed data. Those differences are referred to as "fit" or "goodness of fit," namely, how similar the hypothesized model is to the observed data. As the solution is estimated, regardless of whether the approach used is a variant of least squares or maximum likelihood, the goal of the solution process is through an iterative process to reduce discrepancies between observed and predicted matrices.

At this point, readers should realize that a part of the structural equation process has been left unexplained. That part is how to generate the matrix predicted by the model so that the relationship between the matrix of the observed data and the matrix for the predicted model can be compared. For path modeling, reconstructing the predicted matrix was straightforward but somewhat cumbersome. It required using any one of the methods for decomposition of effects to specify relationships between variables in terms of different paths and then substituting in the values of those paths to generate predicted matrices. The approach that most readily generalized across models (see Chapter 3) was the one that involved multiplying the matrix of path coefficients by itself and summing.

For latent variable SEM, the process is similar but more complicated due to having both measurement and structural models. The process also requires multiplying matrices but specifically requires using the set of matrices described in the measurement and structural models. As is true for even the simplest (overidentified) path model, the goal is to determine the relationships predicted among the observed measures based on the hypothesized model. Some of the parts of the predicted matrix already have been presented, although not as part of an approach for generating a predicted matrix.

Because being able to generate the predicted matrices is not critical to using SEM techniques, the algebra is not repeated here. It has been worked out and presented in many of the earlier articles on SEM (e.g., Wiley, 1973). Insofar as the components that make up the predicted matrix are simplest to understand when the structural and measurement models are separated, demonstration of how the process works first focuses on the structural model and then goes to the measurement model.

For the structural model, the goal is to generate a predicted covariance matrix for all the latent variables. Thus, we begin with a vector:

$$\begin{vmatrix} \eta \\ \xi \end{vmatrix}.$$

Postmultiplying the vector by its transpose, $[\eta \mid \xi]'$, and presenting the matrix as partitioned into submatrices gives

$$\Sigma_{(\eta\xi(\eta\xi)')} = \begin{vmatrix} \Sigma_{\eta\eta'} & \Sigma_{\eta\xi} \\ \Sigma_{\xi\eta'} & \Sigma_{\xi\xi'} \end{vmatrix}.$$

where

$$\Sigma_{\eta\eta'} = \begin{vmatrix} (I-B)^{-1} \Gamma \Phi \Gamma'(I-B)^{-1'} + (I-B)^{-1} \Psi (I-B)^{-1'} \end{vmatrix}$$
$$\Sigma_{\eta\xi'} = (I-B)^{-1} \Gamma \Phi$$
$$\Sigma_{\xi\eta'} = \Phi \Gamma'(I-B)^{-1'}$$
$$\Sigma_{\xi\xi'} = \Phi.$$

In other words, paralleling path analysis, in SEM the predicted matrices are a function of the relationships among the exogenous variables, the relationships of exogenous with endogenous variables and of endogenous variables with themselves, and the residuals of the endogenous variables.

To reproduce the matrix of observed measures, we need the components from the partitioned matrix just presented plus the weight and residual matrices from the measurement model. Together, they yield a covariance matrix in terms of X and Y:

$$\Sigma_{(YX(YX)')} = \begin{vmatrix} \Sigma_{YY'} & \Sigma_{YX'} \\ \Sigma_{XY'} & \Sigma_{XX'} \end{vmatrix}.$$

We can substitute from the basic measurement model for the Σ_{YY} and Σ_{XX} matrices but have to introduce new terms for the Σ_{XY} and Σ_{YX} terms. The full equation, in terms of the matrices, is

$$\Sigma_{(YX(YX)')} = \begin{vmatrix} \Lambda_Y \Sigma_{\eta\eta'} \Lambda_{Y'} + \Theta_\varepsilon & \Lambda_Y \Sigma_{\eta\xi'} \Lambda_{X'} \\ \Lambda_X \Sigma_{\xi\eta'} \Lambda_{Y'} & \Lambda_X \Sigma_{\xi\xi'} \Lambda_{X'} + \Theta_\delta \end{vmatrix}.$$

Note that the covariances among the latent variables are just pre- and postmultiplied by the weight matrices to determine the total common variance, and then the residuals (uniquenesses) are added on to get the total variance.[15]

The formula used by the maximum likelihood estimation techniques, the most commonly used approach, was described in the final example of Chapter 7 where sigma and S matrices were generated. It is

$$F = \ln|\Sigma| - \ln|S| + \text{tr}(S\Sigma^{-1}) - (p + q),$$

where F is the function to be minimized, Σ is the predicted variance/covariance matrix of the X's and Y's calculated as described in the preceding, S is the observed variance/covariance matrix of the X's and Y's, and p and q are the number of observed exogenous (X) and endogenous (Y) variables, respectively. The operations in the equa-

---

15. If any residuals between the Y's and X's are allowed to covary, as can be done in LISREL 8, AMOS, and EQS, then there also would need to be a $\Theta\varepsilon\delta$ matrix (and its transpose) added to the off-diagonal submatrices. In other words, the $\Sigma_{YX'}$ term would be $\Lambda_Y \Sigma_{\eta\xi'} \Lambda_{X'} + \Theta_{\varepsilon\delta}$, and the $\Sigma_{XY'}$ term would be $\Lambda_X \Sigma_{\xi\eta'} \Lambda_{Y'} + \Theta_{\delta\varepsilon}$.

tions are as follows: ln, taking the natural log; | |, taking the determinants (e.g., $|S|$) of the predicted and observed matrices; and tr, the trace or sum of the diagonal elements of a matrix. As explained earlier, as the predicted (sigma) and observed (S) matrices converge, the first two terms approximate each other and their difference approaches zero. Likewise, the difference between the latter two terms should approach zero. As sigma and S converge, sigma inverse will approximate S inverse and $S\Sigma^{-1}$ will approximate SS^{-1}, which is an identity matrix. Because an identity matrix has ones on the diagonal, the sum of the diagonal elements of an identity matrix is the size of the matrix. In this case, the matrix is of size $p + q$, so the difference between the latter two terms approaches zero as the predicted and observed matrices converge.

As latent variable SEM techniques became available, the initial perspective about them was that, because their significance tests and overall fit statistic provided such valuable information about adequacy of the model, a solution could potentially stand on its own without replication. As researchers gained more experience with the techniques and their shortcomings over time, a different perspective emerged, namely, that the best way in which to establish validity of a model is through cross-validation by sample splitting and through replication. Thus, if data sets are large enough, then samples should be split, with one half used to examine plausibility of a model and perhaps even subtly refine it using modifications to the model that do not change the critical components and are conceptually defensible, and with the second half held to fit to the model from the first half (e.g., Cudeck & Browne, 1983). If the sample is not large enough to split, then replication is highly desirable. Even more recently, Browne and Cudeck (1993) proposed using an expected cross-validation index for small samples to estimate effects of cross-validation.

As suggested in the preceding discussion about sample splitting and cross-validation, one is unlikely ever to obtain a model that fits perfectly, regardless of its veracity. The primary challenge for researchers in evaluating plausibility of the model being examined is to determine whether or not its goodness of fit is good or not. The most direct way in which fit is evaluated is through significance testing of the discrepancies between observed and predicted relationships among measures. The test may seem backward to readers who are used to significance as being good, for the test is of significance of discrepancies that remain after the model is fit. Ideally, a researcher would minimize residuals, namely, leave nothing unexplained; if successful, then there would be no significant residual variance remaining once the model is fitted. Thus, a good fitting model would result in a nonsignificant goodness of fit statistic. In the preceding equation, F for a good fitting model would be very small, for F assesses the size of the residuals rather than the size of the model parameters.

Overall fit is assessed by a chi-square goodness of fit test of the residuals. That test statistic has degrees of freedom as explained earlier in this chapter (the model used, e.g., from Figure 8.2 had 38 degrees of freedom), the total number of variances/covariances (66) minus free parameters to be estimated (28). Chi-square is distributed with a mean equal to its degrees of freedom, so dividing chi-square by its degrees of freedom should provide an index of some value as well (e.g., Marsh, Balla, & McDonald, 1988).

Although having a goodness of fit statistic that assesses the size of the residuals is valuable, unfortunately, that statistic is of limited value. The chi-square statistic is directly a function of sample size, for the function minimized is multiplied times the sample size to determine the chi-square statistic. The general formula is N times the function.[16] For perfectly fitting models ($F = 0$), sample size clearly is of no impact. For imperfectly fitting models, however, sample size can have unwanted effects (for a discussion, see, e.g., Bollen & Long, 1993; Jöreskog, 1969). Thus, if the same model is tested in two samples and produces exactly the same function but the size of one sample is twice that of the other, then the larger sample will have a much poorer fit, for its chi-square will be slightly more than twice as great as that in the smaller sample. Because of this relation of fit to sample size, a number of alternative fit indexes have been developed that are less sensitive to sample size. They will be explained in Chapter 10. Other work not covered in this book is attempting to tease apart lack of fit due to sample size from other sources (e.g., Kaplan, 1990).

In summary, this chapter has laid out the basics of latent variable structural equation models. In addition, issues of model specification and identification were addressed through an illustration, and procedures for setting up either equations or matrices to solve for a model also were illustrated. The logic underlying use of reference indicators

---

16. For LISREL, the exact formula to go from the function to the chi-square statistic is

$$\chi^2 = 2(N - 1)F,$$

was presented and illustrated. Finally, basic issues related to the "how" of model testing were covered. The remaining chapters will provide additional illustrations of SEM models, apply latent variable SEM to a couple of different types of problems and discuss issues that could emerge if readers encounter specific types of situations, and look broadly at SEM approaches.

APPENDIX 8.1

A Guide to Basics of LISREL Terminology

■ *The Measurement Model*

$$Y = \Lambda_Y \eta + \varepsilon,$$

where

Λ_Y is the factor pattern matrix relating observed endogenous variables (observed measures) to latent endogenous variables[a]

η is a vector of latent endogenous variables

ε is a vector of residuals for the observed variables

$$X = \Lambda_X \xi + \delta,$$

where

Λ_X is the factor pattern matrix relating observed exogenous variables (observed measures) to latent exogenous variables[a]

ξ is a vector of latent exogenous variables

δ is a vector of residuals for the observed variables

■ *The Structural Model*

$$\eta = \Gamma \xi + \beta \eta + \zeta,$$

where

Γ is a weight matrix of partial regression coefficients relating exogenous to endogenous variables[a] β is a weight matrix of partial regression coefficients interrelating endogenous variables[a]

ζ is a vector of residuals for latent endogenous variables

■ The Variance/Covariance Matrices

Φ (elements φ) of exogenous latent variables[a]

Ψ (elements ψ) of residuals for latent endogenous variables[a]

Θε (elements ε) of residuals for observed indicators of endogenous variables[a]

Θδ (elements δ) of residuals for observed indicators of exogenous variables[a]

a. One of the matrices that has to be specified in the LISREL program command language.

APPENDIX 8.2

LISREL Control Statements for Figure 8.2

Hypothetical four-factor latent variable model, from Chapter 8:

```
DA NI=11 NO=[number of observations here] MA=CM
LA
'ScWkPop' 'ScPlayPop' 'FrPop' 'MathAch' 'ReadAch'
  'AnalyAch' 'EdParents' 'JobParents' 'FamilyIncome'
  'PPVT' 'Raven'
CM FO FI=[location and name of covariance matrix here]
```

[FORTRAN format for matrix, e.g., 8F10.7]

```
MO NY=6 NX=5 NE=2 NK=2 LY=FU,FI LX=FU,FI BE=FU,FI
  GA=FU,FR PH=SY,FR
PS=SY,FR TE=DI,FR TD=DI,FR
LK
'FAMILY SES' 'STUDENT ABILITY'
LE
'STU PEER STATUS' 'STU ACHIEVEMENT'
FR LY 2 1 LY 3 1 LY 5 2 LY 6 2 LX 2 1 LX 3 1 LX 5 2
ST 1.0 LY 1 1 LY 4 2 LX 1 1 LX 4 2
path diagram (if LISREL8)
OU—THE OUTCOME CARD
```

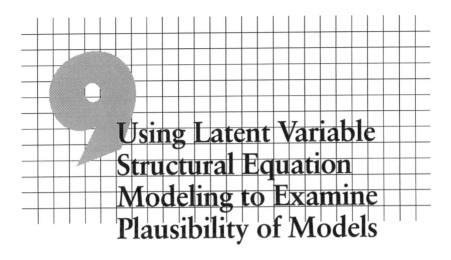

9

Using Latent Variable Structural Equation Modeling to Examine Plausibility of Models

This chapter provides "real data" illustrations of structural equation methods. The three illustrations focus on a single substantive issue and include (a) a unidirectional flow or recursive model constructed from data collected basically at a single point in time, (b) a nonrecursive model based on data from a single time point, and (c) a three-wave, longitudinal, unidirectional flow model that looks at a hypothesized bidirectional relationship across time via a panel design.

Three data sets are used to illustrate different types of latent variable structural models. All three share a single conceptual theme, for they focus on achievement of students in desegregated schools. They also illustrate how a series of studies can address and refine substantive questions about relationships between variables. Because no nonexperimental data study can ever establish causality, replication is more important than it is in experimental work.

First is a relatively simple reanalysis of data, reported in Maruyama and Miller (1979), from a study originally presented as a path analysis (Lewis & St. John, 1974). Included in an appendix to this chapter are files including the control statements using the LISREL, AMOS, and EQS computer programs.

Then, two additional data sets are presented and discussed. These latter two data sets come from different groups within a single large-scale study of school desegregation. The first of these two data sets is used to examine plausibility of a nonrecursive cross-sectional model, whereas the second examines three-wave longitudinal data presented as a panel model. The first data set is reported in Maruyama and McGarvey (1980), whereas the second is presented in Maruyama, Miller, and Holtz (1986) and Maruyama (1993). The latter data set also is used to further illustrate the advantages of having multiple indicators. Finally, these examples were selected not because the models are wonderful or fit extremely well but rather because they illustrate important issues of structural equation models around a single conceptual theme. They also are representative of the kinds of data sets that are available.

Example 1: A Longitudinal Path Model

This simple model illustrates how latent variable structural equation modeling (SEM) approaches can produce findings that differ substantively from ordinary path models. The data and analyses come from reanalyses (Maruyama & Miller, 1979) of data initially reported by Lewis and St. John (1974). The correlation matrix ($N = 154$) appears in Table 9.1. For a sample of African American schoolchildren, the model looks at the relationships between acceptance by white peers and school achievement. We decided to reexamine their study because its conclusions were very different from those we were uncovering using latent variable SEM techniques for parallel models. In our longitudinal analyses, we had not been able to find paths from peer acceptance to achievement that Lewis and St. John reported in their path analyses. Further adding to our interest, findings from their data showed the peer acceptance to achievement path to be inconsistent across alternative measures of achievement that seemingly should have been comparable, if not parallel, to one another. Therefore, we decided to see what would happen if we reconceptualized their hypothesized model using multiple indicators, which would make it more closely resemble our other data sets. Our model appears in Figure 9.1.

In terms of an illustration, Figure 9.1 is of interest for a number of reasons. First, it is not purely a latent variable model, for there are

TABLE 9.1　Correlation Matrix From Lewis and St. John (1974)
(N = 154)

	GPA1-5	OTISIQ	WHPOP	GPA6	RACH	SES	SCHWH
GPA1-5	1.000						
OTISIQ	.570	1.000					
WHPOP	.300	.270	1.000				
GPA6	.770	.580	.360	1.000			
RACH	.520	.560	.160	.530	1.000		
SES	.260	.170	−.020	.210	.220	1.000	
SCHWH	.250	.230	.180	.320	.170	.060	1.000

only single indicators for three of five constructs assessed. Therefore, it provides an opportunity to examine both how models are set up with single indicators and how they are constrained when measurement error cannot be removed. Second, as a reminder of the importance of theory in driving models, the model can be conceptualized in different ways. For example, one could argue that we should have been concerned about the relationship between popularity and grades and that, by combining achievement test performance with grades, this relationship was lost in our analyses. Unfortunately, the data do not allow resolution of the different views, for if we accept that view then we are stymied by the absence of multiple indicators. Our analyses of grade data would replicate the path analyses exactly. Additional data are required to sort out the different views. Third, the model is longitudinal in that data were collected from different points in time, making it superior to a purely cross-sectional design. Yet, it is a fairly weak longitudinal model, for data really were collected at a single point in time but included archival data culled from records. A stronger design is a panel design in which data are collected at several points in time. Fourth, insofar as the model is longitudinal, we definitely should have worked with a covariance matrix, a shortcoming of both the original article and our reanalyses. Because our goal was to compare our findings with the previous ones, we chose simply to reanalyze their data. The shortcoming may be less important in this study than in some others, for the only repeated measure is grade point average. If the variability in grade point average changed markedly, however, then our inferences may be inaccurate because we forced the two grade measures to unit variance and did not allow for "growth."

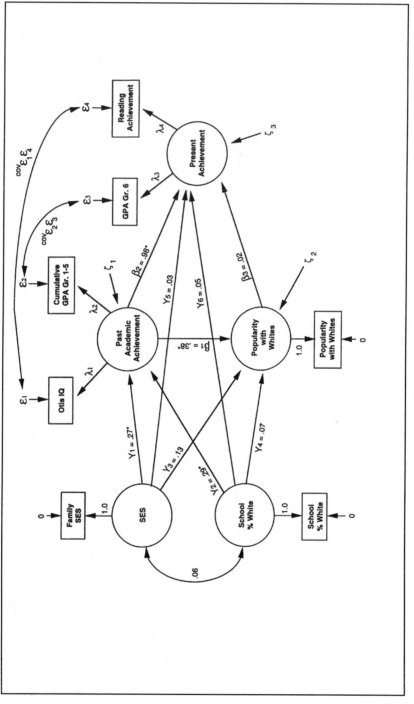

Figure 9.1. Path Diagram for Reanalysis, from Lewis and St. John (1974)
NOTE: Coefficients are from scaled (standardized) solution.

With respect to model specification, the model is constrained by the absence of multiple measures of family social class, percentage of school's children that are white, and popularity with whites. Of the three, school percentage white seems most likely to be highly reliable, although it might imperfectly assess the underlying variable, which may be prior exposure to white peers.[17] In contrast to school percentage white, popularity suffers from reliability problems, as does any measure of social class. Nonetheless, because only single indicators were available, the most defensible methodological decision is to fix the loading to 1.0 and the residual to 0.0, thus making the observed measures and underlying variables identical to one another. (The other alternative is to fix the residual to some nonzero value, which, for reasons described earlier in this book, can be problematic. At the very least, it is likely to be controversial.) For past and present achievement, the two constructs with multiple indicators, fixing a reference indicator allows for identification of both the remaining path and the residuals. Finally, the model includes nonrandom error between the two grade measures and the two standardized test measures. Those residual covariances could tap any subdomain-specific variance that exists separately from common variance on a general achievement domain.

The structural model included all paths that were specified by Lewis and St. John (1974). Their model was fully recursive, for it included all possible paths following a hierarchical order and initially produced a just-identified structural model. Thus, any problems in fitting can be attributed to the measurement model.

Consider again the issue of degrees of freedom. The total possible degrees of freedom for seven measures is $7(8) / 2 = 28$. Degrees of freedom are lost for the four residual variances and two covariances (6), the two lambdas (2), the nine structural paths (9), the three residuals on the endogenous variables (3), and the three elements of the phi matrix (3) given that those directly correspond to the variances and covariances of the single indicators of the exogenous variables. In total, $28 - 6 - 2 - 9 - 3 - 3 = 5$, which should be the degrees of freedom found for the model.

---

17. School percentage white is illustrative of variables that evoke varying interest from researchers from different disciplines. Policy researchers may feel comfortable with such a variable, whereas researchers more interested in uncovering individual student processes are likely to want to recast that variable in psychological terms, as I have done.

The overall fit of the model was acceptable, $\chi^2(5) = 4.88$, $N = 154$. Significant paths were found from socioeconomic status (SES) and school percentage white to past achievement, from past achievement to popularity with whites, and from past achievement to present achievement. Achievement was almost perfectly stable ($\beta_2 = .981$). Standardized values for the significant paths appear with asterisks (*) in Figure 9.1. In contrast to Lewis and St. John (1974) and consistent with our other data, there was no significant path from popularity to achievement. It may be that the increase in stability of achievement in our results compared with theirs prevented other potential predictors from displaying any influence. To the extent that multiple indicators allow for more precise assessment of variables such as achievement, the findings from such models may differ greatly from what would be found if only single indicators were available. This point is illustrated more fully in a later section of this chapter.

The significant paths all are direct effects of variables on subsequent variables. The viable indirect effects in the model are those that include multiple substantial paths. In this model, they all involve multiple significant paths. As can be seen from Figure 9.1, there are no nonsignificant paths strong enough to result in substantial indirect paths. The notable indirect paths are from SES and school percentage white to present achievement (via past achievement) and to popularity with whites (also via past achievement). The magnitude of these effects, as explained in the chapter on path analysis (Chapter 7), is determined by multiplying together the paths connecting the pairs of variables. Thus, the indirect effect of SES on popularity is $.27 \times .38 = .10$ and on present achievement is $.27 \times .98 = .26$. Similarly, the indirect effect of school percentage white on popularity is $.29 \times .38 = .11$ and on present achievement is $.29 \times .98 = .28$. These indirect effects demonstrate that, according to the model, both SES and school percentage white are substantially related to 6th grade achievement despite not displaying a significant direct path. Finally, note that in the model SES and school percentage white can substantially correlate with present achievement without having direct effects on it.

In summary, if the model is specified correctly (the big *if*), then the following conclusions are warranted. Black students higher on achievement during their elementary years were more popular with their white peers in 6th grade. Because this path is significant, the data are consistent with the view that achievement causes peer popularity. On the other hand, there was no evidence that black students who were more popular with their white peers did better in school. Thus, the data are not consistent with the view that popularity causes achievement. Such a view cannot, however, be totally dismissed in the data set, for the path from school percentage white to past achievement could be argued as consistent with a view that peers influence achievement. The processes would, however, have to occur earlier than 6th grade.

■ Example 2: A Nonrecursive Multiple-Indicator Model

This data set has been reported in Maruyama and McGarvey (1980). The correlation matrix appears as Table 9.2. This illustration basically repeats what is contained in more detail in that article, so interested readers might want to look there as well. At the same time, the practice of SEM has changed a lot since 1980, so referring back to that article should be done more for the logic and general methods than for specific details.

Most important for current purposes, this example illustrates the advantages of latent variable SEM approaches for analyzing different types of models. Even though this model (see Figure 9.2) is nonrecursive, it can be handled using the same approach as was used in recursive models such as the preceding example. Readers should pay particular attention to this model and its details, for this illustration will be revisited in Chapter 10 to discuss the different types of statistical tests that are used for latent variable structural equation models and ways in which hierarchical models can be compared. The theoretical variables in the model are socioeconomic status of the family (SES), performance of the child on standardized ability tests (ABL), acceptance by significant adults such as father/mother/teacher (ASA), verbal achievement (ACH), and acceptance by peers (APR). Each theoretical variable is defined by two or more observed measures. The indicators are as follows:

SES: SEI, Duncan socioeconomic index of occupations;
       EDHH, educational attainment of head of house;
       R/P, ratio of rooms in house to people in house;
ABL: PEA, Peabody Picture Vocabulary Test;
       RAV, Raven Progressive Matrices;
ASA: FEV, father's evaluation;
       MEV, mother's evaluation;

TABLE 9.2 Correlation Matrix ($N = 249$)

	SEATPOP	PLAYPOP	SWORKPOP	VACH	VGR	SEI	EDHH	RR/P	RAVEN	PEABODY	FEVAL	MEVAL	TEVAL
SEATPOP	1.000												
PLAYPOP	.593	1.000											
SWORKPOP	.548	.489	1.000										
VACH	.280	.233	.322	1.000									
VGR	.236	.177	.399	.495	1.000								
SEI	.052	.097	.102	.173	.159	1.000							
EDHH	.045	.097	.166	.297	.213	.558	1.000						
RR/P	.021	-.042	-.028	.188	-.040	.172	.098	1.000					
RAVEN	.079	.086	.144	.288	.275	.060	.153	-.001	1.000				
PEABODY	.132	.174	.167	.397	.188	.162	.210	.276	.320	1.000			
FEVAL	.066	.024	.082	.006	.115	.013	-.045	-.041	.095	-.059	1.000		
MEVAL	.152	.081	.174	.134	.271	-.066	-.052	.001	.165	-.067	.424	1.000	
TEVAL	.251	.080	.327	.213	.266	-.018	-.006	.041	.142	.081	.181	.311	1.000

SOURCE: Maruyama and Garvey (1980).

TEV, teacher's evaluation;
ACH: VACH, verbal achievement score;
           VGR, verbal grades;
APR: PPOP, playground popularity;
           SPOP, classroom seating popularity;
           WPOP, schoolwork popularity.

Conceptually, this model examines the same two views of the relationship between peer acceptance and achievement that were introduced in the first illustration. Those views are (a) that being accepted by one's peers enhances one's school achievement (the path from APR to ACH) and (b) that doing well in school achievement enhances one's acceptance by peers (the path from ACH to APR). Of course, both views or neither view may be correct. Remember that, in contrast to the findings originally reported by Lewis and St. John (1974), the prior example found that although achievement influenced peer acceptance, the opposite did not occur. Thus, this model attempts to bring further information to the question addressed by the first example, but with cross-sectional data. Note that one important strength of the model is that it can examine both causal possibilities in a single model, whereas one major weakness is that it cannot control for stability over time of the achievement and peer acceptance variables, which means that it could draw incorrect inferences if one or both of the variables were highly stable.

The sample is 249 white children who attended school in a district about to undergo school desegregation. They were a subsample of a larger group that was tracked as part of the study of desegregation, selected because they had complete data on the measures included in this illustration and because all were measured in pre-desegregation classes. In contrast to the preceding and following samples, both of which are minority children, this particular sample does not focus on acceptance by an out-group. Rather, it allows examination of processes in the mainstream culture of the schools, for the district was predominantly white during this study. In other words, if there is no relationship between peer acceptance and achievement for the main group of children, then there would be little (or at least less) reason to expect that such a relationship would be found across groups.

Aside from the presence of a much better measurement model due to the presence of multiple indicators, the "new" methodological issue illustrated by this example is how to handle nonrecursive models

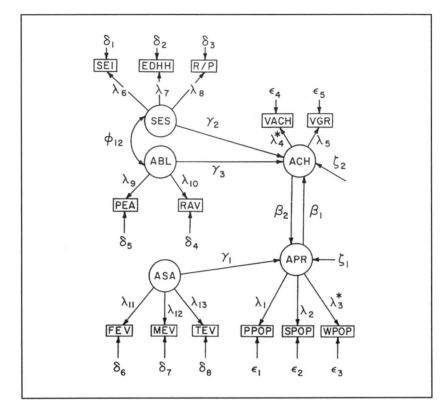

Figure 9.2. Latent Variable Structural Equation Model
SOURCE: Maruyama and McGarvey (1980). Copyright 1980 by the American Psychological Association; reprinted by permission.
NOTE: SES = social class; ABL = academic ability; ASA = acceptance by adults; APR = acceptance by peers; ACH = verbal achievement. Coefficents δ_4 and δ_5 were reversed inadvertently.

and their identification. Unlike recursive models, not all nonrecursive models will be identified. As a review, readers may want to return to the discussion on identification in Chapter 6. Because in this illustration each of the two variables that are reciprocally related has an instrument, the model is identified. As can be seen in Figure 9.2, ASA is an instrument for identifying the paths to the ACH variable, whereas both SES and ABL are instruments for identifying paths to APR. Remember that (a) instruments in the model need to directly cause one of the two variables that are reciprocally related but not the other and that (b) it makes little sense to have instruments that are highly intercorrelated with one another, for if they were, then it would be much more difficult to argue that they have independent effects. In this example, the model specifies that the exogenous variables that act as instruments for different endogenous variables are not intercorrelated.

In contrast to the preceding illustration, each of the conceptual variables has multiple measures available. The primary advantage of multiple indicators is that they allow the conceptual variables to be defined in terms of the commonalities among the measures, thereby *in principle* removing error and unique variance from the constructs. Note that each measure has a nonzero residual attached to it. In practice, the conceptual variables will be only as good as their indicators; if the set of available indicators is poor or the indicators share a single method, then the conceptual variable will be less than ideal. If indicators are poor, then the "correct" conceptual variable may not be assessed; if a single method is used, then the theoretical variable will not have method variance extracted.

The findings from the illustration are somewhat mixed. First, all of the indicators were significantly related to the constructs that they were supposed to represent, and all had significant residuals. In other words, all had significant components of common variance, but also of unique variance. Second, the overall fit of the model was less than ideal, $\chi^2(59) = 138.55$, but the larger sample size compared with that in the first illustration would, of course, produce a larger chi-square statistic even with the same minimum function value. For now, the issue of fit is deferred; it will be reintroduced in the next chapter, when issues of alternative models are introduced. Third, most of the structural paths were significant. SES of the family and ability (ABL) were related (.378), and the paths from ability (ABL) to achievement (ACH) (standardized, .618) and from acceptance by adults (ASA) to acceptance by peers (APR) (standardized, .218) were significant. Finally, the paths of greatest interest, the reciprocal paths between peer acceptance (APR) and achievement (ACH), were as follows: achievement to peer acceptance, significant (standardized, .306); peer acceptance to achievement, marginally ($p < .10$) significant (standardized, .204). In other words, the data are consistent with the view that achievement affects peer acceptance but are somewhat equivocal on whether or not peer acceptance can affect school achievement, leaving open the possibility that it could be found for cross-group contacts but not providing strong grounds for expecting to find such a relationship.

In summary, this example illustrates how nonrecursive models fall under and can be handled by the same general approach as other types of models. At the same time, however, nonrecursive models need to address issues of model identification. Furthermore, the example shows how multiple-indicator models can provide advantages over single-indicator ones. Finally, and hopefully, it reinforces the importance of conceptual models driving the methods; such models require both careful operationalization of constructs and specification of relationships between them. Substantively, the data are generally consistent with those of the first study, but the marginal path from acceptance by peers (APR) to achievement (ACH) leaves some ambiguity about the nature of the relationship between those variables.

Example 3: A Longitudinal Multiple-Indicator Panel Model

As was true for the previous illustration, the data that were used to examine plausibility of the model illustrated in Figure 9.3 were collected as part of a broader study of school desegregation. The sample is the group of Mexican American students in the schools. During the first time period, the students attended segregated schools; during the second and third time periods, their schools had been desegregated. The Mexican American sample was selected for this illustration because, consistent with the conceptual tack that has been taken, it provides a test of out-group acceptance. Although African American students in principle could have done so as well, in fact there were too few students with complete data to estimate a solution for them. Furthermore, there were not enough minority children in any classroom to generate appreciable numbers of minority (out-group) choices for white children, so the analyses are limited to Mexican American children. Finally, in the course of the preliminary analyses of the data set used for these analyses (see Maruyama, 1993), (a) the social class variable turned out to be inconsequential in the Mexican American sample and was dropped and (b) the teacher evaluation variable was found to be highly collinear with ability and was dropped. Therefore, the illustration is simplified compared to white student data presented by Maruyama et al. (1986) and Figure 9.3.

The first five variables in Figure 9.3, which is taken from Maruyama et al. (1986), are the same variables as those in Figure 9.2 except for the teacher dimension. Identical variables are family social class (SES), students' academic ability (AB), acceptance by peers (PAC66), and school achievement (ACH66). Significant adult ratings

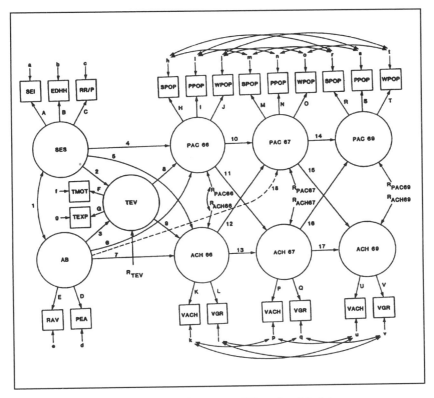

Figure 9.3. Latent Variable Panel Structural Equation Model
SOURCE: Maruyama, Miller, and Holtz (1986). Copyright 1986 by the American Psychological Association; reprinted by permission.
NOTE: The panel model is for examining the relation between peer popularity and achievement. SES = socioeconomic status, measured by SEI (Duncan Socioeconomic Index of Occupations); EDHH = educational attainment of head of household; RR/P = ratio of rooms in home to people living in home; AB = academic ability, measured by RAV (Raven's Progressive Matrices) and PEA (Peabody Picture Vocabulary Test); TEV = teachers' evaluations of students, measured by TMOT (teachers' ratings of students' motivation) and TEXP (teachers' expectations of students' eventual educational attainment); PAC = acceptance by peers, measured by SPOP (seating popularity), PPOP (playground popularity), and WPOP (schoolwork popularity); ACH = school achievement, measured by VACH (verbal standardized test performance) and VGR (verbal grades).

from Figure 9.2 were replaced by evaluations the student received from his or her teacher (TEV). Measurement of the five variables preceded school desegregation during the 1966 school year. Therefore, the peer nominations had to come from other Mexican American students. The longitudinal or panel aspects of the model were available because the achievement and peer acceptance variables were measured again after desegregation, both immediately (in 1967) and

2 years later (in 1969). At those two time points, peer acceptance was acceptance by white peers, and achievement data were from desegregated classes and schools.

As can be seen in Figure 9.3, the model analyzed by Maruyama et al. (1986) examined plausibility of a perspective that views both peer acceptance and student achievement as being influenced by family social class, by students' ability, and by teachers. Teachers are viewed as being able to mediate effects of ability and social class. Because the logic used was that causal effects were lagged; there is no path between acceptance by peers (PAC66) and school achievement (ACH66). Even if we had wanted to construct a reciprocal causation model, instruments were not available to identify a nonrecursive model. That left the three choices of (a) specifying the path one way or the other, (b) omitting paths and assuming that the full relationship between the two variables is due to common causes, or (c) allowing their residuals to covary. This last alternative was chosen as preferable to either trying to argue for predominance of either peer acceptance or achievement or not allowing them to be related over and above their common causes. As discussed earlier, the residual covariance is similar to a covariance between two exogenous variables except that it is between only the unexplained portion of the variance. Also of importance is that in this model the residual covariance explains exactly the same covariance as would either causal path from one to the other.

Once again, the "critical" relationships in the model were the ones between achievement and peer acceptance. They are numbered 11, 12, 15, and 16. As explained in the preceding discussion, there are no causal paths within time periods. Furthermore, at the two later time periods, we hypothesized that the residual covariance between peer acceptance and achievement that was included at Time 1 was not needed because prior measures were available, allowing for a panel model in which stability and cross-lagged effects could be assessed.

Note that as was true for the preceding illustration, each variable has multiple measures; this allows for extraction of measurement error for all measures. In addition, because the same measures were collected repeatedly across time, their residuals were allowed to covary (drawing from the earlier discussion of panel analysis) to pick up measure-specific variance. In contrast to panel analysis, common method variance can be teased apart from trait stability.

Unfortunately, the data from this example also illustrate the major shortcoming of longitudinal sampling, for, despite having a reasonable sample size at the beginning of the study, sample attrition was very great across the 4 years of the study due to both student mobility and missing data scattered throughout the measures. Because we could not assume that attrition was random, we initially attempted to extract a large subsample with complete data, a task that was not possible. As a result, we settled for a data matrix based on the maximum number of observations between each pair of variables, often called a pairwise matrix. This matrix is really appropriate only when data loss is random. Analyses were conducted to compare individuals lost through attrition to those kept in the sample on a number of background variables. These analyses, which compared means and variances, did not yield a clear interpretation. The good news with respect to missing data is that methods for dealing with them have improved (e.g., Graham & Donaldson, 1993; Graham, Hofer, & Piccinin, 1994; Little & Rubin, 1987, 1990; Muthen, Kaplan, & Hollis, 1987). If the analyses of the model of Figure 9.3 were to be done today, then the data source would likely differ from the matrix appearing in Table 9.3, and the sample size would be larger than the nominal 100 that is used for the analyses.

The data for this illustration appear in Table 9.3. The matrix is a scaled covariance matrix in which each measure is standardized the first time it appears, and then changes in variability are calculated (as a ratio) when a measure appears again using the first time that measure appeared as a standard (see, e.g., Meredith, 1964). In other words, the relative size of the variances is preserved for each measure, but the actual variances are changed to a metric in which all variables have similar scales.[18] Furthermore, the metric is similar to a correlation metric, which intuitively is simpler for people. This approach is fine so long as the specific variances are not critical for cross-group comparisons.

Substantively, achievement at Time 1 (Ach66) was related to ability (AB); achievement (ACH) displayed virtually perfect stability over time (standardized coefficients of .98 and 1.00), and peer acceptance displayed no consistency from the segregated to the desegregated classroom (Pac66 → Pac67) and only modest stability within desegregated classrooms over time (Pac67 → Pac69). There were no significant paths between peer acceptance and achievement.

---

18. It turns out that for some models in which variances differ dramatically, rescaling to reduce differences in variances may be needed to obtain meaningful SEM solutions.

TABLE 9.3 Mexican American Student Data Matrix (N = 100)

	Peabody	Raven	WPop 66	SPop 66	PPop 66	VAch 66	VGr 66	WPop 67	SPop 67	PPop 67	VAch 67	VGr 67	Wpop 69	SPop 69	PPop 69	VAch 69	VGr 69	TEval 66	TExpec 66
Peabody	1.000																		
Raven7	.276	1.000																	
WPop66	.165	.100	1.000																
SPop66	.034	.043	.516	1.000															
PPop66	.155	.046	.594	.355	1.000														
VAch66	.314	.238	.082	.098	.165	1.000													
VGr66	.151	.061	.147	.044	.356	.295	1.000												
WPop67	.007	.050	.123	.041	.097	.100	.073	1.000											
SPop67	.024	.025	.157	.055	.076	.106	.001	.675	1.000										
PPop67	.040	.008	.164	.089	.122	.116	.108	.729	.715	1.000									
VAch67	.279	.133	.122	-.008	.174	.331	.362	-.050	.085	.026	.812								
VGr67	.314	.245	.173	.008	.208	.416	.459	.119	.127	.155	.555	.823							
WPop69	-.035	-.010	.002	.106	.160	-.001	.182	.193	.116	.076	-.050	-.040	1.051						
SPop69	-.021	.086	.018	.138	.120	.082	.049	.197	.121	.196	.029	.042	.685	1.100					
PPop69	-.115	-.022	-.051	.043	.044	.043	.015	.196	.110	.224	-.098	-.040	.624	.604	.962				
VAch69	.216	.197	.227	.175	.367	.435	.542	.187	.213	.228	.523	.615	-.008	.035	-.017	1.241			
VGr69	.160	.063	.140	.025	.227	.359	.318	.192	.102	.072	.432	.419	.101	.002	-.058	.506	1.440		
TEval66	.243	.121	.172	.134	.294	.296	.409	.113	.105	.096	.424	.502	.005	-.027	.044	.681	.288	1.000	
TExpec66	.221	.113	.308	.359	.283	.349	.276	.090	.029	.139	.206	.175	.044	.052	.106	.326	.110	.391	1.000

Results of the analyses, presented as the final part of the illustration begun as path analysis and continued as panel analysis and confirmatory factor analysis, appear in Illustration 4.

Overall, then, the longitudinal model seems to suggest that cross-sectional models may, by not taking into account that achievement is highly stable, wrongly infer that other variables, such as acceptance by peers, are affecting it. It also provides less clear information about whether or not achievement shapes peer acceptance. Taken together, the three studies leave some ambiguity but certainly call into question the assertion of Lewis and St. John (1974) that peer acceptance is an important determinant of later achievement.

Before leaving this illustration, it is used to compare models having single indicators to those having multiple indicators. Although these analyses began attempting to fit the full model that appears in Figure 9.3 (see Maruyama et al., 1986), as described earlier, the social class variable and the teacher evaluation variable were dropped (see Maruyama, 1993). The focus on what happens to variables with single versus multiple indicators is accomplished by varying the indicators *on the achievement variables.*

As argued in Maruyama (1993), there are major advantages that accrue from having multiple measures. Ways of trying to simulate having multiple measures seem to provide no effective substitute. Maruyama (1993) provided a comparison that is reported here. For a single data set, the following alternative ways of modeling achievement were examined: (a) a single-indicator model assuming perfect reliability, (b) that same single indicator with its reliability fixed to less than 1.0 (.9) and having a nonzero residual, (c) a single indicator with its reliability fixed to be the same value as was found by the solution for multiple indicators, and (d) the multiple (two-) indicator solution corresponding to Figure 9.3. These changes primarily affected the relationships of achievement with peer acceptance; those relationships varied substantially across the different options.

The paths from the various solutions appear as Table 9.4, which is taken from Maruyama (1993). As can be seen, the different ways of modeling achievement have very different consequences for the inferences drawn from the model. The first column is the data from the multiple-indicator approach, which should be the "best," for it makes use of multiple measures to separate reliable variance from error and unique variance, and it also allows residual covariances across time to capture measure-specific variance separately. In that

TABLE 9.4 Coefficients Interrelating Peer Acceptance and Achievement, Examining Various Assumptions About the Reliability of Indicators of Achievement

Coefficient	Model 1: Multiple Indicators	Model 2: Single Indicator With Perfect Reliability	Model 3: Single Indicator With Reliability of .90	Model 4: Single Indicator With Reliability Set From Model 1
Achievement stability paths				
13 (Ach66-Ach67)	1.00**	.35**	.48**	.75**
17 (Ach67-Ach69)	.98**	.51**	.65**	.95**
Peer acceptance to achievement				
11 (Pac66-Ach67)	−.04	.12	.14	.10
15 (Pac67-Ach69)	.15	.21**	.22**	.24*
Other paths				
6 (AB-Pac66)	.27	.27	.27	.27
7 (AB-Ach66)	.59**	.52**	.59**	.75**
18 (AB-Pac67)	−.08	−.06	−.09	−.13
10 (Pac66-Pac67)	.17	.20	.19	.19
12 (Ach66-Pac67)	.16	.15	.17	.19
14 (Pac67-Pac69)	.22*	.22*	.22*	.22*
16 (Ach67-Pac69)	−.05	−.06	−.07	−.07
Chi-square goodness of fit	87.6	50.1	46.1	42.8
Degrees of freedom	102	67	67	67

SOURCE: Maruyama (1993).
NOTE: Numbers preceding coefficients refer to Figure 9.3. Note that the family social class (SES) and teacher evaluation (TEV) variables are omitted from the model.
*$p < .10$; **$p < .05$.

model, achievement is almost perfectly stable across both time periods (the first two rows of Table 9.4) and is *not* shaped by acceptance by peers (the third and fourth rows of Table 9.4). In each of the other three models, however, the stability of achievement is much lower, and there are at least strong hints that acceptance by peers can influence achievement. Note that even if the reliability of the achievement measure is fixed to the value estimated from the multiple-indicator solution, the data still are quite different and the inferences would likely differ as well.

In summary, this last model illustrates not only what latent variable SEM panel models look like but also the differences that can be found when single-indicator models are compared to multiple-indicator models. It should reinforce the point that latent variable SEM approaches are not particularly powerful when only single indicators are available, for they reduce to path analysis and its variants. Once multiple indicators are added, the capacity to extract nonrandom error, autocorrelation, and, of course, reliability estimates markedly increases the strength and flexibility of SEM approaches.

It is hoped that the examples have helped readers to develop a better understanding of SEM models and how they work. That understanding will be extended in the next chapter, which will look in detail at ways of developing alternative models to compare and a range of techniques for relative model testing.

EXERCISE 9.1

Setting Up Matrices for a Latent Variable Structural Equation Model

Set up the equations and matrices for the measurement and structural models of Figure 9.1. Correct matrices and equations appear in Appendix 9.1. Readers are encouraged to compare the two approaches so that they are able to go back and forth between equations and matrices, for the other examples will be provided only in matrix form. Those matrices and equations can be used to set up the LISREL, AMOS, and EQS programs that appear in Appendix 9.2.

EXERCISE 9.2

Setting Up Figure 9.2 Matrices

Set up the matrices for Figure 9.2. Then calculate the number of degrees of freedom in the model. A summary of degrees of freedom and a LISREL command file appear in Appendix 9.3. In contrast to the first illustration with its small number of measures, the multiple indicators produce a large number of degrees of freedom.

A P P E N D I X   9 . 1

Matrices and Equations for Reanalysis of Data From Lewis and St. John (1974)

Matrices

Lambda X is an identity matrix. **Phi** is a correlation matrix with the correlation between socioeconomic status (SES) and school percentage white (.06) as its off-diagonal element. **Theta** X is null. For the lambda Y matrix, asterisks (*) indicate designated reference indicators that are fixed to 1.0.

$$Y = \Lambda_Y \eta + \varepsilon$$

$$
\begin{vmatrix} \text{OtisIQ} \\ \text{GPA1-5} \\ \text{PopwWhit} \\ \text{GPA6} \\ \text{RdAch} \end{vmatrix}
=
\begin{vmatrix} \lambda_1^* & 0 & 0 \\ \lambda_2 & 0 & 0 \\ 0 & 1.0 & 0 \\ 0 & 0 & \lambda_3^* \\ 0 & 0 & \lambda_4 \end{vmatrix}
\begin{vmatrix} \text{PastAAch} \\ \text{PopwWhit} \\ \text{PresAAch} \end{vmatrix}
+
\begin{vmatrix} \varepsilon_1 \\ \varepsilon_2 \\ 0 \\ \varepsilon_3 \\ \varepsilon_4 \end{vmatrix}
$$

$$\eta = \beta\, a + \Gamma\, \xi + \zeta$$

$$
\begin{vmatrix} \text{PastAAch} \\ \text{PopwWhit} \\ \text{PresAAch} \end{vmatrix}
=
\begin{vmatrix} 0 & 0 & 0 \\ \beta_1 & 0 & 0 \\ \beta_2 & \beta_3 & 0 \end{vmatrix}
\begin{vmatrix} \text{PastAAch} \\ \text{PopwWhit} \\ \text{PresAAch} \end{vmatrix}
+
\begin{vmatrix} \gamma_1 & \gamma_2 \\ \gamma_3 & \gamma_4 \\ \gamma_5 & \gamma_6 \end{vmatrix}
\begin{vmatrix} \text{SES} \\ \text{S\%WH} \end{vmatrix}
+
\begin{vmatrix} \zeta_1 \\ \zeta_2 \\ \zeta_3 \end{vmatrix}
$$

$$
\Theta\varepsilon =
\begin{vmatrix}
\varepsilon^2_1 & & & & \\
0 & \varepsilon^2_2 & & & \\
0 & 0 & 0 & & \\
0 & \varepsilon_{32} & 0 & \varepsilon^2_3 & \\
\varepsilon_{41} & 0 & 0 & 0 & \varepsilon^2_4
\end{vmatrix}
\quad \text{(symmetric)}
$$

$$\Psi\text{diag} = \begin{vmatrix} \zeta^2_1 & \zeta^2_2 & \zeta^2_3 \end{vmatrix}$$

Equations

Otis IQ $= \lambda_1^* \times$ PastAAch $+ \varepsilon_1$

GPA1-5 $= \lambda_2 \times$ PastAAch $+ \varepsilon_2$

PopwWh $= 1.0 \times$ PopwWhit $+ 0$

GPA6 $= \lambda_3^* \times$ PresAAch $+ \varepsilon_3$

RdAch $= \lambda_4 \times$ PresAAch $+ \varepsilon_4$

PastAAch $= \gamma_1 \times$ SES $+ \gamma_2 \times$ S%WH $+ \zeta_1$

PopwWhit $= \beta_1 \times$ PastAAch $+ \gamma_3 \times$ SES $+ \gamma_4 \times$ S%WH $+ \zeta_2$

PresAAch $= \beta_2 \times$ PastAAch $+ \beta_3 \times$ PopwWhit $+ \gamma_5 \times$ SES $+ \gamma_6 \times$ S%WH $+ \zeta_3$

A P P E N D I X   9 . 2

Setups for Figure 9.1

(a) LISREL Setup

```
REANALYSES OF LEWIS & ST. JOHN DATA, SEM BOOK, LISREL
  SETUP
DA NI=7 NG=1 NO=154 MA=KM
LA
'GPA1-5' 'OTISIQ' 'WHPOP' 'GPA6' 'RACH' 'SES' 'SCHWH'
KM FO fi=a:mnmdat
(16F5.3)
MO NY=5 NX=2 NE=3 NK=2 LY=FU,FI FI BE=FU,FI GA=FU,FR
  PS=DI,FR TE=SY,FI
LK
'SES' 'SCHWH'
LE
'PASTACH' 'WHPOP' 'CURACH'
FR LY 2 1 LY 5 3 BE 2 1 BE 3 1 BE 3 2 TE 1 1 TE 2 2
  TE 4 4 TE 5 5 C
TE 4 1 TE 5 2
ST 1.0 LY 1 1 LY 3 2 LY 4 3
OU ad=off PT SE TV rs MR MI FD SS TM=45
```

[File mnmdat, located on A drive, is a long row vector:]

```
1. .57 1. .3 .27 1. .77 .58 .36 1. .52 .56 .16 .53 1.
  .26
.17 -.02 .21 .22 1. .25 .23 .18 .32 .17 .06 1.
```

(b) AMOS Setup

1. Control File

Example from Maruyama and Miller (1979).
First model of relation between popularity and achievement.
Correlations, bogus standard deviations, from Lewis and St. John
(1974).

```
$Mods=4
$Structure
```

```
GPAGR1-5 <- PastAch (1)
GPAGR1-5 <- eps1 (1)
OtisIQ <- PastAch
OtisIQ <- eps2 (1)
WhPop <- PopWH (1)
GPAGr6 <- PresAch (1)
GPAGr6 <- eps4 (1)
RAch <- PresAch
RAch <- eps5 (1)
FamSES <- SES (1)
Sch%Wh <- SchPCWh (1)
SES <-> SchPCWh
PastAch <- SES
PastAch <- SchPCWh
PastAch <- zeta1 (1)
PopWH <- SES
PopWH <- SchPCWh
PopWH <- PastAch
PopWH <- zeta2 (1)
PresAch <- SES
PresAch <- SchPCWh
PresAch <- PastAch
PresAch <- PopWH
PresAch <- zeta3 (1)
eps1 <-> eps4
eps2 <-> eps5
$Include = a:\mnmmatrx.amd
$technical
```

2. Data

```
! REANALYSES OF LEWIS & ST. JOHN DATA.
! Reanalysis of data from Lewis & St. John.
! Correlations.
$Inputvariables
 GPAGR1-5 ! Grade point average grades 1-5
 OtisIQ ! Otis group administered IQ
 WhPop ! Popularity with white peers
 GPAGr6 ! Grade 6 grade point average
```

```
 RAch ! Reading achievement test score
 FamSES ! SES of family of student
 Sch%Wh ! Percent of school that is white
$Samplesize=154
$Correlations
1.000
 .570 1.000
 .300   .270 1.000
 .770   .580   .360 1.000
 .520   .560   .160   .530 1.000
 .260   .170 -.020   .210   .2201.000
 .250   .230   .180   .320   .170 .060 1.000
$Standard deviations
1.0 1.0 1.0 1.0 1.0 1.0 1.0
```

[These last two lines are not needed; they point out that a correlation matrix is being analyzed.]

(c) EQS Setup

```
/TITLE
```

[Example from Maruyama and Miller (1979); reanalysis of Lewis and St. John (1974).]

```
/SPECIFICATIONS
DATA='A:\MNMDAT.EQS'; VARIABLES=7; CASES=158;
METHODS=ML;
MATRIX=CORRELATION;
/LABELS
V1=GPA1-5;  V2=OTISIQ;  V3=WHPOP;  V4=GPA6;  V5=RACH;
  V6=SES;  V7=SCHWH;  F1=PASTACH;  F2=POPWWH;
  F3=PRESACH;  F4=FAMSES;  F5=SCHPCWH;
/EQUATIONS
V1 = 1.0F1 + E1;
V2 = *F1 + E2;
V3 = 1.0F2 + E3;
V4 = 1.0F3 + E4;
```

```
V5 = *F3 + E5;
V6 = 1.0F4 + E6;
V7 = 1.0F5 + E7;
F1 = *F4 + *F5 + D3;
F2 = *F4 + *F5 + *F1 + D4;
F3 = *F4 + *F5 + *F1 + *F2 + D5;
/VARIANCES
F1 = *;
F2 = 1.0;
F3 = *;
F4 = 1.0;
F5 = 1.0;
E1 = *;
E2 = *;
E3 = 0;
E4 = *;
E5 = *;
E6 = 0;
E7 = 0;
/COVARIANCES
F4, F5 = *;
E1, E4 = *;
E2, E5 = *;
```

NOTE: Because I did not have a copy of the EQS program, I could not run this program to ensure that it would work. It conforms to earlier work I did when I had access to EQS.

A P P E N D I X   9 . 3

Analysis of Degrees of Freedom and LISREL Setup for Figure 9.2

1. Analysis of degrees of freedom
Possible degrees of freedom: $N(N + 1) / 2 = 13*14 / 2 = 91$
Parameters to estimate: Total $= 32$
Relations between constructs and indicators: $13 - 2^a = 11$
Residuals on indicators: 13
Structural paths: 5 causal $+$ 1 covariance $= 6$
Residuals on latent variables: 2
Model degrees of freedom: $91 - 32 = 59$

[Note: [a]There are two reference indicators. The variances for the exogenous variables are fixed in the phi matrix to 1.0 each, giving them unit variance.]

2. LISREL commands

[Note: Because of problems estimating a solution in LISREL 8 with a "normal" X and Y setup, the model was set up as if all variables were endogenous. The "all Y" approach to LISREL will be described in Chapter 11. It produces the same solution as an X and Y setup.]

```
CONTROL CARDS, MARUYAMA & MCGARVEY LISREL EXAMPLE,
   ALL Y
DA NG=1 NI=13 NO=249 MA=KM
KM FO SY FI=a:MNMCDAT
(13F6.4)
LA
'SEATPOP' 'PLAYPOP' 'SWORKPOP' 'VACH' 'VGR' 'SEI'
   'EDHH'
'RR/P' 'RAVEN' 'PEABODY' 'FEVAL' 'MEVAL' 'TEVAL'
SE
6 7 8 9 10 11 12 13 1 2 3 4 5/
MO NY=13 NX=0 NE=5 NK=0 LY=FU,FI BE=FU,FI PS=SY,FI
   TE=SY,FI
LE
'SES' 'ABILITY' 'ACCSIGO' 'ACCPEER' 'SCHACH'
```

```
FR LY 9 4 LY 10 4 LY 13 5 LY 2 1 LY 3 1 LY 4 2 LY 6
   3 LY 7 3 C
BE 5 4 BE 4 5 BE 5 1 BE 5 2 BE 4 3 PS 1 1 PS 2 1 PS
   2 2 C
PS 3 3 PS 4 4 PS 5 5 TE 1 1 TE 2 2 TE 3 3 TE 4 4 TE
   5 5 TE 6 6 C
TE 7 7 TE 8 8 TE 9 9 TE 10 10 TE 11 11 TE 12 12 TE 13
   13
ST 1.0 LY 1 1 LY 5 2 LY 8 3 LY 11 4 LY 12 5
OU PT LY=SV2 BE=SV2 PS=SV2 TE=SV2 SE TV MI SS
```

Illustration 4:   Latent Variable Structural Equation Modeling

This is the final illustration drawn from a single data set. At this point, the best possible approach to the model given the existing data is presented. That approach is latent variable structural equation modeling, which adds multiple indicators of each theoretical variable. For this illustration, the social class variable was dropped because it was not related to any of the other conceptual variables, and the teacher evaluation variable was dropped because it was too highly related to the ability and achievement variables, resulting in unwanted collinearity. Dropping variables that should be conceptually distinct or impor-tant is not an easy decision for a substantive article; for the purpose of the illustration, however, the decision is much easier, for the variables are not needed to illustrate the points being made. To again remind readers, the focus is on the paths between peer acceptance and achievement.

The model is described in Figure 9.3, and the matrix (called a:mafullmt.rx in the illustration) appears in Table 9.3.

The LISREL commands for the model are as follows:

Mexican American data, runs for choices of whites, multiple indicators

```
DA NI=33 NO=100 MA=CM
KM FU FO FI=a:mafullmt.rx
(8F10.7)
SD FO
(11F7.5)
1.0 1.0 1.0 1.0 1.0 1.0 1.025 1.049 .981 1.0 1.0
1.0 1.0 1.0 1.0 1.0 1.0 .901 .907 1.114 1.200 .911
.936 .766 .875 .926 1.0 1.0 1.0 1.0 .705 1.0 1.0
SE
```

```
16 17 13 14 15 27 28 4 5 6 18 19 7 8 9 20 21 /
MO NY=17 NE=7 LY=FU,FI BE=FU,FI PS=SY,FI TE=SY,FI
FR LY 2 1 LY 4 2 LY 3 2 LY 7 3 LY 9 4 LY 8 4 C
BE 3 1 BE 2 1 BE 4 1 BE 4 2 BE 4 3 BE 5 2 BE 5 3 BE
   6 5 BE 6 4 C
BE 7 5 BE 7 4 PS 3 2 PS 1 1 PS 2 2 PS 3 3 C
PS 4 4 PS 5 5 PS 6 6 PS 7 7 TE 1 1 TE 2 2 TE 3 3 TE
   4 4 TE 5 5 TE 6 6 C
TE 7 7 TE 8 8 TE 9 9 TE 10 10 TE 11 11 TE 12 12 TE 13
   13 TE 14 14 TE 15 15 C
TE 16 16 TE 17 17 TE 11 6 TE 12 7 TE 13 8 TE 14 9 TE
   16 6 C
TE 17 7 TE 15 10 TE 16 11 TE 17 12
EQ LY 7 3 LY 12 5 LY 17 7
EQ LY 9 4 LY 14 6
EQ LY 8 4 LY 13 6
ST 1.0 LY 1 1 LY 5 2 LY 6 3 LY 10 4 LY 11 5 LY 15 6
   LY 16 7 C
LY 9 4 LY 8 4
path diagram
OU PT AD=OFF SS
```

The results are the same as those described as Model 1 in Table 9.4.
The complete results are as follows:

LISREL ESTIMATES (MAXIMUM LIKELIHOOD)

(a) Relations Between Constructs and Measures (lambda *Y*):

	Ability	*PeerAcc1*	*Achieve1*	*PeerAcc2*	*Achieve2*	*PeerAcc3*	*Achieve3*
VAR 16	1.00	—	—	—	—	—	—
VAR 17	.66	—	—	—	—	—	—
	(.28)						
	2.31						
VAR 13	—	1.35	—	—	—	—	—
		(.27)					
		4.97					
VAR 14	—	.84	—	—	—	—	—
		(.17)					
		4.85					
VAR 15	—	1.00	—	—	—	—	—
VAR 27	—	—	1.00	—	—	—	—

(a) Relations Between Constructs and Measures (continued):

	Ability	PeerAcc1	Achieve1	PeerAcc2	Achieve2	PeerAcc3	Achieve3
VAR 28	—	—	1.02 (.16) 6.26	—	—	—	—
VAR 4	—	—	—	1.01 (.09) 11.78	—	—	—
VAR 5	—	—	—	.98 (.08) 11.61	—	—	—
VAR 6	—	—	—	1.00	—	—	—
VAR 18	—	—	—	—	1.00	—	—
VAR 19	—	—	—	—	1.02 (.16) 6.26	—	—
VAR 7	—	—	—	—	—	1.01 (.09) 11.78	—
VAR 8	—	—	—	—	—	.98 (.08) 11.61	—
VAR 9	—	—	—	—	—	1.00	—
VAR 20	—	—	—	—	—	—	1.00
VAR 21	—	—	—	—	—	—	1.02 (1.16) 6.26

(b) Structural Paths Interrelating Theoretical Variables

	Ability	PeerAcc1	Achieve1	PeerAcc2	Achieve2	PeerAcc3
PeerAcc1	.28 (.19) 1.42	—	—	—	—	—
Achieve1	.50 (.24) 2.06	—	—	—	—	—
PeerAcc2	−.10 (.29) −0.36	.22 (.16) 1.36	.24 (.28) 0.86	—	—	—

(b) Structural Paths Interrelating Theoretical Variables (continued):

	Ability	PeerAcc1	Achieve1	PeerAcc2	Achieve2	PeerAcc3
Achieve2	—	.05	1.35	—	—	—
		(.16)	(.31)			
		−0.30	4.35			
PeerAcc3	—	—	—	.21	−.06	—
				(.11)	(.13)	
				1.89	−0.46	
Achieve3	—	—	—	.12	.97	—
				(.09)	(.12)	
				1.35	7.89	

(c) Residuals

	Ability	PeerAcc1	Achieve1	PeerAcc2	Achieve2	PeerAcc3	Achieve3
Ability	.42						
	(.22)						
	1.94						
PeerAch1	—	.41					
		(.13)					
		3.11					
Achieve1	—	.05	.19				
		(.06)	(.08)				
		0.80	2.47				
PeerAch2	—	—	—	.68			
				(.13)			
				5.31			
Achieve2	—	—	—	—	.01		
					(.11)		
					0.10		
PeerAch3	—	—	—	—	—	.61	
						(.12)	
						5.06	
Achieve3	—	—	—	—	—	—	−.01
							(.11)
							−0.13

Of most prominence are the strong achievement-to-achievement paths, with residuals that are effectively zero (.01 and −.01, the latter an anomalous negative variance called a Haywood case). Most notably, those strong stabilities wiped out any panel relationships, leaving the conclusion that there is no relation between popularity and achievement.

The corresponding fit statistics, which are provided so that readers can look back at them after reading the next chapter, were as follows:

```
GOODNESS OF FIT STATISTICS
CHI-SQUARE WITH 102 DEGREES OF FREEDOM = 87.55 (P =
   0.85)
ESTIMATED NON-CENTRALITY PARAMETER (NCP) = 0.0
90 PERCENT CONFIDENCE INTERVAL FOR NCP = (0.0 ; 9.94)
MINIMUM FIT FUNCTION VALUE = 0.88
POPULATION DISCREPANCY FUNCTION VALUE (F0) = 0.0
90 PERCENT CONFIDENCE INTERVAL FOR F0 = (0.0 ; 0.10)
ROOT MEAN SQUARE ERROR OF APPROXIMATION (RMSEA) = 0.0
90 PERCENT CONFIDENCE INTERVAL FOR RMSEA = (0.0 ;
   0.031)
P-VALUE FOR TEST OF CLOSE FIT (RMSEA < 0.05) = 0.99
COURIER = EXPECTED CROSS-VALIDATION INDEX (ECVI) = 1.91
90 PERCENT CONFIDENCE INTERVAL FOR ECVI = (2.06 ;
   2.16)
ECVI FOR SATURATED MODEL = 3.09
ECVI FOR INDEPENDENCE MODEL = 7.08
CHI-SQUARE FOR INDEPENDENCE MODEL WITH 136 DEGREES OF
   FREEDOM = 666.46
INDEPENDENCE AIC = 700.46
MODEL AIC = 189.55
SATURATED AIC = 306.00
INDEPENDENCE CAIC = 761.75
MODEL CAIC = 373.41
SATURATED CAIC = 857.59
ROOT MEAN SQUARE RESIDUAL (RMR) = 0.063
STANDARDIZED RMR = 0.061
GOODNESS OF FIT INDEX (GFI) = 0.91
ADJUSTED GOODNESS OF FIT INDEX (AGFI) = 0.86
PARSIMONY GOODNESS OF FIT INDEX (PGFI) = 0.61
NORMED FIT INDEX (NFI) = 0.87
NON-NORMED FIT INDEX (NNFI) = 1.04
PARSIMONY NORMED FIT INDEX (PNFI) = 0.65
COMPARATIVE FIT INDEX (CFI) = 1.00
```

INCREMENTAL FIT INDEX (IFI) = 1.03
RELATIVE FIT INDEX (RFI) = 0.82

In summary, the path, panel, confirmatory factor analysis, and latent variable structural equation modeling analyses yielded differing interpretations. The differences point out the importance of having multiple measures of theoretical variables so that issues such as measurement error can be addressed adequately.

As a final activity, look back at the different conclusions that one might draw from the different analytical approaches. This point is the same one as is made, perhaps even more strongly, in the illustration that appears in Table 10.4. The point is that the results from a single data set diverge.

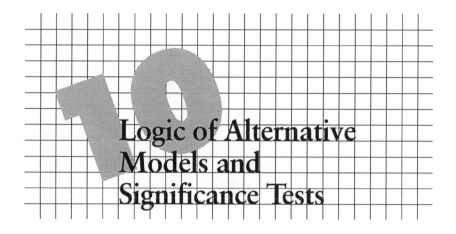

Logic of Alternative Models and Significance Tests

This chapter provides one important and fundamental piece of structural equation modeling (SEM) that still needs to be addressed. That piece is how to use various tests of model plausibility to complement parameter significance tests. As pointed out in Chapter 8 when the basic latent variable SEM model was presented, the chi-square goodness of fit test, although valuable, is limited because it is a direct function of sample size. In small samples even poor models may fit fairly well, whereas in very large samples even trivial differences between the hypothesized model and the observed data will result in models that do not fit by traditional criteria of significance testing.

This chapter discusses aspects of model fitting. First, it discusses what it means to call models nested and the advantages for model fitting that exist when models are nested. Second, it describes and explains general measures of overall model fit and fit indexes for comparing nested models. Third, it presents indexes of fit that allow comparison of non-nested models. Fourth, it describes two approaches for setting up a series of nested models so that readers can see how they might need and use the indexes described in the second section. Finally, the issues covered in this chapter are illustrated through an example. The Maruyama and McGarvey (1980) data set (Figure 9.2; Table 9.2) is used to illustrate a series of nested models plus the array of overall fit indexes.

■ Nested Models

Generally speaking, models can be said to be **nested** whenever one model has all the same free parameters as does a second model but also has other free parameters not shared by the other model. In other words, the two models are equivalent except for a subset of free parameters in one model that are fixed or constrained in the other.

Imagine that we want to test plausibility of a three-wave model in which peer acceptance influences achievement as in Figure 9.3. First, we could compare two models, one with and the other without the peer acceptance to achievement paths. The two models would differ only with respect to those particular paths; their measurement models would be identical, and their structural models would differ only by two parameters that are free in one model but fixed to 0 in the other, so they fit the definition of nested. In other words, the differences, as well as the difference in degrees of freedom, between the two models result from parameters being free in one model and fixed in the other. In this case, those are the two paths from peer acceptance to achievement.

In some instances, nesting of models may not be immediately apparent, for example, comparing a two-factor confirmatory factor model with an alternative one-factor model. In that case, provided that no indicator is related to both factors (e.g., Figure 7.4 provides a simple illustration), the two alternative models are nested even though their nesting is not as readily apparent as in the previous example. A one-factor model actually just assumes that the correlation between the two factors is unity, which makes the factors the same and the loadings on the two factors the same as they would be on a single factor. The two- and one-factor models thus fit the definition of nested, for the freely estimated factor correlation is the only difference between them. Note that, in contrast to the first illustration, the fixed parameter is fixed not to 0 but rather to 1.

The preceding examples describe common types of situations in which variations of a model are pitted against one another to examine plausibility of some hypothesized paths and/or plausibility of alternative views about relationships. The alternative models can be compared for overall fit. Before getting too carried away by the possibility of generating large numbers of nested models to test different paths, however, it is prudent to remember that each parameter estimated has its own standard error and therefore a confidence interval. In other words, significance of each parameter estimate (the difference of that parameter estimate from 0) can be assessed without using nested models. Furthermore, examination of plausibility of alternative views can be done by inspecting confidence intervals around and significance levels of critical parameters. In the two illustrations just described, plausibility can be assessed by examining (a) the significance (difference from a path of 0) of the paths from peer acceptance to achievement and (b) the difference of the correlation between the two factors from a correlation of unity. Looking at confidence intervals is far simpler than setting up a series of nested models to "test" specific parameters. Alternative models should be viewed as testing changes at the model level rather than at the level of the individual parameter. That is, models would be compared that differ with respect to a number of different parameters.

An appealing feature of setting up nested models is that they are directly comparable by a test statistic. If the difference between the chi-square statistics for two nested models is calculated by simple subtraction (e.g., $\chi^2 M1 - \chi^2 M2$, where M1 and M2 are the two nested models), then that difference also is distributed as chi-square with degrees of freedom equal to the difference in degrees of freedom between the models ($df M1 - df M2$). Thus, there is available a simple and straightforward chi-square test of the overall differences between models.

Although using the chi-square goodness of fit statistic to compare models is appealing, it shares the general shortcoming of all chi-square goodness of fit tests for structural models, namely, that it is directly affected by sample size and therefore is somewhat limited in value for assessing differences between alternative models. By contrast, within the range of acceptable sample sizes for latent variable SEM (i.e., large samples), standard errors for estimated parameters do not change much. That is why the approach of choice for examining significance of individual paths is to use standard errors to build confidence intervals rather than constructing chi-square difference tests of overall fit. At the same time, however, nested models can be used as alternative models for the different fit indexes presented in the next section of this chapter. Those indexes are less prone to complications due to changes in sample size than is the chi-square difference test.

A second class of nested models is the type in which equality constraints are imposed. Imposing such constraints can be done in any model, but they make the most sense in either longitudinal or multiple group analyses (see Chapter 11). For longitudinal panel models, the same indicators collected across time can have their loadings constrained so that they are the same at each time point. (This is the variation on tau equivalent tests described in Chapter 7.) The constrained and unconstrained models are nested, for they differ only with respect to the parameters that are constrained in one model and free in the other. When researchers have available multiple groups (e.g., a male sample and a female sample), they may want to examine whether or not parameters are the same in the different samples. As will be described in Chapter 11, SEM techniques allow constraining paths to be equal across samples. Once again, the constrained and unconstrained models are nested.

Regardless of how similar two models are to one another, if they free alternative parameters such that one model no longer is the second with some free parameters added, then the models no longer are nested and therefore no longer are directly comparable. As a result, a chi-square test of difference to compare them is no longer possible. There certainly are many instances in which the different theoretical models are not, cannot be, and should not be made a series of nested models. In those instances, ways of choosing between the alternative models need to be based on something other than the chi-square fit statistic (Akaike, 1987; Browne & Cudeck, 1989).

As a note, just-identified models (sometimes also called **fully saturated** models) will be nested with all possible models, for they have no degrees of freedom and fit the data perfectly. Their nesting with other models, however, is trivial, for all variations of just-identified models fit the same, regardless of their conceptual sensibility. On the other hand, the fact that all sets of variables eventually can be perfectly represented in a model points out the importance of the **principle of parsimony** in model construction. That principle is that tests of model fit ought to give some value to models that approximate the just-identified model while still having many degrees of freedom. That principle has been used in developing a set of indexes of model fit.

SEM researchers also speak of fully saturated or **just-identified structural** models. These have been discussed in previous chapters. They have no degrees of freedom tied to the relations among the latent variables, so all degrees of freedom in such models are tied to the relations of measures with latent variables. Just-identified structural models have as many paths linking latent variables as there are covariances among those latent variables. For example, the model of Figure 9.1 has a just-identified structural model, for there are 5 latent variables and 10 paths among them. *Just-identified structural models are nested with all other models sharing their measurement structure.* This type of nesting is more interesting and important than nesting tied to the just-identified model, for *just-identified structural models are guaranteed to have the best possible fit of any models sharing a particular measurement structure.* If their fit is poor, then no way of specifying relations among the conceptual variables would fit any better.

Because there can be many variants of a structural model that are just identified, just-identified structural models provide another case in which nesting of models may not be immediately apparent. For example, a confirmatory factor model with all latent variables free to covary with one another is identical in overall model fit to any fully recursive path model (and also any just-identified structural model) linking those same latent variables.

To summarize, alternative models that are nested can be directly compared with one another in overall fit through the chi-square statistic and SEM fit indexes. They provide a way in which to engage in direct comparison of competing models and complement the significance information that is available for individual parameter estimates.

▮ Tests of Overall Model Fit

In the past decade, a wide array of tests of overall fit of SEM models has emerged. Although the various tests, or **fit indexes** as they are commonly called, are in the process of being sorted out and compared, at present there is no agreement about a single optimal test or even a set of optimal tests. The unfortunate result is that different articles present different indexes, and different reviewers of articles ask for various indexes that they know about or prefer. Even though there is an entire book focused on model testing (Bollen & Long, 1993), providing readers with cookbook-like guidance in this complex area is not possible (an article that comes close to providing such guidance is that of Hoyle & Panter, 1995). Furthermore, current versions of popular SEM programs such as LISREL, AMOS, and EQS provide a large number of fit indexes—more, in fact, than anyone would want to report. (Look back, for example, at the fit indexes in Appendix 9.4 under the heading of "goodness of fit statistics.")

Basically, the array of writings on overall tests of model fit is extensive and not altogether consistent (e.g., Bentler, 1990; Bollen, 1990; Bollen & Long, 1993; Hu & Bentler, 1995; Marsh, Balla, & McDonald, 1988; Mulaik et al., 1989). The different fit indexes differ with respect to dimensions such as susceptibility to sample size differences, variability in the range of fit possible for any particular data set, and valuing simplicity of model specification needed to attain an improved fit. Although many of *these indexes* have been developed to be used for a number of different estimation approaches (e.g., maximum likelihood, generalized least squares), they *will be presented here in terms of the chi-square statistic that corresponds to maximum likelihood estimation* (see also Table 10.1).

The different indexes have been classified in a number of ways. The most widely cited and followed classification approach is one presented by Marsh et al. (1988). As amended by Hu and Bentler (1995), it provides the framework for the discussion of basic indexes and indexes for nested models presented here. That framework presents "absolute" indexes and then four different subtypes of "relative" indexes. One also could add to that framework yet another dimension for classifying fit, which would be labeled "adjusted" indexes. This additional dimension typically has not been included as a separate category because it does not provide an independent classification scheme.

Absolute indexes address the question: Is the residual or unexplained variance remaining after model fitting appreciable? Thus, they are absolute insofar as they impose no baseline for any particular data set. If a data set, for example, has only small relationships across measures, then almost any model potentially could fit fairly well.

Relative indexes address the question: How well does a particular model do in explaining a set of observed data compared with (a range of) other possible models? Most of these relative fit indexes establish as a baseline a "worst fitting" model. The most common worst-fitting model is one that models only the variances from the variance/covariance matrix. That model is also called the "null model." Because it fits only the variances and assumes that all covariances are 0, it fits only if there are negligible covariances between measures. Then, theoretical models are viewed as falling along a continuum between the null model (the worst possible fitting model) and a best fit model

TABLE 10.1 Fit Indexes Summary

Types (classes) of fit indexes

1. *Absolute*: Is the residual (unexplained) variance appreciable? (e.g., chi-square, chi-square/df, RMR, GFI)
2. *Relative*: How well does the model do compared with (a range of) other possible models with the same data? (e.g., Type 1: NFI; Type 2: TLI, IFI; Type 3: BFI or RNI)
3. *Adjusted*: How does the model combine fit and parsimony? (e.g., LISREL's PGFI, PNFI, TLI)

Specific indexes

In the following, F stands for the function that is minimized, and $\chi^2 = (N - 1)F$. The subscript key is as follows: t = theoretical; n = null; s = saturated; a and b = alternative models. The symbol k = number of measures in the model.

Root mean residual

This statistic is simply the square root of the mean of the squared discrepancies between all the elements of the predicted (Σ) and observed (S) matrices.

LISREL goodness of fit index:

$$GFI = 1 - [tr(\Sigma^{-1}S - I)^2 / tr(\Sigma^{-1}S)^2]$$

The GFI measures the proportion of weighted information in S that fits weighted information in Σ, such as the coefficient of determination. The ratio part of the formula is like a ratio of residual to total variance.

LISREL adjusted goodness of fit index:

$$AGFI = 1 - [k(k + 1) / 2\ df_a] \times (1 - GFI)$$

The AGFI is not recommended (see Mulaik et al., 1989).

Bentler and Bonett's (1980) normed fit index:

$$NFI = (F_a - F_b) / F_n, \text{ or } (\chi^2_a - \chi^2_b) / \chi^2_n$$

Implicitly, the denominator is $F_n - F_s$, but $F_s = 0$).

Tucker-Lewis index (Tucker & Lewis, 1973):

$$TLI = \frac{(\chi^2_n/df_n - \chi^2_t/df_t)}{(\chi^2_n/df_n - 1)} = \frac{((F_n/df_n) - (F_t/df_t))}{(F_n/df_n) - (1/N-1))}$$

where N is the sample size. This also is the Bentler and Bonett non-normed fit index formula.

---

that perfectly fits the observed data (typically attained only by the fully saturated or just-identified model). Different conceptual models can be directly compared only if they are nested.

TABLE 10.1 Continued

Bollen's (1989) incremental fit index:

$$IFI = (\chi^2_n - \chi^2_t) / (\chi^2_n - df_t)$$

Note that df_t = expected value of χ^2 with t degrees of freedom.

Bentler's (1990) and McDonald and Marsh's (1990)
relative noncentrality index:

$$RNI \text{ or } BFI = [(\chi^2_n - df_n) - (\chi^2_t - df_t)] / (\chi^2_n - df_n)$$

James, Mulaik, and Brett's (1982) parsimonious fit index:

$$PGFI = \{df_t / [k(k + 1) / 2]\} \, GFI,$$

where df_t is degrees of freedom of the model, k = size of input matrix, $k(k + 1) / 2$ = total possible degrees of freedom, and GFI is the index defined above.

Mulaik et al.'s (1989) parsimonious normed fit index:

$$PNFI = (df_t / df_n) \, NFI \text{ or } \{df_t / [k(k - 1) / 2]\} \, NFI$$

Mulaik et al.'s parsimonious normed fit index, Type 2:

$$PNFI2 = (df_t / df_n) \, IFI \text{ or } \{df_t / [k(k - 1) / 2]\} \, IFI$$

Akaike information criteria (Akaike, 1987):

$$AIC \text{ (Joreskog)} = \chi^2_t - 2df_t$$

$$AIC \text{ (Tanaka)} = \chi^2_t + 2(\text{number of free parameters})$$

Bozdogan's (1987) modified AIC:

$$CAIC = \chi^2_t - (1 + \ln N)df_t$$

Browne and Cudeck's (1989) expected cross-validation index:

$$ECVI =$$
$$[\chi^2_t / (N - 1)] + 2[\text{number of free parameters} / (N - 1)]$$

Steiger's (1990) root mean square error of approximation:

$$RMSEA = SQRT(F_t / df_t)$$

NOTE: RMR = root mean residual; GFI = goodness of fit index; NFI = normed fit index; TLI = Tucker-Lewis index; IFI = incremental fit index; BFI or RNI = relative noncentrality index; CFI = comparative fit index; PGFI = parsimonious GFI; PNFI = parsimonious NFI; AGFI = adjusted GFI; AIC = Akaike information criteria; CAIC = modified AIC; ECVI = expected cross-validation index; RMSEA = root mean square error of approximation.

Some of the relative indexes, called **Type 1** by Marsh et al. (1988), directly compare the fit of two different models. Other indexes, called **Type 2** by Marsh et al., compare models but also include information from the expected value of the models under a central chi-square distribution. Hu and Bentler (1995) add Type 3 and Type 4 indexes;

Type 3 indexes compare models including information about expected value under a noncentral chi-square distribution, and Type 4 indexes compare models while including information from other distributional forms. At present, there has been little work done on Type 4 indexes (e.g., Hu & Bentler, 1995).

Finally, **adjusted** indexes explicitly address the question: How does the model combine fit and parsimony? The point, mentioned earlier in this book, is that many models could fit the data if enough parameters were estimated, so value ought to be given to models that account for variability with a relatively small number of free parameters. What makes this category nonindependent of the others is that some of the model indexes just described inherently adjust in their formulas for the degrees of freedom in the various models that are being compared, which means that they already build in a control for parsimony. In other words, some of the model indexes described in the previous categories are in fact already adjusted indexes.

▌ *Absolute Indexes*

These indexes include those that use the function that is minimized (the maximum likelihood fitting function or the scaled likelihood ratio), the root mean residual (RMR), the chi-square test and χ^2/df ratio, and the goodness of fit index (GFI) and adjusted goodness of fit index (AGFI) from the LISREL program. They provide information about how closely the models fitted compare to a perfect fit. At the same time, they ignore variability between data sets in how poorly any model could possibly fit.

Of the absolute indexes, the chi-square and χ^2/df ratio indexes already were described earlier in this book. Both look at the absolute size of the residuals. As a reminder, the distribution of chi-square is such that its expected value is equal to its degrees of freedom, so an "ideal" fit would have a χ^2/df ratio of 1.0. "Ideal" is in quotes because (a) in fact a perfectly fitting model would have a chi-square statistic of 0 and (b) for any given level of model fit short of perfect, the chi-square and, consequently, the χ^2/df ratio change as sample size changes. The third absolute index, the RMR, also does not require much explanation, for it is straightforward. It is the square root of the mean squared difference between elements of the predicted and observed matrices. (Differences are squared because the sign of the difference is inconsequential; a discrepancy is a discrepancy regardless of its sign.) The RMR makes most sense when measures are standardized, for then they have a common metric and their residuals have parallel meaning. Of the other indexes mentioned, only the GFI is described here; the AGFI is skipped, for Mulaik et al. (1989) argued that it has problems that make it less desirable.

The GFI has been presented in two different ways. More recent versions of the LISREL manual use the terminology of Tanaka and Huba (1984), but the earlier terminology is more consistent with other indexes and with terms used previously in this book, so it is presented here.

$$GFI = 1 - [tr(\Sigma^{-1}S - I)^2 / tr(\Sigma^{-1}S)^2].$$

GFI assesses the relative amount of the variances and covariances jointly accounted for by the model and thus typically ranges between 0 and 1. As sigma and S converge, the numerator of the term in brackets goes to 0, resulting in GFI going to 1.

Relative Indexes

A Type 1 index widely used but currently not recommended (Hu & Bentler, 1995, recommended *no* Type 1 indexes), because it is affected by sample size and does poorly for small samples, is the Bentler and Bonett (1980) normed fit index (NFI). That index compares fits of two different models to the same data set. One of the models may be a baseline/null model. The NFI can be expressed in terms of either the fit function (F) or the χ^2 statistic, for they yield equivalent results.

$$NFI = [F_a - F_b] / F_n \qquad \text{or}$$
$$[\chi^2_a - \chi^2_b] / \chi^2_n,$$

where a and b are alternative models and n is the null model.

Consistent with the logic presented here in which models are viewed as falling along a continuum from worst possible to best possible fit, the denominator implicitly is $F_n - F_s$, where s is the saturated model and has a fit function of 0. Remember, even though in the NFI equation two competing models are compared, the null model can be one of the two models compared. If it is, then the resulting index provides information about the proportion of possible improvement from null to best fit model that is attained by the conceptual model. Because the NFI is bounded by 0 and 1, it is an appealing index. Bentler and Bonett (1980) recommended accepting NFIs of .90 or greater in comparison to the null model as indicative of a good fit for a theoretical model.

There are several different Type 2 indexes that are widely used. Most important, these indexes are much more consistent across sample size (e.g., Marsh et al., 1988) than are either absolute or Type 1 indexes. The most prominent is the classic Tucker and Lewis (1973) formula, which was expanded by Bentler and Bonett (1980) to compare alternative models rather than comparing one model with a null model. The Tucker-Lewis index (TLI) is

$$\text{TLI} = \frac{(\chi^2{}_n/df_n - \chi^2{}_t/df_t)}{(\chi^2{}_n/df_n - 1)} = \frac{((F_n/df_n) - (F_t/df_t))}{(F_n/df_n) - (1/N - 1))},$$

where N is the sample size, F is the function that is minimized, n is the null model, and t is the theoretical model. The 1 in the denominator results from the fact that the expected value of $\chi^2 = df$, which makes the ratio of expected χ^2 / df for any model t equal to 1. Thus the TLI is a Type 2 index, based on the expected value of χ^2 / df under the central chi-square distribution. The 1 on the far right is divided by $N - 1$, which is the value that the fitting function (F) is multiplied by to get the chi-square value. In other words, the other three ratios from the formula presented in terms of chi-square all are divided by $N - 1$ to go from a chi-square to an F, so the 1 term needs to be as well so as to maintain equivalence.

The TLI is robust across sample size changes (Hu & Bentler, 1995; Marsh et al., 1988) but, unfortunately, is not bounded by 0 and 1, making it more difficult to interpret than an index such as NFI. The Bentler and Bonett (1980) non-normed fit index (NNFI) is identical to the TLI except that Bentler and Bonett allow the null model in the numerator to be replaced by an alternative model, for example, $(\chi^2{}_b / df_b)$ rather than $(\chi^2{}_n / df_n)$.

A second recommended (e.g., Hoyle & Panter, 1995) Type 2 index is Bollen's (1989) incremental fit index (IFI). The IFI looks much like the NFI, but in its denominator it subtracts degrees of freedom of the theoretical model from $\chi^2{}_n$. The degrees of freedom of the theoretical model is the expected value of $\chi^2{}_t$. The formula is

$$\text{IFI} = (\chi^2{}_n - \chi^2{}_t) / (\chi^2{}_n - df_t).$$

Type 3 indexes have not been as widely used in the SEM literature as have Types 1 and 2. Again following recommendations of Hoyle and Panter (1995) as well as Hu and Bentler (1995), only two are mentioned here. First is a statistic developed both by Bentler (1990), called the Bentler fit index (BFI), and by McDonald and Marsh (1990), called the relative noncentrality index (RNI). Like the TLI, it is not bounded by 0 and 1. Its formula is

$$\text{RNI or BFI} = [(\chi^2_n - df_n) - (\chi^2_t - df_t)] / (\chi^2_n - df_n).$$

The second index, also developed by Bentler (Bentler, 1990; Hu & Bentler, 1995) and called the comparative fit index (CFI), adjusts the RNI/BFI so that it falls within the range of 0 to 1. Because that index uses a formula that differs greatly from those presented in this section, its formula is not presented here. In most instances, the RNI (BFI) will fall between 0 and 1, and CFI = RNI (BFI).

▌ Adjusted Indexes

Finally, there are variations of some of the indexes just described that add to them a direct assessment of parsimony of the models being compared. Typically, what these variations do is multiply the indexes by a ratio of degrees of freedom in the theoretical model to degrees of freedom either in the matrix (which for v measures is $v(v + 1) / 2$), used in absolute models, or in the null model (which is $v(v - 1) / 2$), used in relative models. For models that use a lot of degrees of freedom in model specification, the adjusted or parsimonious fit indexes look much worse than do the relative fit indexes. James, Mulaik, and Brett (1982) presented a parsimonious fit index for the LISREL GFI (PGFI):

$$\text{PGFI} = \{df_t / [v(v + 1) / 2]\} \text{ GFI}.$$

Because the GFI is an absolute index, the denominator of the parsimonious adjustment is the total number of available degrees of freedom from the variance/covariance matrix. Mulaik et al. (1989) presented two different parsimonious indexes for relative indexes, one for the normed fit index (PNFI),

$$\text{PNFI} = (df_t / df_n) \text{ NFI} \qquad \text{or}$$
$$\{df_t / [v(v - 1) / 2]\} \text{ NFI},$$

and the other for a Type 2 model (PNFI2) that, although unstated, happens to be for Bollen's IFI. The IFI is inserted into their equation to simplify the formula:

$$\text{PNFI2} = (df_t / df_n) \text{ IFI} \qquad \text{or}$$
$$\{df_t / [v(v - 1) / 2]\} \text{ IFI}.$$

Note that because both indexes are relative indexes, the denominator is the degrees of freedom of the null model.

Fit Indexes for Comparing Non-Nested Models

Researchers who have alternative models that cannot be made nested are faced with a different challenge, for it is difficult to compare models that make different assumptions about patterns and relationships. One could, of course, compare absolute fit indexes such as the chi-square or the GFI. Direct comparison is complicated because no direct statistical comparison is possible. For such models, there are other fit indexes that are useful primarily because of their ability to order models from best fitting to worst fitting. In general, these do not have ideal values to attain but provide a relative ordering of different models for a single data set. These statistics are the Akaike information criteria (AIC) (Akaike, 1987), Bozdogan's (1987) variation, the CAIC, and Browne and Cudeck's (1989) expected cross-validation index (ECVI). Finally, there is Steiger's (1990) root mean square error of approximation (RMSEA), which is a discrepancy per degree of freedom test much like a root mean square (e.g., Browne & Cudeck, 1993).

The AIC is complicated by the fact that the formula is given in different forms that do *not* yield identical values. They do, however, yield parallel findings. The forms presented by Jöreskog (1993) and Tanaka (1993) are presented here:

$$\text{AIC (Jöreskog)} = \chi^2_t - 2df_t$$

$$\text{AIC (Tanaka)} = \chi^2_t + 2(\text{number of free parameters}).$$

Bozdogan's (1987) modified AIC is

$$CAIC = \chi^2_t - (1 + \ln N)df_t.$$

Browne and Cudeck's (1993) ECVI gives a value that would be expected if a cross-validation sample were available:

$$ECVI = [\chi^2_t / (N - 1)] + 2(\text{number of free parameters} / N - 1).$$

The AIC and ECVI will give the same rank order of the models being compared.

Finally, Steiger's RMSEA is calculated by the formula

$$RMSEA = sqrt(F_t / df_t).$$

The suggested level for a good fitting model is an RMSEA of less than .05.

Setting Up Nested Models

Now that a range of indexes for comparing alternative and null models have been described, ways of setting up a series of nested models are described so that readers can see how all these indexes are actually used. Two logical approaches for setting up a series of models are presented. These approaches are those of Bentler and Bonett (1980) and James et al. (1982). The approaches are summarized in Table 10.2.

Bentler and Bonett (1980) suggested that readers should have at least three actual models and that two other models requiring no model fitting also help in thinking about quality of overall fit. First, they suggested the importance of fitting a model of full independence, which is the null or baseline model discussed in the preceding section of this chapter. The null model specifies the variances but estimates all the covariances as 0 (for a critique of null models, see Sobel & Bohrnstedt, 1985). The most recent versions of LISREL, AMOS, and EQS automatically calculate the null model; in earlier versions, the null model would have to be estimated as a separate model.

Second, fit the theoretical model of greatest interest. Third, fit any alternative theoretical models. Fourth, implicitly all researchers estimate a "saturated" model, which is just identified and fits the data

TABLE 10.2 Approaches for Setting Up Alternative Nested Models

---

Bentler and Bonett (1980)

1. Null = full independence (diagonals only)
2. Theoretical = your model
3. Alternative = other viable model(s)
4. Saturated = just-identified, $df = 0$, perfect fit
5. "Ideal" (hypothetical): Take the best fitting statistic from Model 2 or 3 above and give it df = null − 1. If it does not fit, then no model will, for other models will have larger functions and smaller degrees of freedom.

James, Mulaik, and Brett (1982)

1. Null model (same as above)
2. Measurement model with independent latent variables
3. Your model (same as Model 2 above)
4. Just-identified structural model (any lack of fit is due to the measurement model)
5. Fully saturated model, $df = 0$ (same as Model 4 above)
6. Similar to Model 5 of Bentler and Bonett; take degrees of freedom 1 less than from the null model and χ^2 from Model 4

Relative normed fit index for Model 3:

$$\text{RNFI} = [(\chi^2_{M2} - \chi^2_{M3}) / ((\chi^2_{M2} - \chi^2_{M4}) - (df_{M3} - df_{M4}))]$$

Parsimonious relative normed fit index for Model 3:

$$\text{PRNFI} = [(df_{M3} - df_{M4}) / (df_{M2} - df_{M4})] \, \text{RNFI}$$

NOTE: RNFI = relative normed fit index; PRNFI = parsimonious RNFI.

---

perfectly ($\chi^2 = 0$). It is the best fitting model. Finally, Bentler and Bonett (1980) suggested a "quasi-test" or hypothetical test in which the chi-square from the best fitting theoretical model is taken and examined as if it had degrees of freedom 1 less than that of the null model, namely, $[v(v - 1) / 2] - 1$. If that model does not fit well, then none of the models will fit, for they all will have larger functions and fewer degrees of freedom. At that point, a conceptual rethinking may be in order. Assuming that the hypothetical test is not too discouraging, one could use the various indexes to compare the second and third types of models against the null model and against one another.

James et al. (1982) suggested a similar procedure but did not mention the hypothetical test and added a couple of additional alternative models that are helpful. First, they began with the same null or independence model. Second, they fit a measurement model that specifies all latent variables as uncorrelated. One, of course, would not want this model to fit, for a good fit would mean that the latent variables all are independent of one another. Third is the theoretical model or alternative models if there is more than one. Fourth, they estimated a just-identified structural model in which there are no degrees of freedom in the relationships among the latent variables. In such a model, all lack of fit is due to inadequacies of the measurement model. If one were to do a hypothetical test parallel to Bentler and Bonett (1980), taking the fit of the just-identified structural model with 1 less degree of freedom than the null model would be the best test of whether or not any model could fit. Finally, they also anchored the various models with a saturated model that fits perfectly.

James et al. (1982) used Models 2, 3, and 4 (see Table 10.2) to calculate an additional fit index, which they called the relative normed fit index (RNFI). Its formula is

$$\text{RNFI} = (\chi^2_{M2} - \chi^2_{M3}) / [(\chi^2_{M2} - \chi^2_{M4}) - (df_{M3} - df_{M4})].$$

If the difference between Models 3 and 4 $(\chi^2_{M3} - \chi^2_{M4})$ is the same as their expected value $(df_{M3} - df_{M4})$, then RNFI is 1, for the denominator reduces to be the same as the numerator. They also have a parsimonious version (PRNFI):

$$\text{PRNFI} = [(df_{M3} - df_{M4}) / (df_{M2} - df_{M4})] \text{ RNFI}.$$

To summarize, either of the recommended approaches for setting up a series of nested models is worthwhile. They are basically similar, and there is no reason not to use the best elements of each. It seems to me that the just-identified and independent structural models are particularly important, for they provide two valuable anchors for assessing how much different structural paths could affect the overall fit. Using hypothetical tests is also worthwhile, for they might quickly send researchers "back to the drawing board."

Why Models May Not Fit

Cudeck and Henly (1991) provided one framework in which to think about why models may fail to match observed data. They described four types of discrepancy, each of which could be used to select from among competing models. Two of them warrant discussion in the context of fit indexes. First is the **discrepancy of the sample**, which is the minimized difference between the sample covariance matrix and the restricted population covariance matrix for the model. This is what is produced by the minimization function. By contrast, the second type, **overall discrepancy**, is the discrepancy between the underlying population covariance matrix and the estimated covariance matrix for the model. To get a good estimate of this type of discrepancy, Cudeck and Henly recommended the single-sample cross-validation index, the ECVI (e.g., Browne & Cudeck, 1989).

Cudeck and Henly (1991) also noted that models with many parameters to estimate will fit the best provided the sample size is large—and, of course, a large sample size is highly desirable. In large samples, therefore, it is important not to rely only on overall discrepancy and Type 2 indexes; one should use other information as well. Type 3 indexes may help handle model complexity, and cross-validation is useful as well. Finally, Cudeck and Henly went further and noted that the best-fitting model may not be the model closest to the true model, which ought to remind readers that there is much more to SEM than assembling a large-sample complex model that "fits." Their perspective is supported by a discussion in Chapter 12 of post hoc model modification.

Illustrating Fit Tests

At this point, the Maruyama and McGarvey (1980) data set is used to illustrate the different indexes. Five models are compared: a null model, a structural model with independent latent variables, a just-identified structural model, the original model presented by Maruyama and McGarvey, and a modified model that adds residual covariances among five pairs of residuals of measures. Those residual covariances are between father's and mother's ratings; between the Peabody ability measure and the standardized reading achievement measure; and three paths interrelating residuals among verbal grades, schoolwork popularity, and teachers' evaluations (the original model appeared in Figure 9.2).

Results of the various indexes appear in Table 10.3. The top section of the table provides the "absolute" tests that are available in the LISREL program. The second section of the table contains information about the "relative" tests that are widely used; in all indexes, the null model is used as a baseline. I have calculated these indexes by hand even though many programs provide them as part of the program output. Readers have available in Table 10.3 all the information needed (i.e., the χ^2 statistics, the degrees of freedom of the various models, and the minimum value of the function from maximum likelihood estimation) to calculate all the indexes. The third section of Table 10.3 provides information comparing different models with one another. Finally, the bottom section of the table provides the different indexes comparing relative fit for the different models. This last section would provide valuable information even if the models were not nested.

Assume now that one has available this array of indexes and statistics. How can they be interpreted? It is the case that calculating the indexes is the easy part and is done in current versions of most SEM programs. Unfortunately, at this point there is little guidance other than general rules of thumb about overall fit (e.g., NFI > .90, RMSEA < .05), so at this point personal judgment comes into the picture. Also, interpretation is complicated by the fact that, in addition to overall fit, there is the issue of particular paths and their significance. If a model is built to examine a particular relationship of interest, then it could be that plausibility of that relationship can be assessed even without an overall fit that measures up to the usual requirements of a "good" fit.

For the data and models presented in Table 10.3, we might draw the following interpretations. First, as would be expected, the various models do much better than the null model. At the same time, the fit of the null model is not all that bad (RMR = .206), so many of the relationships across measures must be pretty modest. Second, and fortunately, it is not plausible (from the independent latent variables model) to assume that the latent variables are unrelated to one another. Third, the array of different indexes all seem to suggest that although the original hypothesized model does not fit the data poorly, the model could be improved on. As will be described in the following chapter, current versions of SEM programs provide direction about how best to improve the fit of a model by freeing fixed parameters; the information is provided by what are called **modification indexes**. Rather than attempting to improve on the model by relying on modification indices or some other nontheoretical means, however, this model's attempts at improvement are focused on measures that

TABLE 10.3 Illustration of Fit Indexes for Maruyama and McGarvey (1980) Data ($N = 249$)

Description of models

M_0 NULL	Models only diagonal elements of covariance matrix, MODEL 0
M_A INDEP.LVs	Latent variables unrelated to one another, MODEL A
M_B JUST.ID	Just-identified structural model, MODEL B
M_1 M&MCPAPER	As in Maruyama and McGarvey article, MODEL 1
M_2 MOD.M&MC	Modified Maruyama and McGarvey model, residual covariances, MODEL 2

(a) Basic Output Provided by All Versions of the LISREL Program (all are absolute indexes; the χ^2/df ratio was calculated by hand)

Model	χ^2	df	χ^2/df	Function	GFI	AGFI	RMR
NULL	738.94	78	9.4736	1.4898	.627	.565	.206
INDEP.LVs	256.10	65	3.9400	0.5163	.851	.792	.147
JUST.ID	123.74	55	2.2498	0.2495	.927	.880	.067
M&MCPAPER	138.55	59	2.3483	0.2793	.920	.876	.079
MOD.M&MC	104.51	54	1.9354	0.2107	.940	.898	.069

(b) Additional Indexes (all except the first are relative indexes)

Model	PGFI	NFI	PNFI	TLI	IFI	PNFI2 (PIFI)	RNI
NULL	.537	—	—	—	—	—	—
INDEP.LVs	.608	.653	.544	.618	.716	.597	.711
JUST.ID	.560	.833	.587	.853	.899	.634	.896
M&MCPAPER	.596	.813	.615	.841	.883	.668	.880
MOD.M&MC	.558	.859	.595	.890	.926	.641	.924

Bentler and Bonett pseudo-chi square–best fit with most degrees of freedom: $\chi^2(77) = 104.51$

might be expected to share additional sources of common variability beyond the specified factor structure.[19] Those efforts seem to have

---

19. Readers might want to keep in mind a couple of points in reviewing this example. First, the model was intended primarily to illustrate the methods, and we felt that using a nonrecursive model would enhance the illustration. Thus, certain paths cannot be freed, for they would lead to identification problems. Second, the versions of LISREL available when the article was prepared did not readily allow residual covariances for measures; the residuals would have had to be modeled as separate latent variables because the theta matrices had to be diagonal. Unnecessarily complicating the illustration would not have served its purpose.

TABLE 10.3 Continued

(c) Comparisons of Different Models

Comparison	χ^2 Difference	df	NFI	PNFI	NNFI
M_0-M_1	600.39	19	.813	.615	.841
M_0-M_2	634.43	24	.859	.595	.890
M_1-M_2	34.04	5	.046	—	.049

RNFI (compares Model 1 to Models A and B) = (FA – F1) / [FA – FB – (df1 – dfB)] = .916

PRNFI = .366

(d) Tests Applicable to Non-Nested Models

Model	AIC (Jöreskog)	AIC (Tanaka)	CAIC	ECVI	RMSEA
NULL	582.9	764.94	230.58	3.085	0.138
INDEP.LVs	126.1	308.1	–167.53	1.243	0.089
JUST.ID	13.74	195.74	–234.72	0.789	0.067
M&MCPAPER	20.55	202.55	–245.98	0.817	0.069
MOD.M&MC	–3.50	178.51	–247.43	0.719	0.062

NOTE: GFI = goodness of fit index; AGFI = adjusted GFI; RMR = root mean residual; PGFI = parsimonious GFI; NFI = normed fit index; PNFI = parsimonious NFI; TLI = Tucker-Lewis index; IFI = incremental fit index; PIFI = parsimonious IFI; RNI = relative noncentrality index; NNFI = non-normed fit index; RNFI = relative NFI; PRNFI = parsimonious RNFI; AIC = Akaike information.

been somewhat successful, for the modified model fits better (e.g., the chi-square of the difference, which assesses improvement gained by the modifications, is $\chi^2(5) = 34.04$). At the same time, however, the parsimonious indexes do not improve, so there are arguments for going back to the original model. The failure of the parsimonious indexes to improve probably occurs because not all of the residuals specified were significant, so they in aggregate did not improve the fit enough to offset the loss of degrees of freedom.

The final set of indexes provides a fairly consistent ordering from worst to best. The only variability is between the theoretical and just-identified models, and it reflects slightly different weighting between fit and parsimony. In this case, the indexes yield conclusions generally consistent with the ones in the upper parts of Table 10.3.

On balance, this illustration probably is much like many actual studies in not being straightforward or simple to interpret. First, on the plus side, in general the model seems plausible, for the general

factor structure seems reasonable, there were no out-of-range estimates, the different indexes seem generally consistent with one
another, and the fit, although less than ideal, is not bad. Yet, on the
negative side, because the fit is less than perfect, there could be ways
in which to improve the model. At the same time, it is not clear how
much the central theoretical issue, the significance and magnitude of
the paths from acceptance to achievement and vice versa, might be
changed by model modification, so "model improvement" may not
really be an improvement. Furthermore, modifications might not
improve fit when judged by the parsimony criterion.

In summary, a number of different fit indexes are available. When
a sampling of different types of indexes is examined (see, e.g., Hoyle
& Panter, 1995), researchers should have available enough information to feel fairly confident that they understand how well their
models fit. Yet, as can be seen from the example, the indexes do not
necessarily provide clear guidance about plausibility of models, for
the information may be somewhat ambiguous.

To summarize, at this point, readers have been exposed to all the
basic tools they need to be "intelligent" users of structural equation
techniques. This knowledge begins with logic of partialing and path
analysis, and it adds to the blend an understanding of problems of
regression approaches, of issues related to method variance, of the
logic of longitudinal or panel analysis, and of the logic of factor
analysis. Together, these ingredients should give readers the skills
needed to design latent variable structural equation models. Effective
users of latent variable SEM techniques couple these skills with
theoretical knowledge that generates the models to be tested using
SEM techniques.

EXERCISE 10.1

Calculating Fit Indexes

Using the chi-square, the function, and the degrees of freedom, calculate the following indexes and check them against
what is reported: normed fit index, incremental fit index,
Tucker-Lewis index, relative noncentrality index, and the
parsimonious versions of goodness of fit index, normed fit
index, and incremental fit index.

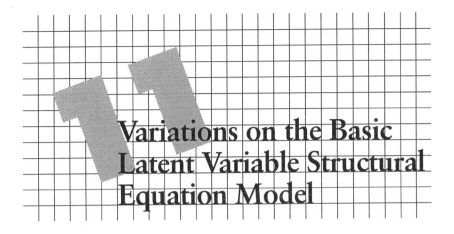

11

Variations on the Basic Latent Variable Structural Equation Model

As noted at the end of Chapter 10, readers at this point should have a technical understanding of how to use latent variable structural equation techniques. A set of basic issues has been covered. Those issues include the roots and fundamentals of decomposition of covariances or correlations into causal and noncausal effects for any particular structural equation model, value and shortcomings of regression techniques with respect to path models, complications of models due to random and nonrandom errors including method variance, the logic of reciprocal causation and/or lagged effects, the value of factor analytic logic for path modeling, and general issues related to the use of latent variable structural equation models.

If readers have acquired a reasonably good understanding of the issues covered, then they should be ready to use the techniques effectively and, perhaps more important, to read the structural equation modeling (SEM) literature and understand it. In other words, hopefully they are ready to work with real data and theoretical models of their own making rather than my making. Structurally, this chapter introduces three variations on SEM approaches.

First, in many instances researchers want to compare structural models in different populations. For example, in the examples of achievement processes presented in Chapter 9, it would have been nice to be able to directly compare achievement processes of white and minority students (e.g., white vs. African American vs. Mexican American). The initial section of this chapter discusses options available in SEM programs for models in which data are collected from multiple populations. Although there have not been as many studies testing comparability of fit across several populations as one might expect, possible uses are many. As examples in addition to analyses of different racial/ethnic groups, one also might want to compare antecedents of sexual behaviors for males with those for females, compare the health behaviors of college graduates with those of nongraduates or the health behaviors of an at-risk group with those of a group not at risk, or compare attitude-behavior links for young children with those same links for older children. In all of these instances, the different samples could, of course, be fitted separately to a single model.

SEM programs have options that allow simultaneously estimating a single solution across a number of samples. The solution can estimate each sample separately or impose constraints across samples that force parts of the model to be fitted to a single solution. By comparing fits of different solutions, researchers are able to draw additional inferences about overall model comparability.

Second, this chapter illustrates how SEM approaches can be used to model second-order factor structures (see, e.g., Liang & Bollen, 1983; Marsh & Hocevar, 1985; Rindskopf & Rose, 1988). Such models hypothesize that the latent variables share common variance due to one or more higher- (second-) order factors that lead to common variance. Perhaps the most widely used example of a second-order factor is general intelligence, or G, which presumably leads to commonalities across different ability variables. Although using SEM programs to set up higher-order factor models is not particularly difficult, there have not been many applications in the literature.

Third, an approach called "all-Y" models is described. Although a functional reason for presenting this approach is so that persons with access to matrix SEM programs can allow residuals of exogenous variables (X's) to covary with indicators of endogenous variables

20. This approach soon should become unneeded for matrix approaches. For example, it has been made moot in LISREL 8 by the addition of an expanded residual matrix, but it still is needed by persons using earlier versions of LISREL, including LISREL 7.

(Y's),[20] it is of conceptual importance because it presents the underlying matrix model used to solve models with X-Y covariances for all programs. For equation-based SEM programs, this discussion can enrich readers' understanding of how the programs work but is irrelevant to using those programs. The approach requires setting up all variables as endogenous variables (i.e., exogenous variables are modeled along with endogenous variables). For example, in the Maruyama and McGarvey (1980) article discussed in Chapter 10, a reasonable argument can be made for allowing the residual of the Peabody ability test (PEA) to covary with the residual of the standardized verbal achievement (VACH) test. But PEA is an X variable, whereas VACH is a Y variable, and in many computer programs residuals of measures of X variables are not allowed to covary with residuals of Y measures, for the two measures are located in different matrices. For such problems, only by combining X and Y variables can their residuals covary. (Note that in Appendix 9.3, the Maruyama and McGarvey LISREL control statements are set up as an all-Y model.)

Analyzing Structural Equation Models When Multiple Populations Are Available

Overview of Methods

One of the most common opportunities, yet one not used all that frequently thus far in the social science literature, is to compare structural models from different groups. This procedure involves the same logic as is used for comparing the magnitude of a relationship between two variables in different samples. For example, we might be interested in asking about the relationship between time spent at a computer and interest in mathematics for boys versus girls or in comparing that same relation for students in the United States versus students in some other country. The comparisons for single relationships are straightforward; they look at the covariances found in the two different groups. The approaches described in this section simply extend the logic of that comparison to greater numbers of relationships and more complex structural models.

For the discussion of multiple groups, even though the goal is to compare models for different populations, in fact what are being compared are models fitted to samples from different populations.

Thus, the language used in this chapter talks about comparing "samples" with the understanding that the samples discussed come from different groups or populations.

An important point is that in multiple-sample comparisons, working with correlations is wrong; correlations yield accurate findings only when the variances in the different samples being compared are identical. When variances differ, the comparison needs to be between covariances (or nonstandardized regression coefficients) in the different samples. *Multiple-sample comparisons always should work with covariance matrices, for only such matrices can deal adequately with differences in variability across samples.* An additional complication can come in setting the metric or scale of latent variables when working with multiple samples (see, e.g., Williams & Thomson, 1986).

Researchers new to SEM frequently carry with them ways of thinking about variables such as gender or ethnicity drawn from analysis of variance and regression approaches, namely, thinking of them as dummy-coded variables to put into their models as additional variables. It certainly is possible to construct models with dummy variables for gender or ethnicity, for differences between means would show up as covariances between the dummy variables and other variables in the models.

Capturing mean differences, however, is not the same as asking about similarity of processes. The latter questions would remove mean differences and compare magnitudes of specific relationships across groups, as was presented earlier in the example of time spent at a computer and interest in mathematics. The issue is not whether or not boys spend more time at computers than do girls, which comes from a mean comparison. If boys spent more time at computers than did girls, then the dummy variable of gender would correlate with the time spent at computers variable and in a model there could be a path between them. By contrast, the cross-sample comparison is whether boys who are some degree above the boys' mean in time spent at computers display an interest in mathematics that reflects their more frequent use of computers *and* whether or not girls who are comparably above the girls' mean display a comparable higher interest in mathematics.

Furthermore, from a methodological perspective, using dummy-coded variables seems risky. First, the dichotomous dummy variables may lead to problems in meeting assumptions of multivariate normality. Second, issues of collinearity can be particularly bothersome. Imagine, for example, a model in which every variable is related to gender. Sorting out causal influences is particularly difficult in such a model. Apparent effects of gender (significant paths from gender to other variables) can vary greatly from sample to sample, due only to fluctuations in the size of relationships that would occur by chance. In summary, if a sufficient sample size is available, then modeling groups as multiple populations is a superior alternative to dummy coding.

Comparing Processes Across Samples

Comparing models across samples provides information that allows researchers to talk about comparability of causal processes in different populations. The focus on processes means attention directed toward relationships, namely, covariance structure comparisons. As an aside, latent variable SEM approaches can be used to compare means as well as covariance structures. Therefore, it is possible to talk about comparability of levels as well as of relationships or processes (e.g., Sörbom, 1974). This text, however, does not focus on the mean comparison issues, for they require introducing a number of new issues, for example, generating for input into the computer programs what is called an augmented moment matrix rather than a covariance or correlation matrix (interested readers can see, e.g., Browne & Arminger, 1995; Byrne, Shavelson, & Muthen, 1989; Sörbom, 1974, 1982).

The most basic way in which to compare solutions across samples is to fit the exact same model with data from different samples and to compare the goodness of fit and the model parameter estimates. Each data set is fitted separately to the model. This solution can be valuable, for comparability of models can be assessed in different ways. For example, all nonsignificant paths could be dropped from the model and "trimmed" models containing only remaining paths compared across the samples to see whether the basic processes seem to be the same. Second, for all paths, confidence intervals could be calculated and compared, and whether or not the confidence intervals for each path overlap in the different samples could be assessed. Where confidence intervals fail to overlap, the models differ.

Although the two approaches just described can be valuable, they also are limited. First, both focus only on comparing individual parameter/path estimates and do not provide a direct comparison of goodness of fit for the different samples. Overall model fitting statistics could be compared only if the sample sizes are identical, and even then differences in fit between samples may not be due to conceptually interesting issues. In other words, the comparison of fit is imprecise, both in its focus and in its capability of detecting conceptually important differences. Second, even when the comparisons attempt to focus on parameters of greatest conceptual interest, the individual tests are tests of significant differences between estimates, rather than of equality of estimates, so finding estimates not to be significantly different does not mean that they are the same.

Many SEM programs have as an option the capacity to analyze more than one sample simultaneously. In its simplest form, this allows an overall fit test of two or more separately estimated samples fitted to a single theoretical model. Because the chi-square goodness of fit test automatically is weighted by the sample size, the overall fit will reflect the different sample sizes. That is, the overall fit is a weighted sum of the fit statistics of the different samples. Said differently, it is the sum of the individual fit statistics, which means that it is not really very different from estimating each sample separately.

The SEM computer programs set up for multiple samples, however, also can allow researchers to force the different samples to be fitted to a single solution. The solution can force estimates of various parameters to be the same across samples (in the language of SEM, constrained to be equal), so a single estimate is generated for each one of any number of specified parameters. That estimate maximizes fit (or minimizes discrepancies) across all the samples simultaneously. As an illustration, look back at Figure 9.2, imagining that there are available two different samples (white and African American student samples). We could decide to constrain the paths between achievement and acceptance by peers (β_1 and β_2) to be equal in the two groups. Equality constraints could be imposed on any part of the model, including the relationships of latent variables to observed measures, the residuals for the observed measures, and the relationships among any of the latent variables. Then the fit of the solution with constraints could be compared with the fit of a solution that allowed the parameters to be estimated separately for each group.

Because actually setting up the cross-sample constraints and running a multisample analysis is tied to the specific SEM program used, this discussion focuses on the logic of the methods. Illustrations of multiple-sample comparisons can be found in manuals for most SEM programs including LISREL (Jöreskog & Sörbom, 1988), AMOS (Arbuckle, 1997), and EQS (e.g., Dunn, Everitt, & Pickles, 1993).

Testing Plausibility of Contraints

As parameters are constrained, additional degrees of freedom are obtained. The critical question is whether or not the fit of the model to the data gets worse as the constraints and degrees of freedom are added. The basic χ^2 fit statistic cannot get better as degrees of freedom are added and would stay the same only if the estimates were identical in the different samples. If the chi-square value stayed the same as more degrees of freedom were added, then other fit indexes would, of course, improve (e.g., χ^2/df). If the overall chi-square increased substantially, then the estimates from the constrained model would not fit as well as those from the unconstrained model. In other words, the samples must differ in terms of the parameters being constrained.

Constraints in the Measurement Model

To compare variables and their relationships across samples, a researcher may decide that he or she needs the relationships between measures and the underlying latent variables they assess to be identical across the samples. That is, by forcing the relationships of measures with variables to be equal, the same latent variables in principle should be assessed in each sample. The equality constraints may help ensure that, by equalizing the loading for each indicator and therefore the relative size of the loadings of the indicators of any particular latent variable, each latent variable will be the same for all samples. In terms of sequencing, constraints in the measurement model may precede other constraints, for they address the issue of comparability of the theoretical variables, irrespective of the relationships among those theoretical variables.

Speaking practically, the free parameters relating observed measures to their underlying constructs (in LISREL, all elements of the lambda matrices) would be constrained to be equal across the samples (analogous to **tau equivalent** tests). In Figure 9.2, these equality constraints would be imposed on the lambda coefficients so that, for example, the estimate for λ_6 linking SEI to SES would be the same in the white and African American samples. Similar constraints would be imposed on all other lambda coefficients.

The constraints also could be extended to the residuals (in LISREL, the theta matrices) if the researcher thought that the total variance would be the same across samples. That variance would then be divided equally into reliable and error variance (analogous to **parallel tests**). Once again returning to Figure 9.2, the focus is on the deltas and epsilons.

Paralleling the preceding discussion, the estimate for δ_1, for example, in the white sample would be constrained to be equal to δ_1 in the African American sample. If the variances of the indicators are not equal, however, then constraining the residuals as well as the relations of indicators to latent variables will result in a poorer fit of the data to the model.

Constraints in the Structural Model

Researchers also could decide to constrain relationships within the structural (latent variable) part of the model. These constraints focus on similarity of hypothesized causal processes, examining whether or not the latent variables displayed the same relationships across samples. Returning to Figure 9.2, constraining β_1 and β_2 would allow us to compare the relationships between acceptance by peers and school achievement for white and African American students. Before imposing constraints in the structural model, however, researchers need to be confident that the measurement models are ensuring that the theoretical variables are the same in the different samples.

When and How to Impose Equality Constraints

Introducing notions about constraints across time and samples draws attention to issues tied to exact versus conceptual replication. Although exact versus conceptual replication issues generally are discussed in the context of experimental work, they are critically important here as well. **Exact replication** refers to situations in which a theoretical variable is operationalized in exactly the same way in different instances. **Conceptual replication** refers to situations in which a theoretical variable is operationalized in different ways in different instances but in which researchers employ some type of validation process to demonstrate that the variable being tapped is the same one.

Issues of exact and conceptual replication in SEM approaches are most prominent in situations where the same measures are being assessed either across time or across samples. Stated most directly, the central issue is how to ensure that the variables are defined the same, either across time or across samples. For example, if we are working with self-concept, how can we be sure that what is being called self-concept at Time 1 or in Sample 1 is the same as what is being called self-concept at Time 2 or in Sample 2?

The primary challenge in ensuring comparability is to determine whether comparability can be better created by trying to produce exact replication or conceptual replication. Exact replication can be done by forcing the loadings across time or samples to be the same via constraints. So, for example, in Figure 11.1 (which is set up to parallel Figure 7.1 but assesses a single variable across time), we could force the following equalities: $p_1 = p_4 = p_7$, $p_2 = p_5 = p_8$, $p_3 = p_6 = p_9$, thereby ensuring that the indicators remain proportionate across time. For multiple samples, imagine that Figure 11.1 has two different samples. In such a case, the parallel issue would be as follows: Should p_1 in Sample 1 be exactly the same as p_1 (which could be called p_1') in Sample 2, that is, $p_1 = p_1'$? The same issue would hold for p_2, p_3, and so on. In complex models, constraints may need to hold both across time and across samples.

Like many latent variable SEM issues, however, forcing equality constraints is the right answer only in context; there are circumstances in which forcing exact replication may result in a *different* conceptual variable being assessed due to the nature of the processes being modeled. For example, in many developmental processes, the dimensionality of constructs may be increasing. In such circumstances, weights representing the best relations of measures to a theoretical variable at one point in time may be a suboptimal weighting of what might be even more than one theoretical variable at a later point in time.

As an illustration, imagine that we are attempting to model a theoretical variable called "academic achievement" in a sample of elementary school-aged children, using as our measures mathematical and verbal achievement test performance. (This discussion parallels an earlier discussion of achievement in panel models in which the comparison is across time rather than across samples.) Imagine further that our study compares processes of children in 1st grade (at which point children have had little, if any, formal instruction in

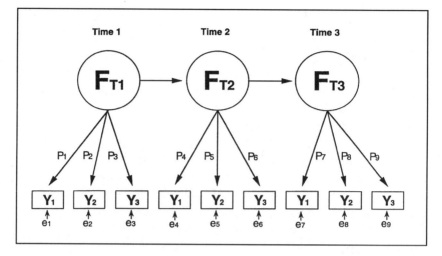

Figure 11.1. Illustration of Equality Constraints for Longitudinal Model

mathematics) with processes of children in 6th grade. If we chose to force the respective weights of verbal and math performance measures to stay the same across the two age groups, then we would likely be taking an indefensible position. As students get older, the results of instruction should be that complexity and diversity in mathematics skills are increasing. (Changes in variability of mathematics skills would not by themselves create a problem, for they should be handled by analyzing a covariance matrix.) Forcing the loadings to be equal across groups has risks. First, we may never tap much of the mathematics achievement domain. Second, if the dimensionality is increasing, then the model may well be misspecified for either or both of the groups and the findings may be meaningless.

The primary point here is that even though exact replication may seem better in many instances, there are times when only through allowing change can conceptual replication be attained. Letting loadings vary across time may be preferable to forcing them to stay the same. Most important, the decision on constraining needs to be driven by theory, not methodological elegance.

Regardless of the decision about constraints, successfully addressing issues of comparability across time and samples is critical for SEM approaches. It is very difficult to speak about comparability of causal processes if the latent variables being compared differ from one another in different samples. Put simply, if the latent variables are different, then the processes being compared cannot be the same.

In summary, then, SEM approaches can be used to compare structural relationships among data collected across two or more groups. By imposing different types of constraints, various assumptions about the relationships can be tested and comparability of latent variables in different samples can be increased. As has been true of every approach described throughout this book, decisions, in this case to analyze data as multiple-group data and to impose restrictive constraints, must be driven by theoretical considerations. Deciding to force relationships between measures and variables to be equal across samples may be necessary in some situations yet wrong in others. In one case, it may be that, without restrictions, the latent variables would be defined so differently in the various samples that the constructs would not be the same. Yet, in another case, it may be that certain constructs display themselves differently in various samples, with the result that constraining loadings to be equal would not allow the same constructs to emerge in different samples. Only from a theoretical basis could these decisions be made with any precision.

In conclusion, multiple-sample comparisons offer a valuable extension of basic latent variable SEM approaches. Yet with the extension comes greater complexity; for multiple-sample comparisons, there are important issues that will have to be resolved a priori about the most likely way in which to ensure comparability of processes across samples.

Second-Order Factor Models

As suggested in the introduction to this chapter, second-order factors are factors of factors. The example mentioned, the *G* factor in ability, posits a higher-order general ability dimension that draws from more specific ability competencies. If those specific competencies are defined as factors, then *G* is a factor defined by those factors or a second-order factor. Each of the more specific ability competencies is a factor that can be assessed through a measurement procedure. By contrast, the general ability dimension is assessed through the specific factors rather than through any measures. If it were directly measured and had its own indicators, then the model would not be a second-order factor model.

Marsh and Hocevar (1985) provided an illustration of second-order factor models for modeling self-concept. They contrasted a first-order factor model for seven self-concept domains (physical ability, appearance, relations with peers, relations with parents, reading, mathematics, and general school self-image) with different second-order models. For example, one model separated academic self-concept from all others as two second-order factors.

Extracting second-order factors can be tricky, for those factors are defined by unmeasured variables whose definitions may be questionable or controversial. Put simply, as one gets to the level of extracting unobservables from unobservables, there is greater potential for error and disagreement. This potential exists even when theorizing allows clear articulation of the processes involved that warrant specification as second-order factors.

The first question for SEM approaches to second-order factoring is a technical one: Is it even possible to model second-order factors? The answer is *yes*, for the model can be adapted to second-order factoring provided conditions for identification are met. In general, identification of those models parallels identification of factor models in which factors correlate; it is the correlations among the factors that are fitted to a particular second-order factor space. Setting up second-order factor models in equation-based programs such as AMOS and EQS is relatively easy, for it just requires additional equations that express second-order factors as a function of first-order factors. For matrix programs such as LISREL, there are special limitations in how to set up the matrices. Second-order factor models require setting up a model as Y only and then to use the gamma, phi, and psi matrices to define the second-order factors.

Assuming, then, that we have a model that warrants specification including second-order factors, how are the details accomplished in a matrix form model? Initially, the first-order factors are set up just like any latent variable confirmatory factor analysis (CFA) model but using the Y measurement model. (For ordinary CFA, either the X side or the Y side of the model can be used.) That is,

$$Y = \Lambda_Y \eta + \varepsilon,$$

yielding

$$\Sigma_{YY} = \Lambda_Y \eta\eta' \Lambda_Y' + \Theta\varepsilon,$$

which is a traditional factor model. The Y side is used because the covariance matrix of the etas has to be specified in terms of other matrices. For a first-order factor model, the eta-eta transpose matrix (ηη′) is specified as psi, with no gamma or phi matrices. For a second-order factor model, however,

$$\Sigma_{\eta\eta'} = \Gamma \Phi \, \Gamma' + \Psi,$$

which is just a factor model paralleling the factor model for the observed measures. The equation combining the first- and second-order factors becomes

$$\Sigma_{YY} = \Lambda_Y(\Gamma \, \Phi \, \Gamma' + \Psi) \, \Lambda_Y' + \Theta\varepsilon.$$

The lambdas relate observed measures to first-order factors, the epsilons are the uniquenesses of observed measures and theta epsilon is their variance/covariance matrix, the gammas relate first-order factors to second-order factors, the phis are the variance/covariance matrix of the second-order factors, and the zetas (the residuals in psi) are the residuals from the first-order factors and psi their variance/covariance matrix.

In summary, second-order factor analysis can be set up with either equation-based or matrix-based SEM programs. The general latent variable SEM approach allows factors of factors to be extracted, casting second-order factor extraction as a straightforward extension of SEM. At this point in time, the matrix approach SEM programs do not allow structural models to causally interrelate second-order factors. For those specific structural models in which the relationships among the second-order factors define a just-identified model, however, the solution to those structural models would be identical in fit to a solution in which all the second-order factors are allowed to correlate with one another. Thus, by extracting the second-order factor matrix in which all factors are allowed to covary with one another and then analyzing that matrix via ordinary regression techniques, structural paths could be estimated. Because the structural part of the model is just identified, the regression estimates would yield the same exact overall fit as the second-order factor model that allows all factors to intercorrelate. In other words, a just-identified second-order structural model would yield a fit identical to extracting a second-order factor variance/covariance matrix.

■ All-Y Models

As mentioned earlier and used in setting up two illustrations in Chapter 9, there are certain instances in which it makes sense when using matrix-based SEM programs to try to "combine" exogenous and endogenous variables. By contrast, equation-based SEM programs such as AMOS and EQS set up the equations and covariances element by element, thus bypassing matrix issues altogether for program users. An important point, however, is that regardless of how the user interface is set up, all programs work with matrices in the parameter estimation process, so the discussion provides a look at how all programs actually estimate relations.

The primary reason for users to select an all-Y model is to allow residual covariances between measures of exogenous and endogenous variables, which cannot be done in some versions of computer programs that set up the free parameters in matrix form. For such a combination to be worthwhile, these programs, of course, produce a solution process identical to what would be found if an equivalent model were calculated separately for exogenous and endogenous variables. That is, if a single model (without residual covariances between X and Y measures) were estimated with X and Y variables and then again as all Y, then the estimates and overall fit would have to be identical regardless of method chosen.

The approach to be presented meets the preceding conditions, for it is exactly the same as the X and Y solution except for the opportunity to add X-Y residual covariates. The matrices from the all-Y model will be bigger in size, for they contain multiple matrices within them. However, as will be shown, there is a direct correspondence between the matrices of the two approaches.

More specifically, looking at the basic model, the measurement model is as follows:

$$Y = \Lambda_Y \eta + \varepsilon \text{ for the endogenous variables}$$
$$X = \Lambda_X \xi + \delta \text{ for the exogenous variables}$$
$$\Sigma_{YY} = \Lambda_Y \eta\eta'\Lambda_Y' + \Theta\varepsilon$$
$$\Sigma_{XX} = \Lambda_X \xi\xi'\Lambda_X' + \Theta\delta.$$

The structural model is as follows:

$$\eta = \beta\,\eta + \Gamma\,\xi + \zeta$$
$$(I - B)\eta = \Gamma\,\xi + \zeta$$
$$\eta\eta' = (I - B)^{-1}\,\Gamma\,\xi\xi'\Gamma'(I - B)^{-1\prime} + (I - B)^{-1}\,\zeta\zeta'(I - B)^{-1\prime}$$
$$\Sigma_{\eta\eta'} = (I - B)^{-1}\,\Gamma\,\Phi\,\Gamma'(I - B)^{-1\prime} + (I - B)^{-1}\,\Psi\,(I - B)^{-1\prime}.$$

Looking at the all-Y variant, the measurement model is as follows:

$$Y^* = \Lambda_Y^*\,\eta^* + \varepsilon^*$$
$$|X| \quad |\Lambda_X\,0| \quad |\xi| \qquad |\delta|$$
$$|Y| = |0\;\Lambda_Y| \quad |\eta| + |\varepsilon|.$$

In other words, what is now being called Y (Y*) is both X and Y and is a vector of size $X + Y$, the new eta (η^*) includes both xi and eta and is a vector of size $\xi + \eta$, the new lambda Y (Λ_Y^*) is now of size $(X + Y) \times (\xi + \eta)$, and the new epsilon ($\varepsilon^*$) is both delta and epsilon and is a vector of size $X + Y$.

The new theta matrix ($\Theta\varepsilon^*$), which is of size $(X + Y) \times (X + Y)$, becomes

$$\Theta\varepsilon^* = |\Theta\delta \;\; \text{symmetric}|$$
$$|\Theta\varepsilon\delta \qquad \Theta\varepsilon\;|.$$

Note that the old theta delta and theta epsilon matrices, although located differently, remain unchanged, but now there are opportunities to allow residuals from X and Y variables to covary in the theta epsilon-delta matrix. The structural model is as follows:

$$\eta^* = \beta^*\,\eta^* + \zeta^*$$

$$|\xi| \quad |0\;0| \quad |\xi| \qquad |\xi|$$
$$|\eta| = |\Gamma\;\beta| \quad |\eta| + |\zeta|.$$

The new model includes only the eta, beta, and psi matrices. Eta (η^*) was defined in the measurement model. As can be seen from the partitioning of the matrices, beta (β^*) includes both gamma and beta, zeta (ζ^*) includes xi (yes, xi appears in two different matrices) and zeta; and, as will be shown, psi (ψ^*) includes both phi and psi. For the "new" psi, even though the exogenous variables are viewed in the model as endogenous, it still is the case that no variable causes any of them (which is, of course, the definition of an exogenous variable), with the result that their total variance is unexplained, and thus their residual variances are their total variances. Their variance/covariance matrix is part of the residual variance/covariance matrix psi. The new psi (Ψ^*) is

$$\Psi^* = \begin{vmatrix} \xi \\ \zeta \end{vmatrix} \begin{vmatrix} \xi\zeta \end{vmatrix} = \begin{vmatrix} \Phi & 0 \\ 0 & \Psi \end{vmatrix}.$$

Finally, paralleling the equations, the covariance structure includes fewer but larger matrices:

$$\Sigma_{\eta^*\eta^{*\prime}} = (I - B^*)^{-1}\,\Psi^*\,(I - B^*)^{-1\prime}.$$

In summary, setting up models as all Y requires only a simple reconfiguring of matrices into a new structure. It changes nothing but allows additional options for programs that require setting the equations up in matrix form.

E X E R C I S E   1 1 . 1

Set up the matrices for the Maruyama and McGarvey (1980) problem illustrated in Chapter 10 as an all-Y model. For LISREL users, set up the control statements. The setup can be compared with the LISREL control statements in Appendix 9.3.

Wrapping Up

This final chapter presents three sets of issues. First, with no intent to squelch any enthusiasm that has been generated, structural equation modeling (SEM) approaches are viewed from perspectives of their critics. This chapter looks at several types of critics of SEM techniques in casting the SEM field within the broader disciplines of the social and behavioral sciences. There are critics within the group of social scientists who could be called users of the techniques as well as critics who would never consider using the techniques because they believe them to be deficient in substantial ways. Second, a "hot" issue in SEM research, that of model modification, is discussed. The issue is determining the extent to which any modification of a theoretical model is appropriate. In other words, it is deciding on a balance between model development and model confirmation. Third, a range of topics not addressed in this book are described briefly. Because this book was intended primarily to provide a general and basic introduction to structural equation techniques, there have been a number of fairly complex or less fundamental SEM issues that have been left out. They are the kinds of issues that a researcher could encounter given a particular type of theoretical model or data set but that are not integral parts of basic SEM approaches.

▌Criticisms of Structural Equation Modeling Approaches

▌ *"Internal" Critics*

One of the most eloquent critiques of SEM approaches is the one given by Cliff (1983). Cliff commended the developers of SEM approaches for the tools they have provided but went on to suggest that few interpretational problems are solved by the approaches and suggested further that use of SEM techniques could be disastrous if social scientists suspended their critical judgments when considering SEM studies and models. He went on to describe four principles of scientific inference that researchers might be enticed to violate.

The first principle is that *data never can confirm a model*; they can only fail to disconfirm it. Hopefully, this point is one that has been made enough times throughout this book to have been deeply embedded into the knowledge readers have acquired about SEM approaches. Cliff (1983) went on to a second point tied to the same principle, also hopefully well entrenched in the understanding of readers: If the data do not disconfirm a particular model, then there are other (alternative) models that are not disconfirmed either. There are important corollaries of this point about alternative models. One is that replication is even more important in SEM research than in experimental work, for it is important to know whether failure to reject is plausible beyond the data set for which a model initially was fitted. A second corollary is that it is critically important to uncover alternative explanations for any finding so that competing models can be tested through inclusion of other variables and replication and extension of the plausible model. A quote of his is particularly cogent: "Much of what characterizes good research is the ability to anticipate, and neutralize with data, potential criticisms of conclusions" (p. 118).

Cliff's (1983) second principle was *post hoc is not propter hoc*. In other words, temporal sequencing of data collection of particular variables is not a guide for inferring causality. Even if correlations are strong, there are many different causal explanations for those correlations. Perhaps the best illustration is the achievement domain in some of the examples presented in this book; even though at any time point achievement was moderately correlated with a number of different variables that temporally preceded it, its stability was so high that in most instances none was a viable cause when the model was specified as longitudinal.

The third principle is another one that has received substantial attention throughout this book. Cliff (1983) called it the *nominalistic fallacy*. The point is that giving something a name does not necessarily make it what we call it or ensure that we understand the thing we have named. Although most obvious in terms of naming factors, the issue basically is one of operationalization or model specification; there always is some gap between theoretical variables and the measures that operationalize them.

For manifest variable models, fundamental issues of validity (What does the measure assess in addition to the theoretical variable of interest?) and reliability (What part of the measure is error, unrelated to any conceptual variable?) for each measure are tied to the nominalistic fallacy. Either poor validity or low reliability causes great problems in trying to interpret paths in a model because one or more variables are not exactly what we think they are and are calling them.

For latent variable models in which multiple indicators are available, one could argue that the problems are substantially lessened, for the theoretical variable always is more than any single indicator. At the same time, however, each conceptual variable is defined by the set of measures or indicators selected to assess it. Researchers assume, often with little justification, that their indicators are representative of the domain defined by the theoretical variable and that a different set of indicators would not change the conceptual variable very much. To the extent that the reasoning is wrong, the results could vary greatly with different measures. Furthermore, because residuals/error is essentially what is left over after a common factor is drawn from the indicators, the residuals also can change as different measures are used as indicators.

An all too common situation is one in which all the indicators of a conceptual variable are collected using a single method. In many of those instances, substantial method variance exists. A likely result is that the common method across indicators becomes "part" of the conceptual variable because method and trait are intertwined. (With "extra" indicators of latent variables, there at least is the opportunity to bootstrap the indicators, dropping them one at a time and reestimating the model to see whether the relationships of the latent variable with other variables change.)

Cliff (1983) illustrated naming problems by discussing a construct of "verbal ability." He suggested that the construct gets defined as what the different tests of verbal ability have in common, which may diverge markedly from the underlying conceptual variable.

Finally, Cliff (1983) addressed the issue of *ex post facto* analysis. His view was a traditional and conservative one that seems to have been relaxed by many SEM researchers, yet one that generally has been advanced by this book. It was that SEM techniques are intended to be used for model confirmation, not model development. Once again, Cliff went further, addressing ways in which inspection of the data (e.g., the correlation matrix of the observed measures) can lead researchers to modify their models even before using SEM programs. In fact, such an approach is implicitly suggested in this book, for use of consistency tests to ensure dimensionality of indicators would allow researchers great insight into their data. Cliff suggested that the fit statistics no longer are meaningful, for the data would have been modified to enhance fit before the SEM analyses are even conducted. Although the problem is not one addressed in this book, the solution proposed by Cliff was one suggested earlier in this book, namely, to split the sample and to use cross-validation of the findings.

Cliff's (1983) criticisms provided a very important context, for they reminded SEM researchers that there is no magic in their methods and that their structural equation models need to stand up to scrutiny on a number of dimensions. Actively working to address the four principles articulated should prepare researchers for the review process, for issues of causal ordering, operationalization, model disconfirmation, and model modification all are central to preparation of a manuscript using latent variable SEM approaches.

A second commonly cited criticism came from Breckler (1990). Breckler focused on five problems that he argued are (or at least were) widespread in the SEM literature. Those problems, which overlap somewhat with Cliff (1983), are (a) problems due to violations of distributional assumptions underlying SEM techniques, (b) problems tied to the existence of alternative models, (c) both developing and "confirming" models with a single set of data, (d) model modification unaccompanied by cross-validation, and (e) poorly justified causal inferences. In part, Breckler's criticisms reflect changing practices within the emerging SEM field, for the field changed rapidly during the time period he covered (1977-1987) in his review. For example, there was a time when "causal modeling" was an accepted description of what now is called structural equation modeling. From my perspective, that issue is not primarily one of beliefs about causality but rather an issue of culture and change—using terminology and style that may be accepted at one time but that is later changed. I would expect that SEM approaches would fare better if more recent studies were examined. Not only are the methods better understood and more carefully used today, but continued development of computer software and SEM methods makes it easier to test for distributional assumptions and to control model modification problems. At the same time, many researchers still are using SEM approaches because they are told they need to use them, even if their understanding is far from perfect.

Breckler's (1990) review of literature in the area of personality and social psychology found many suboptimal uses of SEM methods. According to Breckler, only a small proportion of articles reported examining their data for multivariate normality, many provided only incomplete information on model fit and on prediction of specific variables, and virtually all failed to discuss the existence of equivalent models. Consistent with Cliff's (1983) ex post facto criticism, Breckler found SEM researchers to both develop and test models on a single data set, mostly without cross-validation; many seem to have used post hoc model modifications to improve overall model fit, again without cross-validation. Finally, Breckler found that some researchers used causal language inappropriately. Overall, then, Breckler's criticisms still provide a helpful guide for researchers as they use SEM techniques and prepare SEM manuscripts.

EXERCISE

Readers are encouraged to select articles from their disciplines and see how they fare by Cliff's (1983) four principles and Breckler's (1990) five problems.

▌ *"External" Critics*

As many readers may have discovered in discussing SEM techniques with colleagues and friends, there are many social science researchers who are very skeptical about SEM approaches. Some of these skeptics are simplistic in their views, clinging dogmatically to the phrase "Correlation does not imply causation" or dismissing the techniques due to limitations of manifest path models. Beyond such skeptics, however, is a much more sophisticated group that views SEM techniques negatively (e.g., Baumrind, 1983; Ling, 1982). This group's position can be illustrated by Ling (1982) in his review of Kenny's (1979) book, *Correlation and Causation*. Ling (1982) stated,

> The author of this book holds the view . . . that causal inference from correlational data . . . is a valid form of statistical and scientific inference. My view has been that the methods and techniques, developed and applied under that premise, for causal inference . . . are at best a form of statistical fantasy. (pp. 489-490)

He went on to describe SEM approaches as "a class of pseudo-black-magic methods" (p. 491). Ling's is a very traditional view that still is held by many statisticians.

Baumrind (1983) took a somewhat more moderate position, one driven by traditional conceptions of cause and effect. Her view is that causality claims from SEM techniques markedly exceed the capacity of the methods to speak about causal mechanisms. Her criticisms were driven by (a) failure to dismiss alternative models (SEM theorists agree, e.g., MacCallum, Wegener, Uchino, & Fabrigar, 1993 noted that fit alone never can justify accepting a model, for there will be alternative models that fit the data equally well), (b) incompletely specified models ("First there must be a viable causal hypothesis to model" [p. 1296]), and (c) the often weak nature of relationships uncovered by SEM techniques.

Well, so perhaps I should have warned readers earlier so that they could prepare themselves for the shortcomings of the methods of fantasy that I have been attempting to explain. But, of course, I did; as noted in Chapter 1, there is a range of views about SEM techniques, and many perspectives differ from Ling's (1982) and Baumrind's (1983) views in prominent ways. From my perspective, different views are driven in large part by one's views about the role of methods in supporting and extending theory development. From a view driven purely by methods, Ling's position is not surprising, for methods provide no way in which to distinguish among mathematically equivalent models. Also, from a traditional experimentalist perspective, SEM techniques will not provide what experiments can provide.

When theory is added to the methods, however, a different purpose appears, for there are opportunities (a) to disconfirm a hypothesized model (and its identical alternative models) and (b) to distinguish among competing theoretical models that are nonequivalent. Said differently, the greatest strength of SEM techniques draws from the fact that they need to be driven by theory, not by the statistical techniques that provide methods for the theories.

Most fundamental is that correlational data potentially provide an opportunity to address issues of causation, even if primarily through model disconfirmation. Researchers with correlational data collect those data for reasons tied to implicit conceptual models. They should be encouraged to articulate the causal processes that they think underlie their reasons for selecting the variables that they chose to study and that led them to collect the measures that they did. Once those processes are articulated, their plausibility can be examined.

In general, however, the debate will continue, within both the SEM community and the broader research community. My expectation is that over time, as these techniques are used and corroborated (or not) through complementary methods (e.g., intervention research, experimental designs), their ultimate value will emerge. Then, social scientists can determine whether or not they were a boon, a curse, or somewhere in between.

In summary, there are criticisms of which readers need to be aware, for readers inevitably will encounter them in some form. None of the criticisms provides a reason for SEM techniques to be totally discarded as inappropriate. Rather, they provide different philosophies about ways in which to use available data plus guidance about ways in which to use SEM approaches effectively.

Emerging Criticisms

One area that may well emerge as a new area of controversy for SEM researchers is the balance between overall model fit and significance of particular path coefficients. The emphasis on overall model fit has potentially negative consequences in that, first, it encourages researchers to overfit their data to attain the best possible fit and, second, it distracts attention from the most important coefficients by embedding and judging their worth in broader fit tests. For the first point, there is the distinct possibility that the model that fits best in a single sample will not fit best in a second sample. This is true regardless of how much an investigator tinkers with a model trying to make it fit, due simply to the nature of sampling. Second, often differences among models can have little to do with the relationships that led researchers to look at the data using SEM techniques. That is, lack of fit in some instances may be independent of the primary hypotheses. In the worst possible case, researchers could reject models that accurately specify important relationships because the overall model does not fit. Critics of model fitting might argue that the SEM field has not adapted enough from experimental research about partitioning variance and accepting residual/unexplained variance.

◼ Post Hoc Model Modification

A second issue that has not received a great deal of attention thus far in this book is the issue of modifying models. From one perspective, model modification must not be too bad, for the SEM computer programs typically include first derivatives, modification indices, and Lagrange multiplier tests as part of the output; the information given by these indexes assists researchers in finding ways in which to modify their models that will improve fit (for current thinking about model modification, see, e.g., MacCallum, 1995). The LISREL program even offers unrestricted automatic model modification as an option. Jöreskog (1993), for example, distinguished among three situations— strictly confirmatory, alternative models, and model generating—and suggested that model generating is the most common.

From a perspective more like Cliff's (1983), however, model modification is a substantial shift from the confirmatory intent of latent variable SEM approaches. The most conservative position is that models should be purely confirmatory and not modified except perhaps to help plan the next study. If one begins from a purely confirmatory perspective, then cross-validation through sample splitting and a priori specification of alternative models are ways of allowing some model modification while maintaining the basic confirmatory intent.

Although any discussion attempting to find a preferable course of action can focus on researcher values, there is a second component of this discussion, an empirical one: Can model modification help researchers to find more accurate models? If the answer is a definitive *no*, then the issue is moot. If it is *yes, always*, then the criticism is in principle correct but impractical and counterproductive. If it is somewhere in between, then preferences are likely to be driven by differing researcher values.

The answer to the question of accuracy of model modification in recovering "true" models seems to be that, in general, modifying models is all too likely *not* to be helpful. This answer was provided first by Costner and Schoenberg (1973) for multiple-indicator models, reinforced by MacCallum (1986), and then reaffirmed more strongly by MacCallum, Roznowski, and Necowitz (1992). These studies found that it is difficult to modify misspecified models in ways that move closer to "true" models; their data definitely argue against nontheoretical searches and even for exercising great caution in conducting theory-guided modification. MacCallum et al. (1992) recommended setting forth multiple models a priori to avoid post hoc data fitting modifications. MacCallum (1986), in addition, suggested that any modifications need "rigorous substantive justification" (p. 118) and that, without a good starting model, modification is likely to lead one astray.

From my perspective, a conservative approach to model modification is best. If a researcher anticipates needing model modification due to much uncertainty about causal processes in the literature, then data should be collected with modification in mind. Practically, what that means is that a large enough sample should be collected so that it can be split. Half can be used for model modification and the other half held back to use for cross-validation. MacCallum, Roznowski, Mar, and Reith (1994) provided strategies for cross-validation. Even this approach using cross-validation, however, has weaknesses. The most likely problem (which, based on studies such as Costner and Schoenberg [1973] is a fairly good possibility) is that the modifications will produce improvements in fit from the original model but *not* result in finding the true model. Instead, what is found is one of the many alternative models whose fit approximates the fit of the true model and which may be overfitted. In such instances, examining the modified model on the cross-validation sample will yield a poorer fit than the original sample but one that is improved from the a priori model.

So what should readers conclude? If Jöreskog (1993) was correct, then using SEM techniques for model generation is a common instance, yet one open to potential criticism. If a much more conservative position is taken, then refinement of theoretical models might take many data sets and much time. Clearly, being conservative has fewer pitfalls but may move progress more slowly in a field where modeling is not very sophisticated. If readers opt for speed and decide to risk the greater potential for incorrect inferences and inaccurate models, then they should follow a procedure such as the one suggested by Jöreskog (1993). That procedure includes cross-validation through sample splitting and use of Cudeck and Browne's (1983) expected cross-validation index.

Topics Not Covered

What remains is an array of topics and issues that range from ways of operationalizing different types of models to ways of dealing with different types of data. Many of these issues defy short and simple description and will only be mentioned (and references that address them cited) so that readers facing these situations can find the resources that will help them.

Power Analysis

Research on power analysis of covariance structures still is developing. Cohen (1992) addressed general issues of power in a straightforward fashion. MacCallum, Browne, and Sugawara (1996) focused specifically on power and sample size for structural equation analysis.

Nonlinear Relationships

Readers may encounter circumstances in which they want to posit relationships that are other than linear, for example, that are hypothesized to take a quadratic form. MacCallum and Mar (1995), for example, discussed multiplicative and quadratic models and ways in which to distinguish between them. At a more general level, Kenny and Judd (1984) provided a discussion of how to model nonlinear effects in latent variable models (see also Yalcin & Amemiya, 1993). Kenny and Judd (1984) also addressed a related issue, that of how to model interaction effects. More recently, Jaccard and Wan (1996) provided an accessible source for modeling interactions in latent variable models (see also Jaccard & Wan, 1995; Ping, 1995).

Interaction effects are of particular interest in SEM approaches, for there are many instances in which moderator effects have been hypothesized and moderator effects are modeled as interactions, namely, as product terms (see also Baron & Kenny, 1986).[21] To test for moderator effects, the interaction of two variables is included along with the two variables that interact in the structural model. For observed variable models, inclusion of interaction terms is fairly straightforward, but interactions become more complex when multiple indicators are present. For an approach dealing with interactions for multiple-indicator latent variables, see Jaccard and Wan (1996). One potential concern to attend to when including nonlinear components or interactions in models is collinearity; in many instances, interaction terms are strongly related to the two variables whose interaction is included in the model.

Alternative Estimation Techniques

This book has focused on the basic methods of SEM, assuming ordinary least squares and maximum likelihood estimation. There are a number of alternative ways in which to estimate coefficients from latent variable SEMs (for an illustration, see, e.g., Stein, Smith, Guy, & Bentler, 1993). They include generalized least squares, unweighted least squares, generally weighted least squares, diagonally weighted least squares, and asymptotic distribution-free estimators. The first two are, in general, similar to maximum likelihood in their requirements and properties but yield fit statistics that perform less well than maximum likelihood statistics (e.g., Hu & Bentler, 1995). The latter three differ in that they provide estimation procedures that do not require multivariate normality in the data. At the same time, work on fit statistics has found that the distribution-free estimators, in comparison to maximum likelihood estimates, have not produced estimates with desirable properties, particularly in small samples (Hu & Bentler, 1995). Therefore, at the present time, assuming that one's data do not strongly violate an assumption of multivariate normality, one seems to lose little by staying with maximum likelihood estimates (see also Bentler & Dudgeon, 1996). The caveat, however, is that

---

21. In certain circumstances, moderator variables also may be modeled as nonlinear effects (see Baron & Kenny, 1986).

there currently is substantial research being done on fit statistics that may change the recommended course of action.

Analysis of Noncontinuous Variables

The approaches described have assumed that the variables collected have been continuous. If they are dichotomous, ordered categorical, or polychotomous, then regular covariance matrices should not be analyzed, but parallel methods exist. (Readers may want to think back to the discussion of using demographic variables such as race/ethnicity or gender in models; those will be dichotomous.) These techniques have been developed primarily by Muthen (1984, 1993). Options now provided by the mainstream computer programs for SEM analysis can analyze tetrachoric or polychoric matrices, but the sample size needed tends to be greater than that needed with continuous data. For example, in LISREL the PRELIS program will generate different matrices for analysis. Researchers with these types of data are strongly encouraged to read the articles of Muthen and others.

Adding Analysis of Means

In an earlier chapter, the possibility of adding analysis of means to SEM programs was mentioned. As also noted then, adding means to the analysis requires a different type of matrix to be analyzed, namely, one that has information about the means of the observed measures as well as the covariance structure. That type of matrix is called an augmented moment matrix and contains a vector of means along with a covariance matrix. Recent versions of SEM programs (e.g., PRELIS with LISREL 8) will generate such a matrix, making it much easier to model means. A recent treatment of how to use SEM as an alternative to multiple analysis of variance for modeling multivariate means was provided by Cole, Maxwell, Arvey, and Salas (1993).

Multilevel Structural Equation Modeling

Recently, there has been work on approaches that parallel hierarchical linear modeling (e.g., Bryk & Raudenbush, 1992). These approaches attempt to partition variance at different levels. For example, in a study of student performance, there are impacts at the level of teachers (class level) as well as at the level of students (individual level). This work still is emerging and may change appreciably as it is developed (see, e.g., McArdle & Hamagami, 1996; Muthen, 1994).

Writing Up Papers Containing Structural Equation Modeling Analysis

In addition to looking at existing papers and articles in one's field for guidance in selecting statistical information to report and to present results, there are two articles that should prove helpful to readers new to SEM. For technical issues, see Hoyle and Panter (1995). For more general issues, see Raykov, Tomer, and Nesselroade (1991) as well as Hoyle and Panter (1995).

Selecting a Computer Program to Do Latent Variable Structural Equation Modeling

An ever-increasing number of SEM programs are available. I admit that, like an old dog with new tricks, I have been content to try to keep up with the changes in the program I first learned to use— LISREL. Changes have been fairly frequent, most recently with the introduction of an equation-based version, SIMPLIS, in LISREL 8. Unfortunately, I have not stayed abreast of the array of alternative programs. I recently looked at a demo copy of EQS, the other program I had used at various times in the past. For me, the conclusion was the same as my earlier one, namely, that it still seems easier to use for some problems and harder for others. Its nicest feature is the capacity to work off diagrams created within the program in a drawing program. My most recent version of LISREL provides a diagram and allows one to work off it once the program runs but does not start with a drawing option.

A number of other programs are available varying in ease of use, flexibility, options offered, and, perhaps of greatest importance to many, price. Readers who use SPSS may want to learn AMOS (e.g., Arbuckle, 1994, 1997), for it will be replacing LISREL in the SPSS line of products. It is equation based like EQS and also runs from a diagram created by users. I have used the AMOS diagramming options to prepare many of the figures presented in this book, and I recommend it highly. It was easy to pick up and produce diagrams of high quality. AMOS will read SPSS system files, providing a nice interface for SPSS users. Readers who want to compare the command statements from LISREL, EQS, and AMOS should revisit Appendix 9.2. In so doing, they need to remember that if the diagramming option is chosen for EQS or AMOS, then the control statements are not needed. MX is another SEM program. I have not used it because I already have an SEM program. For new users, however, one advantage is that it can be downloaded for use from a World Wide Web site (http://opal.vcu.edu/html/mx/mxhomepage.html). Finally, one other frequently used SEM program is EZPATH (Steiger, 1989), which is tied to the statistical package SYSTAT.[22]

For readers who want to peruse the full range of alternatives, a review of seven different SEM programs is provided by Waller (1993) for confirmatory factor analysis. Another recent review of EQS, LISREL, and AMOS can be found in Hox (1995), and a very recent and comprehensive discussion of various programs appears in the preface of Hayduk (1996). Waller also is working on a current review. Another source of information is the Internet group SEMNET, which carries a range of information, varying from basic to advanced, about SEM issues. Beware, however, that the group is very active and will deluge you with e-mail.

As readers work with SEM techniques, they will likely need to update and broaden their knowledge about SEM techniques and applications. SEM techniques currently are very popular, and there is a very active group of methodologists and statisticians who are continuing to refine and develop structural equation methods. Readers might follow the work of names that have come up repeatedly through this book. Although listing names inevitably will be incomplete due to omissions and my ignorance, examples of names to track include Jöreskog, Sörbom, Muthen, Bentler, Arbuckle, Miller, Browne, Bollen, Hayduk, Byrne, Cudeck, and Mulaik. Finally, there is a fairly new journal devoted to structural equation models called *Structural Equation Modeling*. It includes a teacher's corner with information and annotated bibliographies of SEM literature.

Good luck, structural equation modelers!

---

22. As I was making final revisions, Michael Browne provided me with a copy of Kano's 1997 *Behaviormetrika* paper (24, 85-125) titled "Software." It provides descriptions by program authors of seven SEM programs—AMOS, COSAN, EQS, LISREL, MECOSA, RAMONA, and SEPATH—and is highly recommended for readers trying to select a program to use.

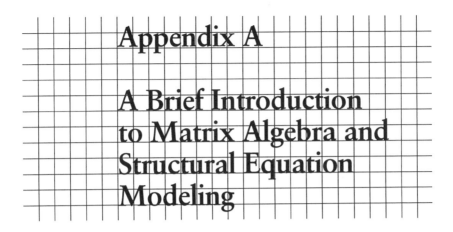

Appendix A

A Brief Introduction to Matrix Algebra and Structural Equation Modeling

$\mathbf{M}$atrix algebra provides a way in which to represent multiple equations in a form that both consolidates information and allows efficient data analysis. By working with matrices, mathematical operations can be expressed in a compact fashion. Finally, with respect to structural equation modeling (SEM) and regression approaches, matrix algebra simplifies and makes more accessible the mathematic operations that are used. (Readers searching for a second source on matrix algebra could see Kerlinger & Pedhazur, 1973.)

▌ What Is a Matrix?

A matrix is an $m \times n$ rectangle containing numbers, symbols that stand for numbers, or variable names. The order of the matrix is m rows by n columns. For example, a 2×3 matrix has two rows and three columns. To illustrate,

	Column 1	Column 2	Column 3
Row 1	(1,1)	(1,2)	(1,3)
Row 2	(2,1)	(2,2)	(2,3)

The pairs of numbers in parentheses are *not* intended to be values; rather, they represent the coordinates of each element of the matrix. For example, the (row 1, column 1) element will be located where (1, 1) is in the matrix. In other words, the coordinates first give the number of the row of any element and then give the number of the column of that element. The coordinates of elements are important for a number of reasons, including (a) they often may be used as subscripts for unknown coefficients (e.g., b_{12}), (b) they can be used to identify the variables that are being related (e.g., r_{21}), and (c) they are used in some SEM programs to specify parameters to be estimated in matrices used by those programs.

A 2 × 3 matrix with values rather than coordinates would look like

$$\text{Matrix } B = \begin{vmatrix} 5 & 3 & 7 \\ 6 & 2 & 8 \end{vmatrix}.$$

With labels for rows and columns, it would look like

$$\begin{array}{l} \text{Column: 1 2 3} \\ \text{Row: } 1 \begin{vmatrix} 5 & 3 & 7 \\ 2 & 6 & 2 & 8 \end{vmatrix}. \end{array}$$

So, for example, the value of the (row 1, column 2) element, namely, (1, 2) in the preceding instance, is 3. A special case of a matrix is one called a **null matrix**, which contains only 0's.

Sometimes the matrix may totally contain algebraic representations of the elements, for example, using subscripts ij where i represents the row coordinate and j the column coordinate. The preceding 2 × 3 matrix could be presented as

$$\text{Matrix } B = \begin{vmatrix} b_{11} & b_{12} & b_{13} \\ b_{21} & b_{22} & b_{23} \end{vmatrix}$$

In the example, $b_{21} = 6$ and $b_{23} = 8$.

In SEM analyses, each row corresponds to a **dependent** or **endogenous** variable. That is, each dependent variable has its own equation, which is a row. By contrast, columns correspond to predictor variables, which may be either exogenous or endogenous. Thus, if we have a system of structural equations containing three dependent variables, then matrix representations of those equations would require matrices with three rows. The number of columns in a matrix containing the SEM path (regression) coefficients would be the sum of the number of (a) exogenous or independent variables that were in the equations and (b) endogenous variables (sometimes limited to endogenous variables that are used to predict other endogenous variables).

If a matrix has either one row or one column, then it is called a **vector**. Vectors are used regularly to present variables and residuals. If, for example, our endogenous variables were peer popularity and achievement, then a vector for those variables would be

$$\left| \begin{matrix} \text{Peer Popularity} \\ \text{Achievement} \end{matrix} \right|.$$

The vector has two rows and one column. Vectors also can have only a single row plus multiple columns.

A common matrix operation is one that turns a matrix on its side by turning rows into columns and columns into rows. It is called taking the **transpose** of a matrix. If we were to take the transpose of Matrix B in the preceding, then the new matrix (B'), using the elements as labeled previously, would be

$$\text{Matrix } B' = \left| \begin{matrix} b_{11}\, b_{21} \\ b_{12}\, b_{22} \\ b_{13}\, b_{23} \end{matrix} \right| = \left| \begin{matrix} 5\ 6 \\ 3\ 2 \\ 7\ 8 \end{matrix} \right|.$$

Note that the elements with two identical subscripts do not move, whereas the others move "around the diagonal." What formerly was the (row 1, column 3) element (b_{13}) now is found in the third row but first column. It has kept its "old" coordinates, so it still is b_{13}. Of course, if we were to give the elements of the transpose new coordinates, then those would correspond to the new rows and columns and b_{13} would become b_{31}, reflecting its new row and column coordinates.

Square matrices. If the numbers of rows and columns are identical, then the matrix is called **square**. For square matrices, the set of elements running from the upper left-hand corner of the matrix to the lower right-hand corner is called the **diagonal**. In terms of coordinates, the diagonal is made up of elements that have two identical coordinates (e.g., r_{11}). If the only nonzero elements of a matrix are found on the diagonal, then the matrix is called a **diagonal matrix**.

Symmetric (square) matrices. Matrices like correlation and covariance matrices are called **symmetric**. Rows and columns are defined by the same variables in the same order, and the matrices have the same elements above the diagonal as below the diagonal except that the elements are transposed. All correlation matrices or covariance matrices have to be both square and symmetric. Here is an example of a symmetric matrix:

$$R = \begin{vmatrix} 1.00 & .71 & .45 \\ .71 & .00 & .32 \\ .45 & .32 & 1.00 \end{vmatrix}.$$

Note that (2, 1) equals (1, 2), that (3, 1) equals (1, 3), and that (3, 2) equals (2, 3).

Identity matrices. A special form of a diagonal symmetric matrix is an **identity matrix**. It contains 1's on the diagonal and 0's (by its definition as diagonal) everywhere else. It is designated by I. A 3×3 diagonal matrix would be

$$I = \begin{vmatrix} 1 & 0 & 0 \\ 0 & 1 & 0 \\ 0 & 0 & 1 \end{vmatrix}.$$

The identity matrix serves the same function as the number 1; anything multiplied by I equals itself. So, if Matrix A were to be multiplied by I, then the result would be A. In other words,

$$AI = IA = A.$$

▌ Matrix Operations

There are three basic matrix operations.

1. Multiplying a Matrix Times a Single Number (or **scalar**)

The result is that each element of the matrix is multiplied times that number. So, if Matrix B in the preceding discussion were multiplied times the number 3, then each element would be three times larger. For example, b_{12} would now be $3 \times b_{12}$, or $3b_{12}$.

2. Taking the Sum of (or difference between) Two Matrices

For two matrices to be summed, those matrices have to be the same size, that is, have identical numbers of rows and columns. If they are the same size, then each will have the same number of elements. Addition and subtraction are done by combining corresponding elements of the matrices on an element-by-element basis. So, for example, imagine that we want to add together Matrices C and D, where

$$C = \begin{vmatrix} 4 & 3 & 6 \\ 1 & 5 & 7 \end{vmatrix} \text{ and } D = \begin{vmatrix} 2 & 1 & 8 \\ 0 & 9 & 3 \end{vmatrix}$$

$C + D =$

$$\begin{vmatrix} 4 & 3 & 6 \\ 1 & 5 & 7 \end{vmatrix} + \begin{vmatrix} 2 & 1 & 8 \\ 0 & 9 & 3 \end{vmatrix} = \begin{vmatrix} (4+2) & (3+1) & (6+8) \\ (1+0) & (5+9) & (7+3) \end{vmatrix} = \begin{vmatrix} 6 & 4 & 14 \\ 1 & 14 & 10 \end{vmatrix}.$$

If we were subtracting D from C, then we would be doing the equivalent of multiplying each element in D by a -1 (described earlier as Operation 1), which would change the signs of each of the elements of D, and then adding the corresponding elements together. So, $(1, 1)$ would be $4 + (-2)$ rather than $4 + 2$ when C and D are summed. For addition and subtraction, the rules are simply that (a) the matrices have to be the same size and (b) corresponding elements in the two matrices must be combined.

3. Multiplying Two Matrices Together

Multiplication of matrices is addressed in two steps. First, the conditions under which multiplication can be done are described. Second, the mechanics of matrix multiplication are explained.

When multiplication is possible. To be able to multiply two matrices together, the first matrix (or that which appears on the left) needs to have a number of columns equivalent to the number of rows of the second (or right) matrix. The rows of the first matrix and columns of the second matrix define the size of the resulting matrix. If we were trying to multiply Matrix E $(r \times s)$ times Matrix F $(t \times u)$, E with r rows and s columns and F with t rows and u columns, then s must equal t, and the resulting matrix has dimensions of r by u. Ordering of the matrices is very important, for Matrix E times Matrix F is not the same as F times E. To multiply F times E, r would have to equal u. If they are not equal, then even though it is possible to compute $E \times F$, it is not possible to compute $F \times E$ using matrix algebra. One way in which to do notation is to put the number of rows in a matrix to the left of the matrix name and the number of rows to the right, as $_rE_s \times _tF_u$. In such notation, s and t can be compared readily.

For example, can we multiply E (3×2) times F (2×3), or $_3E_2 \times _2F_3$? Yes, for E has two columns and F has two rows, so the requirement is met. As stated, the matrix that is the product $E \times F$ will have the same number of rows as E and columns as F and will be 3×3, the "outside" numbers in $_3E_2 \times _2F_3$. Illustrating the differences between $E \times F$ and $F \times E$ is simple; $F \times E$ also could be computed, but the result would be a 2×2 matrix. If G were substituted for F and was 2×4, then $E \times G$ could be calculated, for the two columns of E correspond to the two rows of G. By contrast, $G \times E$ cannot be computed, for G's four columns do not align with E's three rows.

Computations for matrix algebra. In matrix multiplication, the row elements from the first matrix are multiplied by their corresponding column elements from the second matrix. What that means concretely can best be explained through illustration. Matrix E (3×2) and Matrix F (2×3) will be multiplied:

$$E = \begin{vmatrix} 1 & 2 \\ 2 & 3 \\ 4 & 1 \end{vmatrix} \text{ and } F = \begin{vmatrix} 3 & 4 & 2 \\ 2 & 5 & 1 \end{vmatrix}.$$

For any element (i, j) of the resulting product matrix, the elements of row i from E are combined with the elements of column j from F. So,

$$\begin{vmatrix} 1 & 2 \\ 2 & 3 \\ 4 & 1 \end{vmatrix} \times \begin{vmatrix} 3 & 4 & 2 \\ 2 & 5 & 1 \end{vmatrix} = \begin{vmatrix} 7 & 14 & 4 \\ 12 & 23 & 7 \\ 14 & 21 & 9 \end{vmatrix}.$$

For example, element $(1, 1)$ in the product matrix is determined by multiplying the elements of the first row of E by the elements of the first column of F. Element $(1, 1)$ is $[(1 \times 3) + (2 \times 2)] = 7$, where (1×3) is (first row, first element of first matrix) times (first column, first element of second matrix) and (2×2) is (first row, second element of first matrix) times (first column, second element of second matrix).

$$
\begin{vmatrix} 1\ 2 \\ 2\ 3 \\ 4\ 1 \end{vmatrix} \times \begin{vmatrix} 3\ 4\ 2 \\ 2\ 5\ 1 \end{vmatrix} = \begin{vmatrix} 7\ 14\ 4 \\ 12\ 23\ 7 \\ 14\ 21\ 9 \end{vmatrix}.
$$

Elements of row 1 in the resulting matrix all use the first-row elements from Matrix E but combine with the corresponding values from the columns of F.

Illustrations are done for elements (2, 2) and (3, 1) of $E \times F$. Element (2, 2) uses the second row of E and the second column of F; thus, $23 = (2 \times 4) + (3 \times 5)$, where 2 is the first element of the second row of E, 4 is the first element of the third column of F, 3 is the second element of the second row of E, and 5 is the second element of the third column of F.

$$
\begin{vmatrix} 1\ 2 \\ 2\ 3 \\ 4\ 1 \end{vmatrix} \times \begin{vmatrix} 3\ 4\ 2 \\ 2\ 5\ 1 \end{vmatrix} = \begin{vmatrix} 7\ 14\ 4 \\ 12\ 23\ 7 \\ 14\ 21\ 9 \end{vmatrix}.
$$

Element (3, 1) uses the third row of E and the first column of F; thus, $14 = (4 \times 3) + (1 \times 2)$.

$$
\begin{vmatrix} 1\ 2 \\ 2\ 3 \\ 4\ 1 \end{vmatrix} \times \begin{vmatrix} 3\ 4\ 2 \\ 2\ 5\ 1 \end{vmatrix} = \begin{vmatrix} 7\ 14\ 4 \\ 12\ 23\ 7 \\ 14\ 21\ 9 \end{vmatrix}.
$$

Up to this point, nothing has been said about division of matrices, and for good reason. In fact, division cannot be done. The closest thing to division is multiplying a matrix times the inverse of some matrix, where the inverse is analogous to a reciprocal of a number. The discussion of collinearity in this book centers around issues tied to invertibility, for correlation or covariance matrices with perfect collinearity have no inverse (are not invertible), and regression approaches cannot produce a valid solution.

Inverting Matrices

By definition, an **inverse** of a Matrix H, written as H^{-1}, is the matrix that, when multiplied times another matrix, yields an identity matrix. That is, $H^{-1}H = I$. Because I matrices always are square, only square matrices can have inverses. At the same time, as already noted, many square matrices do not have inverses. Those that do not have inverses cause problems for SEM analyses.

Specifically, if there exists a Matrix B such that $A \times B = I$, then A is said to be **nonsingular** or invertible and B is the inverse of A. Similarly, B is nonsingular and A is its inverse (in this case, $A \times B = B \times A = I$). Because calculating inverses is complicated and tedious, details are not provided here. Most important, standard statistical packages calculate inverses in regression and factor analysis programs, and often they offer inverses and **determinants**, which are described next, as optional output. As is explained in the text, the diagonal elements of inverses of correlation matrices provide information about collinearity among variables.

▌ *Determinants*

Determinants are a single numerical value associated with any square matrix. Mathematics of calculating inverses is not covered here, for as matrices get larger, the calculations get more complex and more difficult to illustrate. Readers interested in attaining a fuller understanding should consult a book on matrices or matrix algebra (e.g., Marcus & Minc, 1964).

For the simplest case, a 2×2 matrix, calculation is fairly simple. Consider Matrix A:

$$A = \begin{vmatrix} a & b \\ c & d \end{vmatrix}.$$

The determinant is $(a \times d) - (b \times c)$.

$$\text{So, if } A = \begin{vmatrix} 3 & 1 \\ 2 & 5 \end{vmatrix},$$

then its determinant is $(3 \times 5) - (2 \times 1) = 13$.

For correlation matrices, the determinant will range between 1 (if all variables are totally uncorrelated) and 0 (if there is perfect collinearity between one or more variables). If a determinant is very close to 0, then there must be substantial relationships between variables, and the data should be examined to look for problems tied to collinearity.

▌ *Matrices and Rules*

Finally, a brief reminder about how some common rules apply to matrices:

Commutative: $A + B = B + A$; however, $A \times B$ and $B \times A$ are not
    equal except in special circumstances
Associative: $A + (B + C) = (A + B) + C$; $A(BC) = (AB)C$
Distributive: $A(B + C) = AB + AC$; $(B + C)A = BA + CA$
Distributing Transposes: $(AB)' = B'A'$
    (note that the order of elements is reversed).

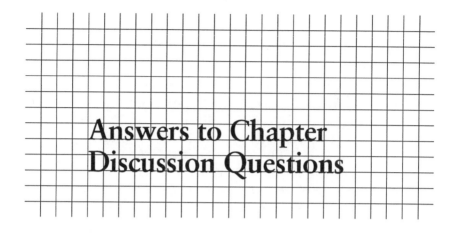

Answers to Chapter Discussion Questions

■ CHAPTER 1

1. Yes, remembering that dichotomous and ordered categorical measures can fall under the class of quantitative data.
2. Yes, provided sample size issues are addressed. That is, some time series analyses and other analyses at aggregated levels can have samples too small for these methods.
3. No, moderation implies an interaction type of effect between variables. Chapter 12 will address moderating effects.
4. Equivalent models are those that predict the exact same pattern of relationships between measures. For example, Job— Success— Family is mathematically equivalent to Figure 1.2, as is Success causing both Family and Job, for they predict the relationship between Family and Job to be the product of the other two correlations. Because the models always start with theory, one should have chosen a model from among equivalent ones that matches the hypothesized relationships. That of course does not make the model correct, but it affirms plausibility of the theory.

■ CHAPTER 2

1. Yes, technically speaking, path analysis always uses standardized data.

2. Yes, for identified or over-identified models, multiple regression yields optimal estimates. Yes, path coefficients are partial regression coefficients.

3. Again speaking technically, *no*, for when data are longitudinal, covariance matrices need to be analyzed. On the other hand, if nonstandardized coefficients are examined, then regression techniques can be used to analyze longitudinal data. (Those coefficients sometimes were called path regression coefficients in the path analysis literature.).

4. Degrees of freedom for path models are determined by the number of pieces of information that are available to use for solving for path coefficients. In the same way that subjects are bits of information for many analyses, each correlation (covariance) is one piece of information for path models. Each path to be estimated "uses up" a degree of freedom, so eliminating a path "puts back" a degree of freedom in the model. Degrees of freedom provide the opportunity for models to diverge from the data, and therefore allow the possibility of model disconfirmation.

5. Under-identified models *cannot* be solved. If their plausibility is of interest, they need to be reconceptualized to make them identified.

6. Surprisingly, the answer is Yes, even though there are few cases in which they are appropriate, for they are far inferior to the latent variable structural equation techniques described later in this book.

■ CHAPTER 3

1. Because path analysis is regression analysis, it analyzes correlation or covariance matrices that are used in regression analysis.

2. Partial correlation attempts to completely eliminate the relationships of the controlled variable with the remaining variables and their relationships with one another, while partial regression attempts to spread common variance across the various predictors. Partial correlation would be picked to look at residual relationships after removing some variable or variables.

3. Although path analysis approaches do not formally talk about working with partial correlation matrices, there may be instances in which, due to sample size limitations, control variables like age or gender would need to be partialed out so the sample is sufficient for SEM techniques. Remember, however, that decisions to partial need to be guided theoretically, and therefore likely should not be done if the variable to be partialed is expected to display different causal structures at different levels.

4. The signs of the nonstandardized coefficients will be the same as the standardized coefficients, and the nonstandardized values are very descriptive insofar as they describe the relationship in raw score units. For example, we could say that for every year (1 raw score unit) of education "produces" an X dollar (raw score units) increase in expected annual earnings.

5. Stepwise regression can be guided by theory, and is when used for decomposing effects. If it is not, yes, it can be misleading. Remember, however, that at the last step of the regression analysis, if all variables are entered into the equation, the order of entry used does not matter; all orders of entry yield the same final outcome provided the same variables are in the equation.

6. Yes, the logic of decomposition of effects is the same across all different types of SEM techniques.

7. The matrix form is very appealing, for it works for over-identified as well as just-identified models. The other approaches work as well, requiring that coefficients that are omitted from the model take on a value of 0.

8. ANOVAs are not used, although path analysis can be used to model experimental studies. Path modeling can be particularly effective if some variable is viewed as a mediating variable. There it can be used to test plausibility of a mediation model. It also can be valuable if there are questions about the conceptual variable that is being assessed by some independent or dependent variable. It may be possible to use SEM techniques to aggregate measures into conceptual variables.

CHAPTER 5

1. The information on variability within the sample is very important, and it is lost in converting to correlations. Of course the tradeoff is that a correlation metric (ranging from −1 to 1, the meaning of r^2, etc.) is so intuitive.

2. Here, if we are talking about assumptions of regression, viz., independence of residuals, then we are thinking only about path analysis models. Other path models can allow residuals to covary, which is why it is tricky to talk about "too much non-random error" as a violation of an assumption. Whether or not assuming residuals to be independent is reasonable is a question that begins with theory but then is "tested" by data. As will be explained later, tests of fit are all based upon residuals, the part of relationships that are not accounted for by models. Sometimes, it will be obvious by looking at a correlation matrix that a hypothesized model will not fit. For example, if a set of four measures is hypothesized as assessing a single construct, but two of the measures have a correlation twice that of all the others, it is clear that a single factor model will not work well. Other times, the pattern of relationships will be more complicated, and can be examined only through looking at the residual matrix and the measures of model fit.

3. To go from standardized to nonstandardized coefficients or vice versa, it is the standard deviations, not the standard errors, that are used. Yes, there is a fairly simple conversion from one to the other that requires only dividing by (or multiplying by) a ratio of two standard deviations. There has been a controversy in the literature about the meaning of standardized versus nonstandardized coefficients and how to explain that difference. From my perspective, it is most important to think of it conceptually. Standardized coefficients describe relations in standard deviation units, whereas nonstandardized coefficients describe relations in real raw score units.

4. Decisions about relationships between methods should be driven at the data collection stage. It seems to me that the ideal answer is "*no*," that it would be simpler if there was no method variance. At the same time, one needs to trade off difficulty in collecting data where methods do not exert influence on

answers versus simplicity in getting needed data. If one decides that the best decision is to collect data from measures that have method variance, then that variability needs to be modeled so variability can be adequately partitioned.

5. Systematically attending to method variability is clearly as important today as it was in the past. Using multiple methods is highly desirable. Yet, as will be described in Chapter 7, MTMM matrices produce problems of estimation in certain types of models, which reduces somewhat their value.

▌CHAPTER 6

1. Lag refers to the passage of time. The exact amount of time varies with the nature of the conceptual issues.

2. I suspect that I am guilty of accepting ways of talking about stability that do not fit with some other uses of terms, and, more importantly, I have not been as clear in my usage as I should have been. To clarify (hopefully): Stability as I have used it refers only to single variables. In the absolute sense, stability means absence of change in some variable across some time period. With respect to covariances, however, stability means only that the relative position of a group of individuals on some dimension does not change. For example, if all children in a class grew at a common rate, their height scores would all increase by a constant, and their heights at the first time (before growing) would correlate perfectly with their heights at the second time (after growing), and height would be perfectly stable. Said differently, height at time 1 perfectly predicts height at time 2. Finally, if a relationship between 2 variables is called stable, then their covariance should not have changed from some point in time to some later time.

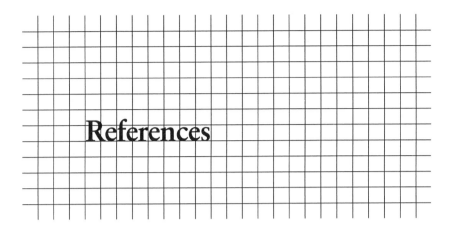

References

Akaike, H. (1987). Factor analysis and AIC. *Psychometrika, 52,* 317-332.

Arbuckle, J. L. (1994). AMOS: Analysis of moment structures. *Psychometrika, 59,* 135-137.

Arbuckle, J. L. (1997). *AMOS users' guide: Version 3.6.* Chicago: SPSS.

Bagozzi, R. P. (1991). On the use of SE models in experimental designs: Two extensions. *International Journal of Research in Marketing, 8,* 125-140.

Baron, R. M., & Kenny, D. A. (1986). The moderator-mediator variable distinction in social psychological research: Conceptual, strategic, and statistical considerations. *Journal of Personality and Social Psychology, 51,* 1173-1182.

Baumrind, D. (1983). Specious causal attributions in the social sciences: The reformulated stepping-stone theory of heroin use as exemplar. *Journal of Personality and Social Psychology, 45,* 1289-1298.

Bentler, P. M. (1989). *EQS: Structural equation manual.* Los Angeles: BMDP Statistical Software.

Bentler, P. M. (1990). Comparative fit indexes in structural models. *Psychological Bulletin, 107,* 238-246.

Bentler, P. M., & Bonett, D. G. (1980). Significance tests and goodness of fit in the analysis of covariance structures. *Psychological Bulletin, 88,* 588-606.

Bentler, P. M., & Dudgeon, P. (1996). Covariance structure analysis: Statistical practice, theory, directions. *Annual Review of Psychology, 47,* 563-592.

Blalock, H. M., Jr. (1964). *Causal inferences in non-experimental research.* Chapel Hill: University of North Carolina Press.

Bollen, K. A. (1989). A new incremental fit index for general structural equation models. *Sociological Methods & Research, 17,* 303-316.

Bollen, K. A. (1990). Overall fit in covariance structure models: Two types of sample size effects. *Psychological Bulletin, 107,* 256-259.

Bollen, K., & Lennox, R. (1991). Conventional wisdom on measurement: A structural equation perspective. *Psychological Bulletin, 110,* 305-314.

Bollen, K., & Long, J. S. (1993). *Testing structural equation models.* Newbury Park, CA: Sage.

Bozdogan, H. (1987). Model selection and Akaike's information criteria (AIC): The general theory and its analytical extensions. *Psychometrika, 52,* 345-370.

Breckler, S. J. (1990). Applications of covariance structure modeling in psychology: Cause for concern? *Psychological Bulletin, 107,* 260-273.

Brophy, J. E., & Good, T. L. (1974). *Teacher-student relationships: Causes and consequences.* New York: Holt, Rinehart & Winston.

Browne, M. W. (1984). The decomposition of multitrait-multimethod matrices. *British Journal of Mathematical and Statistical Psychology, 37,* 1-21.

Browne, M. W., & Arminger, G. (1995). Specification and estimation of mean- and covariance-structure models. In G. Arminger, C. C. Clogg, & M. E. Sobel (Eds.), *Handbook of statistical modeling for the social and behavioral sciences* (pp. 185-249). New York: Plenum.

Browne, M. W., & Cudeck, R. (1989). Single sample cross-validation indices for covariance structures. *Multivariate Behavioral Research, 24,* 445-455.

Browne, M. W., & Cudeck, R. (1993). Alternative ways of assessing model fit. In K. A. Bollen & J. S. Long (Eds.), *Testing structural equation models* (pp. 136-162). Newbury Park, CA: Sage.

Bryk, A. S., & Raudenbush, S. W. (1992). *Hierarchical linear models: Applications and research methods.* Newbury Park, CA: Sage.

Byrne, B. M. (1989). *A primer of LISREL: Basic applications and programming for confirmatory factor analysis models.* New York: Springer-Verlag.

Byrne, B. M. (1994). *Structural equation modeling with EQS and EQS/Windows: Basic concepts, applications, and programming.* Thousand Oaks, CA: Sage.

Byrne, B. M., Shavelson, R. J., & Muthen, B. (1989). Testing for the equivalence of factor covariance and mean structures: The issue of partial measurement invariance. *Psychological Bulletin, 105,* 456-466.

Byrne, D., & Griffitt, W. (1973). Interpersonal attraction. *Annual Review of Psychology, 24,* 317-336.

Calsyn, R. J., & Kenny, D. A. (1977). Self-concept of ability and perceived evaluation of others: Cause or effect of academic achievement? *Journal of Educational Psychology, 69,* 136-145.

Campbell, D. T., & Fiske, D. W. (1959). Convergent and discriminant validation by the multitrait-multimethod matrix. *Psychological Bulletin, 56,* 81-105.

Campbell, D. T., & O'Connell, E. J. (1967). Methods factors in multitrait-multimethod matrices: Multiplicative rather than additive? *Multivariate Behavioral Research, 2,* 409-426.

Cliff, N. (1983). Some cautions concerning the application of causal modelling methods. *Multivariate Behavioral Research, 18,* 115-126.

Cohen, J. (1992). A power primer. *Psychological Bulletin, 112,* 155-159.

Cole, D. A. (1987). Utility of confirmatory factor analysis in test validation research. *Journal of Consulting and Clinical Psychology, 55,* 584-594.

Cole, D. A., Maxwell, S. E., Arvey, R., & Salas, E. (1993). Multivariate group comparisons of variable systems: MANOVA and structural equation modelling. *Psychological Bulletin, 114,* 174-184.

Cooley, W. W. (1978, October). Explanatory observational studies. *Educational Researcher,* pp. 9-15.

Costner, H. L. (1969). Theory, deduction, and rules of correspondence. *American Journal of Sociology, 75,* 245-263.

Costner, H. L., & Schoenberg, R. (1973). Diagnosing indicator ills in multiple indicator models. In A. S. Goldberger & O. D. Duncan (Eds.), *Structural equation models in the social sciences* (pp. 167-199). New York: Seminar Press.

Crandall, C. S. (1994). Prejudice against fat people: Ideology and self-interest. *Journal of Personality and Social Psychology, 66,* 882-894.

Cudeck, R. (1988). Multiplicative models and MTMM matrices. *Journal of Educational Statistics, 13,* 131-147.

Cudeck, R. (1989). Analysis of correlation matrices using covariance structure models. *Psychological Bulletin, 105,* 317-327.

Cudeck, R., & Browne, M. W. (1983). Cross-validation of covariance structures. *Multivariate Behavioral Research, 18,* 147-167.

Cudeck, R., & Henly, S. J. (1991). Model selection in covariance structures analysis and the "problem" of sample size: A clarification. *Psychological Bulletin, 109,* 512-519.

Darlington, R. B. (1978). Reduced-variance regression. *Psychological Bulletin, 85,* 1238-1255.

Darlington, R. B. (1990). *Regression and linear models.* New York: McGraw-Hill.

Duncan, O. D. (1966). Path analysis: Sociological examples. *American Journal of Sociology, 72,* 1-16.

Duncan, O. D. (1975). *Introduction to structural equation models.* New York: Academic Press.

Dunn, G., Everitt, B., & Pickles, A. (1993). *Modelling covariances and latent variables using EQS.* London: Chapman & Hall.

Ford, J. K., MacCallum, R. C., & Tait, M. (1986). The application of exploratory factor analysis in applied psychology: A critical review and analysis. *Personnel Psychology, 39,* 291-314.

Gerbing, D. W., & Hamilton, J. G. (1996). Validity of exploratory factor analysis as a precursor to confirmatory factor analysis. *Structural Equation Modeling, 3,* 62-72.

Goldberger, A. S. (1964). *Econometric theory.* New York: John Wiley.

Gordon, R. A. (1968). Issues in multiple regression. *American Journal of Sociology, 73,* 592-616.

Gorsuch, R. L. (1983). *Factor analysis* (2nd ed.). Hillsdale, NJ: Lawrence Erlbaum.

Graham, J. W., & Donaldson, S. I. (1993). Evaluating interventions with differential attrition: The importance of nonresponse mechanisms and use of follow-up data. *Journal of Applied Psychology, 78,* 119-128.

Graham, J. W., Hofer, S. M., & Piccinin, A. M. (1994). Analysis with missing data in drug prevention research. In L. M. Collins & L. Seitz (Eds.), *Advances in data analysis for prevention intervention research* (pp. 13-53). Washington, DC: American Psychological Association.

Green, B. F. (1977). Parameter sensitivity in multivariate methods. *Multivariate Behavioral Research, 12,* 263-288.

Hayduk, L. A. (1996). *LISREL issues, debates, and strategies.* Baltimore, MD: Johns Hopkins University Press.

Hox, J. J. (1995). AMOS, EQS, and LISREL for Windows: A comparative review. *Structural Equation Modeling, 2,* 79-91.

Hoyle, R. H. (1995). *Structural equation modelling: Concepts, issues, and applications.* Thousand Oaks, CA: Sage.

Hoyle, R. H., & Panter, A. T. (1995). Writing about structural equation models. In R. H. Hoyle (Ed.), *Structural equation modelling: Concepts, issues, and applications* (pp. 158-176). Thousand Oaks, CA: Sage.

Hu, L., & Bentler, P. M. (1995). Evaluating model fit. In R. H. Hoyle (Ed.), *Structural equation modelling: Concepts, issues, and applications* (pp. 76-99). Thousand Oaks, CA: Sage.

Jaccard, J., & Wan, C. K. (1995). Measurement error in the analysis of interaction effects between continuous predictors using multiple regression: Multiple indicators and structural equation models. *Psychological Bulletin, 117,* 348-357.

Jaccard, J., & Wan, C. K. (1996). *LISREL approaches to interaction effects in multiple regression* (Quantitative Applications in the Social Sciences, Vol. 114). Thousand Oaks, CA: Sage.

James, L. R., Mulaik, S. A., & Brett, J. M. (1982). *Causal analysis: Assumptions, models, and data.* Beverly Hills, CA: Sage.

Jöreskog, J. G. (1969). A general approach to confirmatory maximum likelihood factor analysis. *Psychometrika, 34,* 183-202.

Jöreskog, K. G. (1971). Statistical analyses of sets of congeneric tests. *Psychometrika, 36,* 109-133.

Jöreskog, K. G. (1973). A general method for estimating a linear structural equation system. In A. S. Goldberger & O. D. Duncan (Eds.), *Structural equation models in the social sciences* (pp. 85-112). New York: Seminar Press.

Jöreskog, K. G. (1993). Testing structural equation models. In K. A. Bollen & J. S. Long (Eds.), *Testing structural equation models* (pp. 294-316). Newbury Park, CA: Sage.

Jöreskog, K. G., & Sörbom, D. (1988). *LISREL 7: A guide to the program and applications.* Chicago: SPSS.

Jöreskog, K. G., & Sörbom, D. (1993). *LISREL 8: Structural equation modeling with the SIMPLIS command language.* Mooresville, IN: Scientific Software.

Kaplan, D. (1990). Evaluating and modifying covariance structure models: A review and recommendation. *Multivariate Behavioral Research, 25,* 137-155.

Keesling, W. (1972, June). *Maximum likelihood approaches to causal flow analysis.* Unpublished doctoral dissertation, School of Education, University of Chicago.

Kenny, D. A. (1979). *Correlation and causation.* New York: John Wiley.

Kenny, D. A., & Judd, C. M. (1984). Estimating the nonlinear and interactive effects of latent variables. *Psychological Bulletin, 96,* 201-210.

Kenny, D. A., & Kashy, D. A. (1992). Analysis of the multitrait-multimethod matrix by confirmatory factor analysis. *Psychological Bulletin, 112,* 165-172.

Kerlinger, F. N., & Pedhazur, E. J. (1973). *Multiple regression in behavioral research.* New York: Holt, Rinehart & Winston.

Land, K. C. (1969). Principles of path analysis. In E. F. Borgatta (Ed.), *Sociological methodology, 1969* (pp. 3-37). San Francisco: Jossey-Bass.

Lewis, R., & St. John, N. (1974). Contribution of cross-race friendship to minority group achievement in desegregated classrooms. *Sociometry, 37,* 79-91.

Liang, J., & Bollen, K. A. (1983). The structure of the Philadelphia Geriatric Center morale scale: A reinterpretation. *Journal of Gerontology, 38,* 181-189.

Ling, R. F. (1982). Review of "Correlation and Causation." *Journal of the American Statistical Association, 77,* 489-491.

Little, R. J. A., & Rubin, D. B. (1987). *Statistical analysis with missing data.* New York: John Wiley.

Little, R. J. A., & Rubin, D. B. (1990). The analysis of social science data with missing values. *Sociological Methods & Research, 18,* 292-326.

Loehlin, J. C. (1992). *Latent variable models: An introduction to factor, path, and structural analysis* (2nd ed.). Hillsdale, NJ: Lawrence Erlbaum.

MacCallum, R. C. (1986). Specification searches in covariance structure modelling. *Psychological Bulletin, 100,* 107-120.

MacCallum, R. C. (1995). Model specification: Procedures, strategies, and related issues. In R. H. Hoyle (Ed.), *Structural equation modelling: Concepts, issues, and applications* (pp. 16- 36). Thousand Oaks, CA: Sage.

MacCallum, R. C., & Browne, M. W. (1993). The use of causal indicators in covariance structure models: Some practical issues. *Psychological Bulletin, 114,* 533-541.

MacCallum, R. C., Browne, M. W., & Sugawara, H. M. (1996). Power analysis and determination of sample size for covariance structure modeling. *Psychological Methods, 1,* 130-149.

MacCallum, R. C., & Mar, C. M. (1995). Distinguishing between moderator and quadratic effect in multiple regression. *Psychological Bulletin, 118,* 405-421.

MacCallum, R. C., Roznowski, M., & Necowitz, L. B. (1992). Model modifications in covariance structure analysis: The problem of capitalization on chance. *Psychological Bulletin, 111,* 490-504.

MacCallum, R. C., Roznowski, M., Mar, C. M., & Reith, J. V. (1994). Alternative strategies for cross-validation of covariance structure models. *Multivariate Behavioral Research, 29,* 1-32.

MacCallum, R. C., Wegener, D. T., Uchino, B. N., & Fabrigar, L. R. (1993). The problem of equivalent models in application of covariance structure analysis. *Psychological Bulletin, 114,* 185-199.

Marcus, M., & Minc, H. (1964). *A survey of matrix theory and matrix inequalities.* Boston: Allyn & Bacon.

Marsh, H. W., Balla, J. R., & McDonald, R. P. (1988). Goodness-of-fit indexes in confirmatory factor analysis: The effect of sample size. *Psychological Bulletin, 103,* 391-411.

Marsh, H. W., & Byrne, B. M. (1993). Confirmatory factor analysis of MT-MM self-concept data: Between-group and within-group invariance constraints. *Multivariate Behavioral Research, 28,* 313-349.

Marsh, H. W., & Grayson, D. (1995). Latent variable models of multitrait-multimethod data. In R. H. Hoyle (Ed.), *Structural equation modeling: Concepts, issues, and applications* (pp. 177-198). Thousand Oaks, CA: Sage.

Marsh, H. W., & Hocevar, D. (1985). Application of confirmatory factor analysis to the study of self-concept: First- and higher order factor models and their invariance across groups. *Psychological Bulletin, 97,* 562-582.

Maruyama, G. (1977). *A causal model analysis of variables related to primary school achievement. Dissertation Abstracts International, 38,* 1470B. (Doctoral dissertation, Department of Psychology, University of Southern California)

Maruyama, G. (1982). How should attributions be measured? A reanalysis of data from Elig and Frieze. *American Educational Research Journal, 19,* 552-558.

Maruyama, G. (1993). Models of social psychological influences in schooling. In H. J. Walberg (Ed.), *Advances in educational productivity* (Vol. 3, pp. 3-19). Greenwich, CT: JAI.

Maruyama, G., & McGarvey, B. (1980). Evaluating causal models: An application of maximum likelihood analysis of structural equations. *Psychological Bulletin, 87,* 502-512.

Maruyama, G., & Miller, N. (1979). Re-examination of normative influence processes in desegregated classrooms. *American Educational Research Journal, 16,* 272-283.

Maruyama, G., & Miller, N. (1980). Physical attractiveness, race, and essay evaluation. *Personality and Social Psychology Bulletin, 6,* 384-390.

Maruyama, G., & Miller, N. (1981). Physical attractiveness and personality. In B. Maher (Ed.), *Progress in experimental personality research* (Vol. 10, pp. 203-280). New York: Academic Press.

Maruyama, G., Miller, N., & Holtz, R. (1986). The relation between popularity and achievement: A longitudinal test of the lateral transmission of values hypothesis. *Journal of Personality and Social Psychology, 51,* 730-741.

McArdle, J. J., & Aber, M. S. (1990). Patterns of change within latent variable structural equation models. In A. von Eye (Ed.), *Statistical methods in longitudinal research* (Vol. 1, pp. 151-224). New York: Academic Press.

McArdle, J. J., & Hamagami, F. (1996). Multilevel models for a multiple group structural equation perspective. In G. A. Marcoulides & R. E. Schumacher (Eds.), *Advanced structural equation modeling: Issues and techniques* (pp. 57-88). Mahwah, NJ: Lawrence Erlbaum.

McConahay, J. B. (1986). Modern racism, ambivalence, and the modern racism scale. In J. Dovidio & S. L. Gaertner (Eds.), *Prejudice, discrimination, and racism: Theory and research* (pp. 91-124). New York: Academic Press.

McDonald, R. P., & Marsh, H. W. (1990). Choosing a multivariate model: Noncentrality and goodness of fit. *Psychological Bulletin, 107,* 247-255.

McGarvey, B., Miller, N., & Maruyama, G. (1977). Scoring field dependence: A methodological comparison of five rod-and-frame scoring systems. *Applied Psychological Measurement, 1,* 433-446.

Mehrens, W. A., & Lehmann, I. J. (1984). *Measurement and evaluation in education and psychology* (3rd ed.). New York: Holt, Rinehart & Winston.

Meredith, W. (1964). Rotation to achieve factorial invariance. *Psychometrika, 29,* 187-206.

Miller, M. B. (1995). Coefficient alpha: A basic introduction from the perspective of classical test theory and structural equation modeling. *Structural Equation Modeling, 2,* 255-273.

Mulaik, S. A. (1972). *The foundations of factor analysis.* New York: McGraw-Hill.

Mulaik, S. A., James, L. R., Van Alstine, J., Bennett, N., Lind, S., & Stilwell, C. D. (1989). Evaluation of goodness-of-fit indices for structural equation models. *Psychological Bulletin, 105,* 430-445.

Muthen, B. (1984). A general structural equation model with dichotomous, ordered categorical, and continuous latent variable indicators. *Psychometrika, 49,* 115-132.

Muthen, B. (1988). *LISCOMP: Analysis of linear structural equations with a comprehensive measurement model.* Chicago: Scientific Software.

Muthen, B. (1993). Goodness of fit with categorical and nonnormal variables. In K. A. Bollen & J. S. Long (Eds.), *Testing structural equation models* (pp. 205-234). Newbury Park, CA: Sage.

Muthen, B. (1994). Multi-level covariance structure analysis. *Sociological Methods & Research, 22,* 376-398.

Muthen, B., Kaplan, D., & Hollis, M. (1987). On structural equation modeling for data that are not missing completely at random. *Psychometrika, 52,* 431-462.

Namboodiri, N. K., Carter, L. F., & Blalock, H. M., Jr. (1975). *Applied multivariate analysis and experimental design.* New York: McGraw-Hill.

Olkin, I., & Finn, J. D. (1995). Correlations redux. *Psychological Bulletin, 118,* 155-164.

Pelz, D. C., & Andrews, F. M. (1964). Detecting causal priorities in panel study data. *American Sociological Review, 29,* 836-848.

Ping, R. A. (1995). A parsimonious estimating technique for interaction and quadratic latent variables. *Journal of Marketing Research, 32,* 336-347.

Price, B. (1977). Ridge regression: Application to nonexperimental data. *Psychological Bulletin, 84,* 759-766.

Raykov, T., Tomer, A., & Nesselroade, R. J. (1991). Reporting structural equation modeling results in psychology and aging: Some proposed guidelines. *Psychology and Aging, 6,* 499-503.

Rigdon, E. (1995). A necessary and sufficient identification rule for structural equation models estimated in practice. *Multivariate Behavioral Research, 30,* 359-383.

Rindskopf, D., & Rose, T. (1988). Some theory and applications of confirmatory second-order factor analysis. *Multivariate Behavioral Research, 23,* 51-67.

Rogosa, D. (1980). A critique of cross-lagged correlations. *Psychological Bulletin, 88,* 245-258.

Rozelle, R. M., & Campbell, D. T. (1969). More plausible rival hypotheses in the cross-lagged panel correlation technique. *Psychological Bulletin, 71,* 74-80.

Shingles, R. D. (1976). Causal inference in cross-lagged panel analysis. *Political Methodology, 3,* 95-133.

Sobel, M. E., & Bohrnstedt, G. W. (1985). Use of null models in evaluating the fit of covariance structure models. In N. B. Tuma (Ed.), *Sociological methodology, 1985* (pp. 152-178). San Francisco: Jossey-Bass.

Sörbom, D. (1974). A general method for studying differences in factor means and factor structures between groups. *British Journal of Mathematical and Statistical Psychology, 27,* 229-239.

Sörbom, D. (1982). Structural equation models with structured means. In K. G. Jöreskog & H. Wold (Eds.), *Systems under direct observation* (pp. 183-195). Amsterdam: North Holland.

Steiger, J. H. (1989). *EZPATH: A supplementary module for SYSTAT and SYGRAPH.* Evanston, IL: SYSTAT.

Steiger, J. H. (1990). Structural model evaluation and modification: An interval estimation approach. *Multivariate Behavioral Research, 25,* 173-180.

Stein, J. A., Smith, G. M., Guy, S. M., & Bentler, P. M. (1993). Consequences of adolescent drug use on young adult job behavior and job satisfaction. *Journal of Applied Psychology, 3,* 463-474.

Tanaka, J. S. (1993). Multifaceted conceptions of fit in structural equation models. In K. A. Bollen & J. S. Long (Eds.), *Testing structural equation models* (pp. 10-39). Newbury Park, CA: Sage.

Tanaka, J. S., & Huba, G. J. (1984). Confirmatory hierarchical factor analysis of psychological distress measures. *Journal of Personality and Social Psychology, 46,* 621-635.

Tanaka, J. S., Panter, A. T., Winbourne, W. C., & Huba, G. J. (1990). Theory testing in personality and social psychology with structural equation models: A primer in 20 questions. In C. Hendrick & M. S. Clark (Eds.), *Review of personality and social psychology* (Vol 11, pp. 217-242). Newbury Park, CA: Sage.

Thurstone, L. L. (1938). Primary mental abilities. *Psychometric Monographs,* No. 1.

Tucker, L. R., & Lewis, C. (1973). The reliability coefficient for maximum likelihood factor analysis. *Psychometrika, 38,* 1-10.

Waller, N. G. (1993). Seven confirmatory factor analysis programs: EQS, EZPATH, LINCS, LISCOMP, LISREL 7, SIMPLIS, and CALIS. *Applied Psychological Measurement, 17,* 73-100.

Wiley, D. E. (1973). The identification problem for structural equation models with unmeasured variables. In A. S. Goldberger & O. D. Duncan (Eds.), *Structural equation models in the social sciences* (pp. 69-83). New York: Seminar Press.

Willett, J. B., & Sayer, A. G. (1994). Using covariance analyses to detect correlates and predictors of individual change over time. *Psychological Bulletin, 116,* 363-381.

Williams, R., & Thomson, E. (1986). Normalization issues in latent variable modeling. *Sociological Methods & Research, 15,* 24-43.

Wothke, W. (1987, April). *Multivariate linear models of the multitrait-multimethod matrix.* Paper presented at the annual meeting of the American Educational Research Association, Washington, DC.

Wright, S. (1921). Correlation and causation. *Journal of Agricultural Research, 20,* 557-585.

Wright, S. (1934). The method of path coefficients. *Annals of Mathematical Statistics, 5,* 161-215.

Yalcin, I., & Amemiya, Y. (1993). Fitting of a general non-linear factor analysis model. *American Statistical Association Proceedings* (Statistical Computing Section), pp. 118-122.

Author Index

Aber, M. S. 108
Akaike, H., 237, 241, 246
Amemiya, Y., 280
Arbuckle, J. L., 19, 179, 261, 283
Andrews, F. M., 120-121
Arminger, G., 259
Arvey, R., 282

Bagozzi, R. P., 3
Balla, J. R., 200, 239, 241, 244
Baron, R. M., 40, 281
Baumrind, D., 276
Bennett, N., 239-241, 243, 245
Bentler, P. M., 19, 179, 239, 240, 241, 242-245, 247-248, 281
Blalock, H. M. Jr., 17, 106-108
Bohrnstedt, G. W., 247
Bollen, K. A., 12, 81, 106, 189, 200, 238, 239, 241, 244, 256
Bonett, D. G., 240, 243-244, 247-248
Bozdogen, H., 241, 246
Breckler, S. J., 274-275
Brett, J. M., 241, 245, 247-249
Brophy, J. E., 6
Browne, M. W., 73, 81, 97, 199, 237, 241, 246, 247, 250, 259, 280
Bryk, A. S., 282
Byrne, B. M., 31, 149, 195, 259

Byrne, D., 6

Calsyn, R. J., 109
Carter, L. F., 106-108
Campbell, D. T., 92-96, 120-121, 149, 151-152
Cliff, N., 135, 139, 272-275, 278
Cohen, J., 280
Cole, D. A., 149, 282
Cooley, W. W., 3
Costner, H. L., 132, 154, 158, 279
Crandall, C. S., 89
Cudeck, R., 34, 73, 97, 118, 199, 237, 241, 246, 247, 249-250, 280

Darlington, R. B., 61, 73
Donaldson, S. I., 217
Dudgeon, P., 281
Duncan, O. D., 17, 29, 46
Dunn, G., 149, 261

Everitt, B., 149, 261

Fabrigar, L. R., 276
Finn, J. D., 71

Fiske, D. W., 92-96, 120-121, 149, 151-152
Ford, J. K., 136

Gerbing, D. W., 138
Goldberger, A. S., 62
Good, T. L., 6
Gordon, R. A., 66-70, 75
Gorsuch, R. L.,80, 132, 134
Graham, J. W., 217
Grayson, D., 153
Green, B. F.,63
Griffitt, W., 6
Guy, S. M., 281

Hamagami, F., 283
Hamilton, J. G., 138
Hayduk, L. A., 12, 284
Henly, S. J., 249-250
Hocevar, D., 256, 265
Hofer, S. M., 217
Hollis, M., 217
Holtz, R., 5, 204, 214-220
Hox, J. J., 284
Hoyle, R. H., 12,
Hoyle, R. H., 238, 244, 245, 254, 283
Hu, L., 239, 242-245, 281
Huba, G., 81, 243

Jaccard, J., 280, 281
James, L. R., 239-241, 243, 245, 247-249
Joreskog, J. G., 19, 20, 147, 178, 179,
    187-200, 246, 261, 278-280
Judd, C. M., 280

Kano, Y., 284
Kaplan, D., 200, 217
Kashy, D. A., 96, 149, 152-154
Keesling, W., 187
Kenny, D. A., 40, 85, 96, 104-105, 109,
    132, 149, 152-154, 157-160, 276,
    280, 281
Kerlinger, F. N., 285

Land, K. C., 18, 49
Lehmann, I. J., 80, 84

Lennox, R., 81
Lewis, C., 240, 244
Lewis, R., 203-209, 211, 220
Liang, J., 256
Lind, S., 239-241, 243, 245
Ling, R. F., 276
Little, R. J. A., 217
Loehlin, J. C., 136
Long, J. S., 200, 238, 239

MacCallum, R. C., 81, 136, 276, 278, 279,
    280
Mar, C. M., 279, 280
Marcus, M., 292
Marsh, H. W., 149, 153, 200, 239, 241,
    244, 245, 256, 265
Maruyama, G., 5, 6, 63, 94, 102, 113, 153,
    203-220, 221, 234, 250-254, 257,
    270
Maxwell, S. E., 282
McArdle, J. J., 108, 283
McConahay, J. B., 89
McDonald, R. P., 200, 239, 241, 244, 245
McGarvey, B., 5, 94, 102, 209-214, 234,
    250-254, 257, 270
Mehrens, W. A., 80, 84
Meredith, W., 217
Miller, M. B., 136
Miller, N., 5, 6, 63, 94, 203-209, 214-220
Minc, H., 292
Mulaik, S. A., 132, 239-241, 243, 245,
    247-249
Muthen, B., 31, 217, 259, 282, 283

Namboodiri, N. K., 106-108
Necowitz, L. B., 4, 279
Nesselroade, R. J., 283

O'Connell, E. J., 96, 149
Olkin, I., 71

Panter, A. T., 81, 238, 244, 245, 254, 283
Pedhazur, E. J., 285
Pelz, D. C., 120-121
Piccinin, A. M., 217
Pickles, A., 149, 261

Ping, R. A., 280
Price, B., 74-75

Raudenbush, S. W., 282
Raykov, T., 283
Reith, J. V., 279
Rigdon, E., 106, 190
Rindskopf, D., 256
Rogosa, D., 109, 121
Rose, T., 256
Rozelle, R. M., 120-121
Roznowski, M., 4, 279
Rubin, D. B., 217

St. John, N., 203-209, 211, 220
Salas, E., 282
Sayer, A. G., 108
Schoenberg, R., 132, 154, 158, 279
Shavelson, R. J., 31, 259
Shingles, R. D., 109, 121
Smith, G. M., 281
Sobel, M. E., 247
Sorbom, D., 19, 31, 78, 179, 259, 261
Steiger, J. H., 241, 246, 284
Stein, J. A., 281
Stilwell, C. D., 239-241, 243, 245
Sugawara, H. M., 280

Tait, M., 136
Tanaka, J. S., 81, 243, 246
Thomson, E., 258
Thurstone, L. L., 133
Tomer, A., 283
Tucker, L. R., 240, 244

Uchino, B. N., 276

Van Alstine, J., 239-241, 243, 245

Waller, N. G., 284
Wan, C. K., 280, 281
Wegener, D. T., 276
Wiley, D. E., 20, 187, 197
Willett, J. B., 108
Williams, R., 258
Winbourne, W. C., 81
Wothke, W., 152
Wright, S., 9, 15, 16

Yalcin, I., 280

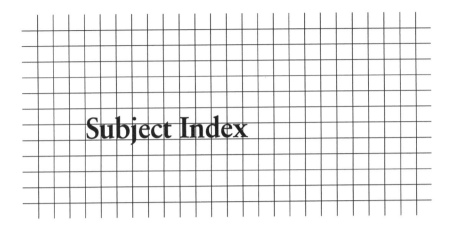

Subject Index

"All-Y" models, 256-257, 267-270
Alternative models, 234-238

Collinearity, 60-70
Computer programs for SEM, 283-284
Conceptual replication, 262-263
Consistency tests, 154-161
Constraints, 147-148, 257-265
Correlations:
    confidence intervals for, 70-71
    partial, 51-52
Criticisms of SEM, 272-278

Decomposition of effects, 30, 35-48
Degrees of freedom, 48
Determinant of a matrix, 292
Direct effect, 36
Distribution free estimation, 281

Exact replication, 262-263

Factor analysis:
    confirmatory, 131,139-147
    exploratory, 136-139
    logic of, 132-136
Finite causal lag, 100
Fit indexes, 238-246
    absolute, 229, 242-243

parsimonious/adjusted, 242, 245-246
    relative, 239-242, 243-245

Identification, 18, 105-108
    of latent variable models, 188-192
    order condition for, 107
    rank condition for, 107
Indirect effects, 36
Instrumental variables, 105
Interaction effects, 281
Illustrations of SEM models, 187-195, 203-220

Just-identified model, 18

Lack of fit, 249-250
Least squares estimation, ordinary, 39
Longitudinal models, 108-122

Matrix:
    addition, 289
    diagonal, 282
    identity, 288
    inverse of, 291-292
    multiplication, 289-290
    nonsingular, 292
    square, 287

309

symmetric, 288
transpose, 287
Matrix algebra, 285-293
Mean differences, analysis of, 282
Measurement error, 29, 79-89
Measurement model, 178-181
Mediation, 10
Method variance, 88-92
Model modification, 278-280
Moderator variables, 281
Modification indices, 251
Model fit, 161, 163-164, 195-201
Multicollinearity, 61
Multilevel modelling, 282
Multiple population analyses, 255, 257-265
Multitrait, multimethod models, 92-97
    and confirmatory factor analysis,
        148-154

Nested models, 235-246, 247-249
Noncausal effects, 36
Noncontinuous variables, 281
Nonlinear relationships, 280
Non-nested models, 246-247
Nonrandom error, 87-89
Nonrecursive models, 100-105

Overall model fit, 238-247
Over-identified model, 18

Panel analysis, 110-112
Panel models:
    analysis of, 120-122
    stability in, 112-115

stability of causal processes, 118-
    120
temporal lag in, 115-118
Path analysis, 9, 15-20, 29
Path modeling notation, 36, 37, 58
Power analysis of SEMs, 280

Random error, 84-87
Recursive model, 16
Reference indicators, 178, 181-184
Regression:
    partial, 49-50
    ridge, 61, 73-75

Second-order factor models, 256, 265-269
Specification error, 29
Structural equations, 6, 10
Structural model, 184-187

Tests:
    congeneric, 148
    parallel, 147
    tau-equivalent, 148

Under-identified model, 18

Variable:
    endogenous, 37
    exogenous, 37
    intervening, 4
    mediating, 4
    moderating, 281
Vector, 287

About the Author

Geoffrey M. Maruyama is Vice Provost for Academic Affairs in the Office of the Provost for Professional Studies at the University of Minnesota. His responsibilities include academic planning, curricular and instructional issues, graduate education, faculty issues including promotion and tenure, and research. He received his Ph.D. in psychology from the University of Southern California in 1977. He has been a faculty member in the Department of Educational Psychology since September 1976. Before his appointment as Vice Provost, he spent 10 years as director of the Human Relations Program in the Department of Educational Psychology, 3 years as director of the Center for Applied Research and Educational Improvement, and 1 year as Acting Associate Dean in the College of Education and Human Development. His academic experience also includes 9 years of active involvement in faculty governance and 4 years as lobbyist for faculty issues at the Minnesota state legislature.

Maruyama has also written another book, *Research in Educational Settings* (with Stan Deno), as well as 13 book chapters and more than 50 articles. His research interests cluster around (a) methodological issues including application of structural equation modeling, action research and its implications for collaborate research, and applied research methods/program evaluation; and (b) substantive issues tied to the interface of psychology and education, including school reform, school achievement processes, and effective educational techniques for diverse schools.